A

PHOTO: SHARON THOMSON

C.J. Taylor worked as Parks Canada historian in
Ottawa and Calgary for thirty-five years before retiring
in 2009. He has had an abiding interest in national parks and
enjoys exploring them both in the archives and in the field.
He currently lives in Calgary from where he enjoys
hiking and skiing in the mountain parks.

JASPER

A History of the Place and Its People

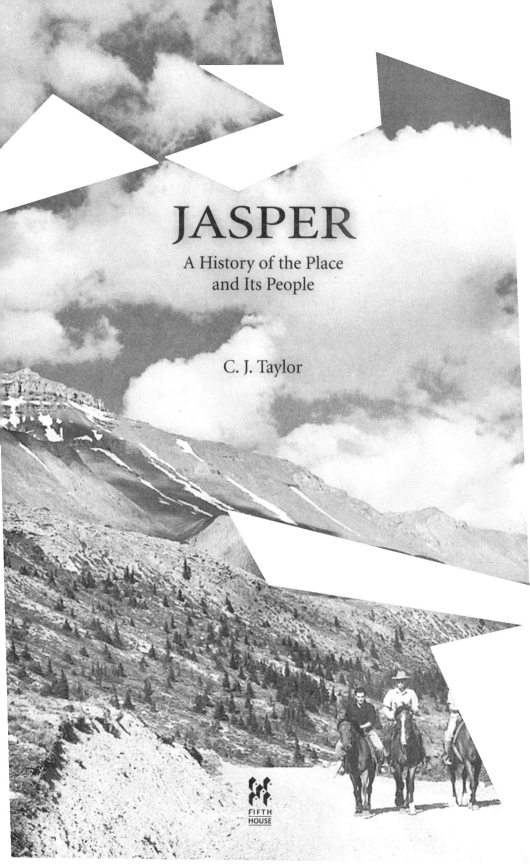

JASPER

A History of the Place and Its People

C. J. Taylor

FIFTH
HOUSE

Cover and interior design by John Luckhurst
Edited by Kirsten Craven
Copyedited by Peter Midgley

The type in this book is set in Minion 11/14 point.

The publisher gratefully acknowledges the support of The Canada Council for the Arts and the Department of Canadian Heritage.

We acknowledge the financial support of the Government of Canada through the Book Publishing Industry Development Program (BPIDP) for our publishing activities. The author and publisher thank the Jasper Yellowhead Historical Society for their financial support.

Printed in Canada on Forest Stewardship Council (FSC) approved paper

2009 / 1

First published in the United States in 2010 by
Fitzhenry & Whiteside
311 Washington Street
Brighton, Massachusetts, 02135

Library and Archives Canada Cataloguing in Publication Data

Taylor, C. J. (Christopher James), 1947- Jasper : a history of the place and its people / C.J. Taylor.
Includes bibliographical references and index. ISBN 978-1-897252-34-5

1. Jasper National Park (Alta.)–History. 2. Jasper (Alta.)–History. I. Title.

FC3664.J3T39 2009   971.23'32   C2009-900557-3

Fifth House Ltd.
A Fitzhenry & Whiteside Company
195 Allstate Parkway
Markham, Ontario
L3R 4T8
1-800-387-9776
www.fitzhenry.ca

Contents

Preface

This is the history of one of Canada's most famous attractions, Jasper National Park. It is the story of a place that has long impressed people for its grandeur and beauty. It is also a case study of the complex organization that looks after Canada's national parks, now known as Parks Canada.

Although this is a history of a national park written by a Parks Canada historian, it is not an official history. Parks Canada commissioned the project but its management did not direct the topics or censor the interpretation. What the outfit offered was a delightfully benign freedom, allowing me unfettered access to the park, its people, and records. The manuscript has been adopted by the Jasper Yellowhead Museum and Archives, which collects the royalties for this book. If there were constraints on the writing, they were professional ones: how to select a meaningful narrative from so many disparate bits, decide what was important for discussion, and leave out what was thought not to be relevant. It reflects the outlook of a Canadian historian at the beginning of the twenty-first century, influenced by current debates and discussions swirling about concerning the meaning of parks and environmental history. No doubt someone could come along in another generation and tell a different story. Still, I have endeavoured to tell the truth as I saw it and I hope that it will be relevant for a while yet.

So many people helped in this project.

I have to thank Jasper wardens Rod Wallace and Mike Wallace for first proposing that I write a history of Jasper. They provided a multitude of advice, assisted in the interviews, read and criticized earlier versions of chapters, and exhibited enormous patience and courtesy when the project went through its fallow stages. Rod took me on horse trips that allowed me to travel almost in the footsteps of Lawrence Burpee, the first historian of the park, and he taught me to read the stories in the peculiar landscape that is Jasper National Park. He remained involved in the project even after his retirement and provided a model of the nostalgic yearner for the good old days. Mike asked many questions that helped ease the manuscript into more interesting waters. And, speaking of waters, pointed out when this city slicker had the Athabasca River flowing in the wrong direction!

Also in Jasper, librarian Kim Forster and interpretive specialist Ken Walker gave me the benefit of their vast knowledge of the place. Kim helped with the photos, including finding an old photo of the Free Camp from her personal archives. Ken read an earlier draft and provided many helpful comments. Former Jasper park naturalist Larry Halverson provided biographical information about the first full-time park naturalist. The late Doug Welleck gave a too brief interview about the beginnings of the park's visitor service function.

The help of the Jasper Museum and Archives was also invaluable. They have been collecting records from the Jasper area for over half a century now and are an important source of Jasper history. I received plenty of assistance and encouragement from Meghan Power, archives manager, and Karen Byers, director of the museum, also supported the project.

Ron Pelletier from Prince George was extremely helpful in helping me understand the history of his Moberly ancestors and provided insight into the nascent Métis community at Jasper.

In the Calgary office of Parks Canada, librarian Katharine Kinnear, archaeologists Peter Francis, Marty Magne, and Jack Porter, clerical staff Phyllis Kennedy and Shirley Leonard, designer Heather Wall, biologist Dave Poll, and town planner Neil MacDonald provided a range of professional services that made the Western and Northern Service Centre such an interesting and enjoyable place to work. Katharine ordered up the microfilm and the interlibrary loans and helped track down elusive photographs that formed an essential part of the research. Heather Wall and Rob Storeshaw drew the maps.

In Edmonton, I was fortunate to get the helpful advice of Alwynne Beaudoin of the Royal Alberta Museum. She gave me a veritable graduate course on palaeoecology of the province.

In Victoria, my former colleague, and still friend, architectural historian Ted Mills, collaborated on an earlier project that studied Jasper Park Lodge and its golf course. In subsequent discussions, he helped me appreciate the traditions of national park architecture and define that illusive style that he has termed Tudor Rustic.

I am grateful to the many former park wardens that gave me interviews: Bob Haney, Toni Klettl, Clarence Wilkins, and Max Winkler. Max and Julie Winkler invited me to a memorable supper one evening at their ranch near Waterton where they regaled me with stories about their life in the Brazeau District. Max, being the wise old man he is, counselled me not to judge the past by the present, advice which caused me to look at the wider context of my research. I would have liked the chance to interview Mike Schintz, a former colleague in the Calgary office and, at the beginning of his career, a Jasper warden, but he died before I could interview him in depth. He sent me a message of encouragement, literally from his death bed. I benefit-ted from conversations with Gerry Israelson, now of Kootenay/Yoho/Lake Louise, but a former public safety warden at Jasper and with my friend Don Mickle, retired Banff park warden, whose family is steeped in the lore and memory of the horse tradition of the mountains.

I am grateful to my historians' network whose members listened to my ramblings and occasionally conversed on the various topics at hand. Mike Payne, formerly of Alberta Historic Resources and now the City of Edmonton Archivist, Bill Waiser at the University of Saskatchewan, Don Smith at the University of Calgary, and Ian MacLaren at the University of Alberta encouraged me to think sharper and write better. Mike gave me lots of advice on the first chapters and I benefitted from his research on the fur trade history of the upper Athabasca. Bill and Don encouraged me to tell stories and Ian encouraged me to start writing on the topic of Jasper history. I am also grateful for the advice of Ted Hart, director of the Whyte Museum in Banff, who allowed me to read a draft of his biography of J. B. Harkin and who passed along words of encouragement and advice.

At Fifth House, I am grateful to Charlene Dobmeier, who showed an early interest in the project, and managing editor Meaghan Craven, who shepherded the manuscript through production.

And lastly, friend, colleague, and wife Janet Wright lived through the Jasper project and provided her usual thoughtful insights on early drafts of chapters. She is, coincidentally, a distant relative of Athol C. Wright, super-intendent of Jasper from 1936 to 1938.

Writing a book is a lonely task: errors of fact and interpretation are mine alone.

People and the Park

Jasper National Park is renowned for its many natural splendours: towering mountains, alpine meadows, pristine rivers and forests, and the wildlife that inhabit these wild places. Less known is the human history that occupies these spaces. Humans have inhabited these lands for many years, sometimes as hunters or explorers, and often also as travellers. Humans also explain the existence of Jasper, for national parks do not spring up by themselves—they are social constructs, established by governments and defined by people's actions. Humans have continued to define the area through the first one hundred years of the park's history.

The earlier history of Jasper is perhaps better known than that of the modern era since the creation of the park. The historical dimensions of Jasper National Park were recognized at the time of its establishment in 1907. Railway surveyors had noted the location of fur-trade posts and "Old Indian Trails" and its romantic past was presented in some of the subsequent publicity for the park. The well-known historian and author Lawrence Burpee wrote two books about Jasper in the 1920s that celebrated its past and introduced the idea that it was possible to travel in the past by following in the steps of the early travellers along routes that had changed little since yesteryear.[1] Around 1930 author Mabel Williams wrote in the tourist booklet *Jasper Trails*:

> The steel rails from Edmonton to the Divide had retraced
> two of the oldest and most traveled trails across the mountain
> fastnesses—the highways of the fur trade in its most glorious
> days, routes rich in history and famous in the literature of a
> century. Here for over fifty years went the explorer and fur
> trader, the pioneer missionary, scientist and artist; fighting their
> way across the snows of the Athabasca Pass to the Columbia, or
> up the stony valley of the Miette to the "Leather" Pass, as the
> Yellowhead summit was first called.[2]

Williams felt that train travellers could bask in the vicarious experience of following these ancient mountain routes. This idea is still valid today. With the construction of new highways largely built during the 1950s and 1960s, travellers can follow the routes navigated by earlier trains, as well as those cleared by the fur trader and explorer of yesteryear.

Jasper's early past continued to be explored and appreciated by subsequent inhabitants of the community of Jasper. As early as the 1950s, a group of local enthusiasts undertook to record the memories of some of the area's oldest inhabitants. Men like Adam Joachim, Lewis Swift, and Fred Brewster could recall events from the first decades of the century. In 1963 the Jasper-Yellowhead Historical Society was formed and, under the able direction of Constance Peterson, the pioneers' stories were collected and saved for future generations. The National Historic Sites program of Parks Canada also recognized the importance of the past. Henry House was designated a national historic site in 1926 and the site of the second Jasper House the following year. Other national historic site markers designate the exploration of David Thompson in 1811 and the passage of the Overlanders in 1862. These designations encouraged the production of several historical studies on Jasper, all focusing on the early period.[3] An early popular history of the area, James MacGregor's *Packsaddles to Tete Jaune Cache*, first published in 1962, paints a picture of the area during the first two decades of the twentieth century through the eyes of an old horse guide and trapper, James Shand-Harvey.[4] Two recent books on the history of the area—*A Hard Road to Travel* and *Culturing Wilderness in Jasper National Park*—offer more selective explorations of the history of the park era.[5] An interesting footnote to this history is that Tom Peterson, one of the authors of *A Hard Road to Travel*, is the son of one of the founders of the Jasper-Yellowhead Historical Society, so continuing a long tradition of interest in the area's past.

The past has also been preserved in the landscape.[6] Charged with protecting natural scenery, Parks Canada has also protected pieces of old trails, abandoned railway rights of way, and old buildings as a kind of collateral benefit to its primary mandate of wilderness protection. Many features of this cultural landscape are evident even during a casual motor tour of the park. If you follow the Yellowhead Highway that enters the park at the East Gate, you find yourself on the route of the old Grand Trunk Pacific Railway. Turn off the highway at Palisades, cross under the railway overpass, and follow a quiet road toward the Snaring River. You will pass the Palisades

Training Centre, part of the pioneer 1890s Lewis Swift homestead. The road is as straight as a railway track, which indeed it once was. You are now on the old Canadian Northern right-of-way built in 1912. The road turns a corner and you leave the old rail bed and drive along a tree-lined gravel road that takes you past Ewan Moberly house, an 1890s Métis homestead. Continuing along past Suzanne Karakonti's grave, you will come to the Celestine fire road. The road itself was developed in the 1950s to provide fire fighting access to the North, but it follows much earlier trails. The railway construction crews used the route as a wagon road, and before this it was used by the fur traders as the main route west. Hidden in the trees along the route are old trappers' cabins, a railway construction camp, and even a prehistoric campsite. Some present-day tourists who are more adventuresome park their vehicles just past the site of the old Devona warden cabin and walk along the Canadian National Railways access road to the railway. Here is a siding track called Devona, one of the original stations of the Canadian Northern. Just across the track is the site of the second Jasper House that served as a staging area for the fur trade routes through the Rocky Mountains. The best way to approach this site is from the other side of the Athabasca River, approaching the riverbanks from Highway 16 to look at the place across the river or, better still, by boat. The site of Jasper House itself is just a clearing in the forest, a meadow with depressions and mounds indicating the few simple buildings that once stood here. But, like many of life's experiences, the real meaning is in the journey, for the trail to the site is part of an ancient route to the northwest, connecting the Athabasca with the Peace River Country. Looking back, one can see the wagon ruts and braided horse trails made by the travellers of long ago. Across from Jasper House is the Rocky River trail, running southeast through a chain of passes and rivers leading to Saskatchewan Crossing and Kootenay Plains, another important prehistoric meeting place. And the Athabasca itself leads to two routes through the Rockies to the west. The site of Jasper House, built in 1830, is on the site of a much more ancient crossroads known to travellers since the end of the ice age.

There are many later signs of human occupation on the landscape as well. The most prominent, perhaps, are the remains near the East Gate of the coal mine and settlement of Pocahontas that were abandoned in 1921. There are many other cultural features along Highway 93A. Following this route out of the town of Jasper, you cross an old Bailey Bridge built in 1914. You pass under a rocky promontory, known since the fur trade era as Old

Fort Point, and along a little-used tree-lined road. At the other end of the bridge from the town is a low-lying area that was once the site of an internment camp during World War I, and which was then reused as a hippy camp in the early 1970s. If you were to continue along this road, you would come to the back entrance of Jasper Park Lodge by the golf course, marked by an elaborate rustic gateway. This was part of the original main road into town until it was replaced in 1940 by the present Athabasca crossing. It follows even older tote roads and fur-trading trails.

Historians have not written much about Jasper's later history; there are few accounts of the park's history in the twentieth century. And yet, Jasper National Park, as one of the largest and most popular pieces of the national park system, has a rich and interesting past that stretches back over a century. Interesting in its own right, Jasper's history provides a worm's-eye view of history of the national parks service. This past is preserved in the records of Parks Canada. Carefully organized correspondence files document the creation of the park and its development through the decades. The files treat the many issues facing the park as it grew into a major tourist destination: townsite development, highway construction, wildlife conservation, campground establishment.

Because of the close relationship between the park and the larger organization that looks after it, some understanding of the nature of that organization is necessary to understanding the park's own history. On the other hand, this is a history of Jasper, not an administrative history of a government organization so here, then, is merely a brief overview of the national parks service to give some necessary background. When Jasper was made a national park in 1907, several parks had already been created in the Rocky Mountains: Rocky Mountains Park (renamed Banff in 1930), Yoho, and Waterton Lakes. Glacier and Mount Revelstoke had been created in the Selkirk Mountains of British Columbia. With the exception of Waterton, these other parks had been created along the line of the recently completed Canadian Pacific Railway. Jasper was created along the twin lines of the Grand Trunk Pacific and the Canadian Northern Railways, so railway companies played an important part not only in the creation of these parks, but in their early development.

In 1911 the federal government created a separate organization within the Department of the Interior to manage this network of parks. This organization evolved into a significant branch of the mighty department that oversaw the opening of the west and north. The first head of the national parks branch developed a structure that, with elaboration and modification, remained largely intact until the 1990s. The head of the outfit was assisted in Ottawa by a group of lieutenants, each looking after a particular specialty, such as administration and finance, engineering, wildlife, publicity, and architecture and town planning. Each park was governed by a superintendent who reported directly to the head of the outfit in Ottawa. He in turn (they were all men until the 1980s), was assisted by a group of lieutenants that paralleled the Ottawa division chiefs. While the superintendent was nominally in charge of the park staff, that is, he oversaw most hiring and the staff was accountable to him, in many cases there was a kind of functional management where the Ottawa lieutenants provided professional direction to their counterparts in the field. Thus the head of administration devised a system of record-keeping that was followed in each park. The administration created duplicate files in both Ottawa and the park, each containing the same correspondence, organized according to identical subjects. The park engineer also followed professional direction from headquarters. Only conservation broke with this model. In the park, the warden service was responsible for conservation, which at first took grudging direction from the chief of the wildlife division. The conflict between the warden service and the wildlife division will be examined in the chapters treating wildlife management in the park. Each park had a superintendent who reported to the head of the parks branch in Ottawa. Other functions were added in the 1960s that followed the functional management model: interpretation and visitor services.

In 1936 the Department of the Interior was abolished and many of its functions were assumed by a new department called Mines and Resources. The parks service did not fare very well in this new organization and it was buried in a multi-function branch whose head had a variety of other responsibilities besides national parks. The Department of Mines and Resources became Resources and Development in 1951 and Northern Affairs and National Resources in 1954. The profile of the national parks program began to rise following the departmental reorganization that created the Department of Indian Affairs and Northern Development in 1966. In this organization it formed a branch of the conservation program alongside the Canadian Wildlife Service (CWS). With the departure of the CWS in 1970, the national parks organization achieved equal footing with the other two branches that managed Indian reserves and the northern territories respectively, finally surpassing the previous high point that had been lost with the dissolution of the Department of the Interior in 1936. In 1973 it became known as Parks Canada. Finally, Parks Canada became a Crown corporation in 1999. Through all of these permutations, the structure of the organization remained similar. The name has been changed from Dominion Parks Service, to National Parks Service, to Canadian Parks Service, to Parks Canada, but it still comprised a dedicated national office overlooking a network of national parks. And, while the head has been called at various times commissioner, controller, assistant director, director, assistant deputy minister, or, most recently, chief executive officer, he has always sat at the top of a distinct organization. Throughout the book the term "national parks service" is used to refer generally to the organization. Parks Canada is used to refer to the outfit after 1973.

The 1911 organization suffered its most serious disruption in the mid-1990s when the centralizing influence of functional management was dismantled. National or regional heads no longer interact directly with their counterparts in the parks. An unfortunate casualty of this decentralization was the loss of any central record keeping. Future historians wishing to reconstruct the post-1995 era will have a difficult time finding the correspondence that tells so much of the issues and thinking of the day. Still, the dynamic interaction between the individual parks and the larger administration continues to be a hallmark of the organization. In this context, the history of Jasper National Park sheds light on the arcane workings of the larger organization through the twentieth century.

Finally, the name Jasper requires some explanation. The name is derived from one Jasper Hawes who was in charge of a fur trade post on the upper Athabasca in the 1820s. The post came to be called Jasper House, and the park was named in honour of the post. The principal settlement of the town was first named Fitzhugh, but in 1914 was also called Jasper. For purposes of simplicity the term Jasper is used to indicate the area occupied by the present park even before its establishment in 1907. Jasper National Park or "the park" is used to refer to the actual park, while the town of Jasper or Jasper townsite signifies the community of Jasper.

CHAPTER ONE

Early Travellers

In prehistoric times people travelled to the Jasper area for many of the same reasons that they come there today: Jasper was their destination or they were passing through on their way to somewhere else. Jasper has always served as a transportation corridor; through time, only the means of travel have changed. In the early days, people travelled down major river systems. On the eastern slopes of the Rockies they came along the Athabasca River from the northwest or down the Smokey and Snake Indian rivers from the north. On the western side of the Rockies, they travelled along the Fraser or Columbia rivers. The upper Athabasca is in the middle of this great natural transportation system and the Athabasca, Yellowhead, and Snake Indian passes are important connectors or portages between these river systems. In the early days, travellers were funnelled to Jasper by the coincidence that it was the centre of a great continental river network. This was where travellers could connect from one river to another, like taking a connecting train.

Between five and six million years ago, sheets of the earth's crust were thrust upwards to form the front and main ranges of the Rocky Mountains. Geologists have identified the southeast striking Pyramid Thrust, located just east of the present town of Jasper, as dividing the front from the main ranges.[7] At this particular part of the Rockies, the mountains lined up in a northeast–southwest direction, forever confusing travellers seeking a straightforward east–west connection. Nothing much happened for the next three or four million years and then, a little over a million and a half years ago, the ice age began, covering much of what is now Canada under a giant sheet of ice. In the Rocky Mountains, two giant ice sheets, one from the west, the Cordilleran, and the other from the east, the Laurentide, converged.

About nine thousand years ago, the ice began to melt and the region began to assume its present topography. The defining elements became the mountains and the rivers. Four drainage areas converged at the heart of Jasper and defined the earliest human use of the area. Imagine a large St. Andrew's Cross and you will get an idea of what it looks like. The Athabasca

River has its origins to the southwest in the Columbia Icefields along the Continental Divide. It flows into Lake Athabasca to the northeast. Tributaries of the Athabasca flow down from the northwest to the south and southeast.

The earliest travellers likely began coming to the upper Athabasca valley at the end of the ice age, about nine thousand years ago. The early visitors travelled from the northeastern woodlands, from the western plateau in what is now British Columbia, and from the plains to the east. They came looking for food in the form of grazing animals, who themselves followed seasonal rounds. Long ago, in the time of the early travellers, the northern Rockies were less forested and covered with more grass than they are today. Grazing herds of buffalo, elk, and deer would migrate into the upper Athabasca valley and its tributaries in search of new grass. The area was favoured by animals in the winter when the warm Chinook winds would have kept the snow away from the nutritious sedges. And where the animals roamed the hunters would follow.

The exact numbers of animals that naturally lived in the Jasper area at that time has posed a mystery to wildlife biologists, historians, and archaeologists, but it seems likely that there were not great numbers of game grazing up the mountain valleys. Archaeological evidence supports this supposition. Archaeologists have not found large prehistoric kill sites like at Head-Smashed-In Buffalo Jump in Alberta, nor have they found settlement sites showing long periods of human habitation. If there had been large numbers of animals, then archaeologists would have found corresponding evidence of a larger human impact on the area than they have. (Anthropologists associate the size of hunting societies with the size of local animal populations; if there were not many people living in the area, it was probably because there were not many animals around to provide sustenance.)

Archaeologists have further speculated that there was an actual decline in the number of people travelling to the area in the late prehistoric period beginning about two thousand years ago. One explanation of this decline is a change in climate that caused the forested areas to spread south into the mountain grasslands and cut the area off from the plains to the east. The forest and marshy area to the east would have created a barrier to migrating plains bison. Moreover, the increased forest cover in the mountains reduced grazing areas in the upper valleys, further reducing the numbers of game. This is borne out by the notes of the early explorers who arrived here at the beginning of the nineteenth century and commented on the general scarcity of large grazing animals.

While large groups of people did not likely travel through the region in early times, there is evidence that small groups of hunters did. A typical prehistoric site sits high atop a one-hundred-metre hill looking down over the Athabasca Valley. On this windswept site archaeologists have found a number of stone points and tool fragments indicating that it was occupied on a regular basis from four to one thousand years ago. This would have been a temporary site, employed for scouting game and for manufacturing stone points.

Early people travelled to Jasper to do more than just hunt. The upper Athabasca funnels several travel routes into two principal mountain crossings. The Athabasca Pass route follows the Whirlpool River over the height of land and down the western slopes of the Rockies to the Columbia River. The Yellowhead Pass route branches up the Miette River, over a low pass and down to the Fraser River on the west. To the east, the Athabasca flows into the lake that shares its name in the northeast while the tributary Snake Indian/Smoky river system connects to the Peace Country to the northwest. Routes south can be taken along the Rocky and Maligne rivers or the Athabasca itself, which veers south down the spine of the Rockies. While the upper Athabasca valley was not home to any single Indigenous people, it was on the edge of several culture areas and seems likely to have been a meeting place for people travelling from hundreds of miles in several directions. Here, they could have traded, exchanged information, or simply gone their separate ways. Besides game, many would have also travelled to gather the quarry rock that was an important material for toolmaking. Other people may have come looking for medicinal plants.

Projectile Points

In describing the pre-contact history of the Rocky Mountains, archaeologists usually distinguish between three main periods: early prehistoric, between 7,500 and 11,000 years ago; middle prehistoric, between 1,750 and 7,500 years ago; and late prehistoric, between 225 and 1,750 years ago. Dating sites can be difficult in the hard mountain environment, where material quickly deteriorates, but archaeologists use commonly found spear- or arrow points, collectively known as projectile points, to date the people who were there. People from the early prehistoric period used thrusting spears with large stone points, those from the middle period used throwing spears with slightly smaller, notched tips, while those from the late prehistoric period used bows that shot arrows with notched stone heads. Variations in style within the three main types of projectile points permit more precise identification of the people who were there. Archaeologists have found examples from all three categories of projectile points in the Jasper area.

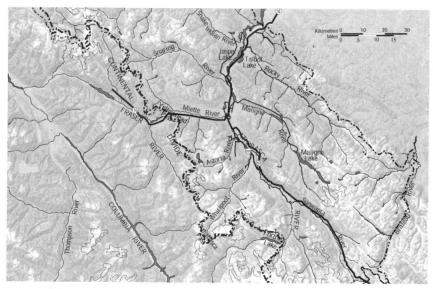

Rivers of the Upper Athabasca Region. ROB STONESHAW, PARKS CANADA

The importance of the upper Athabasca as a travel crossroads led David Thompson to the area in 1810. Thompson was an explorer with the North West Company (NWC), a rival to the mighty fur trading empire of the Hudson's Bay Company (HBC). The Montreal-based NWC sought to compete with the HBC by finding new fur-trading territory in western Canada. It commissioned a group of now-legendary explorers, including Alexander Mackenzie, Simon Fraser, and David Thompson, to search for routes to the Pacific. Thompson spent much of the first decade of the nineteenth century looking for routes over the Rockies to the Columbia. In 1807 he travelled up the North Saskatchewan River and found a portage over the mountains to the Columbia that was later named Howse Pass. However, while the portage was a relatively easy route over the mountains, it was also an important Aboriginal crossroads. Consequently, the established traders did not wish to contend with fur trade trespassers and they warned Thompson against coming back. Thompson then shifted to looking for an alternate route.

Returning to his base on the North Saskatchewan River at Rocky Mountain House, Thompson next ventured north into the Athabasca River valley. There he met a community of independent fur traders and hunters already ensconced in that region. They came from an Iroquois community near Montreal and had travelled to the area in the early 1800s in the wake of Alexander Mackenzie's explorations. Now aligned with neither the HBC nor the NWC, they were called "freemen." Sometime after reaching the Athabasca River in November 1810, Thompson engaged a local guide known as Thomas the Iroquois to lead him over the mountains. He established a base on the shores of Brule Lake where they made their preparations for travelling in winter, stockpiling meat and making snowshoes. To assist his return journey, Thompson had left William Henry behind to provision a camp near the present town of Jasper. This was marked on his map as "Henry's House," and became a generic reference point for future travellers to the area.

Then, still guided by Thomas the Iroquois, Thompson and his group journeyed up the Whirlpool River, over Athabasca Pass, and down to a place that he named Boat Encampment on the upper reaches of the Columbia River. Thompson completed his journey to the Pacific in July 1811, the last of his many epic journeys of exploration. The trip, while important for blazing a route across the mountains, was not completely successful as being the first of its kind. Thompson had been pitted in a race to the Pacific against his American competitors, and he later found out that he had been beaten to the mouth of the Columbia River by the American Fur Trading Company, known colloquially as the Astorians, after their leader John Jacob Astor.

Although Thompson was not the first fur trader to reach the mouth of the Columbia, the route that Thompson discovered nonetheless became hugely important to his employer. The NWC established Fort George at the mouth of the Columbia and developed a string of posts linking it to the Athabasca. In 1813 the company sent François Decoigne to establish a post at Brule Lake near Thompson's old base camp. In 1817 the post was headed by Jasper Hawes who was assisted by two Iroquois and three other hunters. Soon the post became known as Jasper House, forming a pun of the postmaster's name. The post was initially intended to supply the fur trade brigades that crossed the mountains twice a year to and from the Pacific. It was near to where the voyageurs left their canoes and, helped by pack horses, trudged over the mountains. Indeed, the route was initially called the Athabasca Portage and Jasper House would have formed the eastern end of this land route. To supply the brigades, the post therefore tended a herd of horses that grazed on the grassy meadows of the upper Athabasca valley. Gradually, the post also became important for the number of fine furs that were traded there by the travelling Native groups.

Jasper House interacted with three distinct groups of Native people. The Iroquois freemen formed a close attachment to Jasper House and many of them were regularly employed by the post as hunters. These people ranged north into the Grande Cache area, as well as east toward Lac Ste. Anne. As the fur-trading era progressed, they became associated with the northern Cree and many Iroquois men took Cree wives. Besides the Iroquois freemen, the other two groups that hunted and traded in the area of Jasper House included an offshoot of a Shushwap band that travelled from the upper Fraser River and a few families of Assiniboines, also known as Stoneys. Both groups were well established in the area before Thompson's visit. Isolated bands of Carriers, an Athabascan group from west of the Rockies would also have visited the area although they generally traded at Fort George and Fort St. James.

Not much is known of the Shushwap band that existed on the frontier of their peoples' traditional hunting and trading area and they were subsequently displaced or assimilated in the resettlement period during the second half of the nineteenth century. One of the few reliable accounts of the Shushwap people was provided by the late-nineteenth-century ethnologist James Teit, who traced the origins of the small group of Shushwaps who visited Jasper House. In a footnote to his main text on the Shushwap of the upper Thompson, he wrote:

> They were very nomadic and a number of families lived most
> of their time beyond North Thompson River, at the head of the
> Fraser River, and east through the Rocky Mountains to Jasper
> House. Of late years there seems to have been a concentration
> of the people around the latter place.[8]

Teit ended his note with a comment that implies that the Shushwap were being assimilated into the nascent Métis community there. Although Thompson does not mention them directly in his journal, his famous map drawn in 1814 identifies the Snare Indian River, which is now known as the Snaring River. Anthropologists generally agree that the Snare Indians and the offshoot of the Shushwap band described by Teit are one and the same people.[9]

The third local group was a band of Mountain Stoney. This group was also encountered by Thompson who, like other fur traders, called them Assiniboine, acknowledging their roots among the Siouan-speaking people on the eastern plains. One anthropologist has estimated that four Stoney families frequented the Jasper House area in the 1820s.[10] They have given their names to several places in the area. What is now the Snake Indian River used to be called the Stone Indian River on David Thompson's map. Later, Jasper House residents also called it Assiniboine Creek. The Rocky River might also be a corruption of the Stoney name. A main group of Mountain Stoneys gradually migrated south down along the Rocky Mountains throughout the eighteenth century and by the middle of the nineteenth century were ranging south of the Bow River. From their base on the Bow, they hunted north to the hunting and trading areas around Kootenay Plains and farther north into the Brazeau Valley. The American traveller Mary Schäffer used a map drawn by Sampson Beaver of the Stoney Morley Band to find Maligne Lake by way of the Brazeau and Poboktan Pass in 1908. The name "Poboktan" is derived from the Stoney word for owl.

Although the three main groups—Iroquois, Shushwap, and Stoney—were associated with Jasper House, other Aboriginal groups would have occasionally travelled to the area. Father Pierre-Jean de Smet, a Jesuit priest, wrote of meeting some Carrier people during his visit to Jasper House in 1846: "In the neighbourhood of the Miette River, we fell in with one of those poor families of Porteurs or 'Isatem,' of New Caledonia ... The condition of those poor people seemed very wretched; they had no clothes but a few rags and some pieces of skins, and yet, notwithstanding their extreme poverty, they laid at my feet the mountain sheep they had just killed."[11]

Life for all Aboriginal groups was likely precarious, but it was especially so for the Shushwap-Snare, who seemed to be at odds with the other two groups. On 31 January 1828, Jasper House postmaster Michel Klyne noted: "I met they [three] Soushaps [sic] at Mr Laroques House all starving. I traded from them 98 Beaver Skins and 30 martens." His entry for 26 November 1830 read, "Two Assiniboine arrived with nothing. They are starving." On March 25 1831, he wrote, "One soushap [sic] arrived all most Dead of starving." The winter and spring of 1831 seems to have been especially bad. On 10 April Klyne wrote, "A Soushap [*sic*] woman arrived with three of her childrens starving. A few days past two of her childrens and her husband died of hunger at Mr La Roque house." On 21 April Klyne wrote, "Two Iroquois and Dick Conlin, a free man arrived from the Smokey River. The Starvagen [starvation] oblige them to leave their furs in a cache at Batish [Athabasca] River." On 30 April he reported that three Assiniboines had been seen starving.[12]

It is likely that the Shushwap trapping on the west side of the mountains had better access to furs than the other groups but worse access to game, which was not as plentiful in the more heavily forested areas of the western slopes of the Rockies. The Iroquois and Stoneys, on the other hand, were probably used to acting as middle men in the fur trade. They would have been happy to trade food for furs with the Shushwap, but would have discouraged, by violence if necessary, efforts on the part of the Shushwap to trade directly with the fur trade companies at their posts. The Iroquois and Stoneys likely had the advantage of larger numbers living closer to Jasper House and they would have benefitted from early and regular contact with the fur trade by having ready access to muskets and horses. The Shushwap seemed to have neither. While the Jasper House post journal makes no direct reference to violent encounters, there are not many references to healthy Shushwap males. Those who do approach the post appear more like refugees than bona fide traders. The most explicit reference to hostility between the Aboriginal groups is the entry for 11 March 1830, when post-master Klyne noted: "7 Saushap [*sic*] Indians arrived to make piece [*sic*] with the Assiniboins."[13]

There are numerous references in the literature to a massacre of Shushwap Indians carried out by the Stoneys. George Simpson places the event during the NWC's regime, some time between 1813 and 1823, at a peace conference held on the banks of what is now the Snake Indian River. According to Simpson, the Shushwap were attacked at this meeting and most were killed. Some who fled into the forest were hunted down and killed. Henry John Moberly embellished this story by telling of two Shushwap women who were captured with the intention of being made into slaves. Tied up naked in a tepee, they managed to escape and secretly survived in the area for many months until again being captured by an Iroquois hunter. Although Moberly's version resembles the plot of a Victorian bodice-ripper, the broad elements of the massacre have assumed the stuff of local legend and are associated with the name of the Snake Indian River.[14]

The fortunes of the sleepy outpost improved slightly with the amalga-mation of the NWC with the HBC in 1821. Under the direction of Gover-nor George Simpson, the expanded company was reorganized and revitalized to better capitalize on its western assets. As a consequence, Jas-per House became a significant post in what was known in the company as the Saskatchewan District. The Athabasca route became more accessible following the construction of a rough wagon road in 1824 to the river north from Fort Edmonton to where Fort Assiniboine was established.[15] Simpson also opened up a second fur-trading route from Jasper House, over what subsequently became known as the Yellowhead Pass. In the fur-trading era this was called the Caledonia Portage and it connected with the headwaters of the Fraser River and the heart of the fur-trading district known as New Caledonia, served by its posts at Fort George and Fort St. James. As New Caledonia was chronically short of moose, whose hide was important in the manufacture of moccasins and other leather goods, the route was also known as the Leather Pass. Under the Simpson regime, Jasper House not only doubled in size as a trans-shipment depot, where the brigades divided to cross either the Columbia or the Caledonia portage, it also grew as a fur-trading centre and by 1827 it was occupied year-round.

Tete Jaune (d. 1828)

Tête Jaune, French for Yellow Head, was the nickname of an Iroquois trapper and hunter also called Pierre Bostonais. His nickname sug-gests that he was of mixed European ancestry. He came to the Jasper area around 1815 where he joined the small community of Iroquois freemen living there. He hunted and trapped on the west slopes of the mountains, using the pass that now bears his name. He established a cache, or storage place for meat and furs, at the junction of the Fraser and Robson rivers. Indigenous people living on the western slopes resented his incursions into their territory, and in 1828 Tete Jaune, his brother, and both their families were murdered. For many years the area near the eastern end of the Yellowhead Pass was known as Tete Jaune Cache. The Grand Trunk Pacific later established a construction camp there and its name has been adopted by a nearby community. His name influenced the book *Tay Jaune,* written by local author Howard O'Hagan, the son of Thomas O'Hagan, Jasper's first doctor.

In 1830 Jasper House was relocated from its site on Brule Lake farther up the river to a site near Jasper Lake. It is not known exactly why the move occurred. Some people believe that the site was prone to flooding,[16] and that the new location was strategically situated at the crossroads of the Athabasca where the Snake Indian flowed in from the northwest and where, across the river, the Rocky River entered the Athabasca from the southeast. The new post was also closer to the beginning of the two portages at the Whirlpool and Miette rivers. It was also likely that the pasturage for horses was better there, as well as to the west where the Chinook winds kept the snow off the grass. The hunting was likely better, too, and the new post was closer to Talbot Lake, which was important as a source of whitefish.

From the 1820s until the 1850s, Jasper House served as a staging point for the two mountain crossings over the Athabasca and Yellowhead passes. The supply of healthy mounts was an important function of the post at this time. Postmaster Klyne figured that he required at least fifty-four horses for the two portages and many more would have been grazing in the valley to supply this number when required. Moberly wrote that "The Hudson's Bay Company kept some three hundred and fifty mares separated into bands, in the valley along the pass as far as the forks of the river where one branch

Charles Horetzky's photograph of Jasper House, 1872. LAC, NA 382-5

flows into the Fraser and the other to the Columbia."[17] The Iroquois freemen also grazed horses in the Athabasca Valley. The horses would have
grazed along a series of meadows along the river between Brule Lake and
the site of the present town of Jasper. During Klyne's time, there was an
outpost located at the mouth of Cottonwood Creek that he refers to as "La
Roque's House." His journal entry for October 1827, for example, notes:
"Jacques Cardinal and my boy went off to Mr. LaRoque house to bring
down some of his horses and see his mares." This area tended to be kept
free of snow in the winter by the Chinook winds that blew there and so was
a favoured place to winter horses. The grazing of so many horses led to
stringent predator control. Wolves were trapped, shot, or poisoned.

Born in Ontario, the son of a retired Royal Navy officer, Henry Moberly
(1835–1931) joined the HBC at the age of eighteen, looking for adventure
in the West. He was initially based at Fort Edmonton, the area headquarters, but in 1858 he was sent to Jasper House to revive the abandoned outpost and drum up trade with the locals. He made the place his home for
three years, helped by his country marriage to Suzanne Karakonti. She was
ten years older than young Moberly and was the mother of a three-year-old
girl, but Suzanne brought several advantages to the union. It was well
known to fur traders that Native women were indispensable to backcountry living. Samuel Hearne, the famous explorer, gave a widely publicized
account of their use. Quoting Matonabbee, the legendary Chippewyan
chief, he said, "Women were made for labor." Further again, according to
Matonabbee: "They also pitch our tents, make and mend our clothing, keep
us warm at night, and, in fact, there is no such thing as travelling any considerable distance, or for any length of time, in this country, without their
assistance."[18]

As a woman who had lived her whole life in the area, Suzanne Karakonti would have had an intimate knowledge of its people and places. As
the daughter of Louis Karakonti, Suzanne would have brought Moberly
into a network of family relationships that would have helped him profes-
sionally in the area. She also gave him a Native view of the area, which
would have been rather like having his own spirit of place illuminating an
otherwise alien land. When he left Jasper House in 1861, he also left Suzanne
and the two children who he had fathered with her. However, just before
he left he married her in a formal ceremony, possibly to give her and her
children some protection from the HBC. Ron Pelletier gives the following
impression of his great-great-grandfather's departure:

Henry did leave after their marriage but I believe he tried to persuade her to go with him. In his book he talks of getting two pack horses loaded at Fort Edmonton and camping a few miles away from the Fort. He then says he proceeded to Lac Ste. Anne where he spent the night at the Roman Catholic Mission. It is my belief this was his last attempt to persuade Susanne to go with him. He was heading for B.C. to work for his brother Walter, but instead was convinced to take charge of Fraser Lake by Peter Ogden. When Henry left that day he never saw his oldest son ever again, the sad thing is he never saw his unborn son John.[19]

Moberly left for northern British Columbia and later moved to Saskatchewan where he died at the age of ninety-six. Suzanne stayed at Jasper House and later took up with one of Moberly's successors, John McAulay, by whom she had her fourth child in 1867.

The glory years of Jasper House lasted until 1853 when another reorganization of HBC supply routes brought about a decreased use of the two passes and diminished the importance of the outpost on the Athabasca. While the fortunes of the fur-trading post rose and fell, Jasper House remained an obscure but constant landmark in the mountain wilderness. In addition, as the passes it guarded remained relatively safe connections to the Fraser and Columbia routes, the place received a steady stream of travellers not connected with company business. People like the Astorian Gabriel Franchère, botanist David Douglas, artist Paul Kane, missionary Father de Smet, and explorer James Hector brought new perspectives to the upper Athabasca valley.

In 1814 the American Fur Trade Company post at Fort Vancouver was taken over by the NWC, and some of its employees, not liking the new arrangement, chose to return to their homes in Montreal. Gabriel Franchère and his party of Astorians travelled back through the Athabasca portage and by way of revenge, gave names connected to the American company to some of the local landmarks. The Astoria River was named after the company's president, John Jacob Astor, and the Tonquin Valley was named after the company boat that was lost to hostile Natives off the coast of Vancouver Island. Franchère wrote a book on his adventures that gives some very early descriptions of the place we now call Jasper. Coming over the Athabasca Pass, he provides the following description of the route down the Whirlpool River to the Athabasca:

On the 16th of May we started out again, passing through swamps and dense thickets. We killed a partridge. We crossed the little river and our guide led us through the woods to the banks of the Athabasca or La Biche River, which we forded and found shallower than expected. As this crossing was the last, we dried ourselves and went on our way through more attractive country than on previous days, occasionally coming upon Buffalo carcasses, and camped on the edge of a prairie that our guide told us was called Cow Prairie.[20]

The next day Franchère and his companions continued down the trail, climbing a promontory that we now understand to be Old Fort Point. From there, they followed the Athabasca River through the forest to an old house, which historians conjecture was a cabin built by William Henry in support of Thompson's 1811 expedition.[21] Franchère sparked a long tradition of misunderstanding when he referred to the house as a former trading post: "The site of this trading post is the most charming that can be imagined: suffice to say that it is built on the bank of the beautiful river Athabasca, and is surrounded by green and smiling prairies and superb woodlands."[22] Another place that had already been named by this time was the prominent Roche Miette that overlooked the Athabasca near the crossroads of the Rocky River.

Another early traveller not in the employ of the fur trade to pass this way was the British botanist David Douglas, who accompanied a fur-trading brigade over the Athabasca portage in May 1827. The going was difficult as there was deep snow in the Athabasca pass and down the banks of the Whirlpool River, causing Douglas to be extremely tired by the time he and the brigade made camp on the banks of the Athabasca. Yet, he must have been able to draw on a bit of reserve energy, for he recorded that on that day he shot one partridge and collected "two specimens of a handsome Anemone: flowers large, fruit blue and white."

The painter Paul Kane also passed through Jasper House, on his way west in the fall of 1846. Carried along by another fur-trading brigade, he was made fairly despondent by the cold, forbidding environment. But the comfort of the post soon restored his good humour and his journal entry noted: "But I was soon cheered by a blazing fire and five or six pounds of mountain sheep, which I certainly then thought far more delicious than any domestic animal of the same species."[23]

In addition to men of science and art, missionaries were also led toward Jasper House to minister to the needs of the Montreal-based fur traders. Fathers Demers and Blanchet stayed at the post in 1838. The most famous missionary in the area, however, was a Belgian Jesuit named P. J. de Smet. He spent two weeks at Jasper House in 1846 and made many friends as well as converts in the area. Hindered by his immense weight, de Smet was an early dieter and his journal speaks longingly of the large feasts held at the post. One of the people he baptized was the twenty-two-year-old daughter of Louis Karakonti called Suzanne.

All of these early travellers, who were guided by the fur-trading brigades, camped at a number of regular stopping places along the Athabasca portage. Buffalo Prairie was a major stopping place on the Athabasca River as it was just downstream from the mouth of the Whirlpool. It was known as a "campement" in the language of the fur trade. Other campements along the route were also likely meadows influenced by fire and attractive to game. HBC clerk Edward Ermantinger, travelling the route in 1827, described a stopping place near the upper reaches of the Whirlpool River called *campement de fusil*. Farther down river they spent the night at *campement d'orignal*. This last campment likely referred to the presence of moose, as *orignal* means moose in French. *Campement de cardinale* was located on Jasper Lake, likely close to where the second Jasper House was relocated by 1830.[24]

In 1859 two Scotsmen travelled to the area on quite different missions. Dr. James Hector spent two months exploring around the post in 1859 as part of a larger expedition led by Captain James Palliser that had been tasked by the British government to explore the western plains and mountains of British North America and report on the area's potential for settlement. Hector was a physician practicing in London and, having an athletic and adventurous disposition, agreed to accompany Palliser as his second-in-command. Hector undertook much of the difficult exploration of the Rocky Mountains. The year before he had explored the passes to the south and on one bad occasion had been kicked in the chest by a pack horse. This event is memorialized in the name "Kicking Horse," which was given to both the river and the pass. The year 1859 found him in the more comfortable surroundings of Jasper House. He accompanied the postmaster, Henry Moberly, on a lynx hunt up the Snake Indian River. He then explored the Whirlpool River up toward Athabasca Pass with an Iroquois guide named Tekarra.

That same year James Carnegie, the Earl of Southesk, entered what is now Jasper Park by way of Rocky Pass and the Medicine Tent River. He was hunting big game and sought the trophy-sized rams that inhabited the eastern slopes. The country south of the Athabasca was little known to Europeans at this time and Southesk was guided by local hunters into the game-rich Brazeau country. He was perhaps the first real tourist to visit Jasper. Southesk Pass and the Southesk River commemorate his journey.

Although Jasper House was not formally closed until 1884, it had been in decline for many years before that. By the 1870s, it was more of an outpost of Lac Ste. Anne than an independent operation in its own right. But this does not mean that the locals were not still engaged in the fur trade. According to historian Michael Payne, "The local population simply traded their furs at other locations or with the growing number of independent traders operating from Edmonton, Lac La Biche, Lesser Slave Lake and other locations."[25] Still, the absence of a post likely led to a diaspora of the local inhabitants.

Until the 1860s, communication between Jasper House and Fort Edmonton, the main fur-trading post in the district that now forms the province of Alberta, followed the circuitous route of the Athabasca River. This meant that travellers wishing to go from Fort Edmonton to Jasper House first had to travel north to Athabasca Landing or Fort Assiniboine. However, following the establishment of a fur-trading post and mission at Lac Ste. Anne, west of Edmonton, fur traders occasionally journeyed between the two posts by land. Henry Moberly, postmaster at Jasper House, journeyed this way in 1858. By that time, Lac Ste. Anne had become a comparatively large community that comprised four hundred Métis and about thirty families of Iroquois.[26]

Gradually, a hardened trail was pushed west from Edmonton, past Lac Ste. Anne and eventually reaching all the way to Jasper House. This changed the orientation of the people living in the area and Lac Ste. Anne became a social centre as Jasper House declined. Another centre that superseded Jasper House was the Grande Cache area to the north where many of the Iroquois freemen had come to settle. The Snake Indian–Smokey River route had long formed an important hunting area for the post and by the 1850s a significant population was expanding into the Grande Cache area. This is where explorer James Hector described the Iroquois communities making their agricultural experiments in the 1850s.

The Overlanders of 1862

In 1862 several parties from Ontario passed through the upper Athabasca valley and the Yellowhead Pass en route to the gold fields of British Columbia. Their route took them to Fort Garry (now Winnipeg) and across the prairies by Red River Cart to Fort Edmonton. There they traded their carts for pack horses and followed the Athabasca River to Jasper. One party, led by the McMicking brothers, comprised 125 people and a 140-horse pack train. They followed the overgrown fur trade route with difficulty but were helped by local Aboriginals over the pass to Tete Jaune Cache. There they split into two groups, one rafting down the Fraser River to Fort George (present day Prince George) while the other cut a trail to the North Thompson River and then went on to Kamloops. The rafters overturned in the rapids and six men were drowned. The Kamloops party included the only woman of the group and she gave birth to her fourth child upon arriving at her destination. Vestiges of the parts of the Overlanders' trail through Jasper can still be found.

Historic Sites and Monuments Board plaque commemorating the Overlanders of 1862. COURTESY ROD WALLACE

CHAPTER TWO

Standing at the Crossroads of Time

The future president of Queen's University, George Monro Grant, was a Presbyterian minister in Halifax, Nova Scotia, in 1871 when one of his congregation, the engineer Sandford Fleming, invited him along on a cross-country tour. Fleming had been tasked by the government of Canada to find a practical route for a railway across the new country of Canada. British Columbia, the westernmost British colony in North America, had agreed to join Confederation on condition that a railway be built to connect it with the eastern provinces. In between lay the mountains and prairies that had been the domain of the Hudson's Bay Company (HBC) of fur traders. Recently ceded to Canada, it was now known as the North West Territories and it was across this largely uncharted land that one of Canada's foremost engineers turned his attention.

Crossing the Rocky Mountains posed one of the more difficult challenges for a railway route that had to keep its grades below about 5 per cent per mile. Fleming ended up selecting the Yellowhead Pass as the most practical way through the mountains. Ultimately, however, the government overruled Fleming's recommendation and instead ordered him to select a more southerly route, and so the eventual route of the Canadian Pacific Railway (CPR) through the Rockies was by way of the much more difficult Kicking Horse Pass. Yet, in 1872 this decision was still in the future—that year Fleming and Grant travelled through the Rockies by way of the Athabasca Valley, admiring its picturesque qualities. Grant later wrote of the "wonderful combination of beauty about these mountains" in his book *Ocean to Ocean.*[27]

Standing on the banks of Jasper Lake in 1872, Grant also stood at the crossroads of time. There lay the trading post of Jasper House, occasionally opened to trade furs and goods with the Iroquois/Métis hunters and trappers who still frequented the area. But there, too, were the advance scouts of Canadian civilization, planning its westward advance. These two paths existed side by side in the Athabasca Valley and were symbolized by the Métis who emerged as a prominent group in the area toward the end of the nineteenth century.

The Métis stood at the centre of human development in the area. As a group they were not in the Jasper area at the beginning of the nineteenth century and, although they did not come from elsewhere, they were there at the century's end. In a process that some historians have termed "ethno-genesis,"[28] they emerged from the diverse people that lived in the area through the century and absorbed several ethnic identities. They traced their origins to the Iroquois freemen and yet they spoke Cree. They inter-married with Euro-Canadians, taking European names, learning ways of commerce and agriculture, and yet retained their Native identity. Already multicultural, the Jasperites consciously assumed the Métis identity after coming into contact with French-speaking Métis at the Lac Ste. Anne and St. Albert missions in the 1860s. Perhaps no Métis epitomizes this meta-morphosis better than Suzanne Moberly. Born of an Iroquois father, she married a Canadian fur trader named Moberly and, at the time of her death, had taken the traditional Métis surname of Cardinal. Two of her children, John and Evan Moberly, were sons of the fur trader. Moberly descendents still reside in the area.

Death of Suzanne Karakonti (c. 1824–1905)

Albert Norris was the Métis son of Suzette Swift who worked in the Jasper area through the early twentieth century. He gave the follow-ing account of Suzanne's death to George Camp who wrote it down in 1964:

Suzanne was camped on the Miette River with her grandson Adolphus Moberly when she was taken sick, Adolph fixed up a travois for one of their horses and brought his grandmother down country to a cabin formerly owned by Donald McDonald, which stood in the poplars on the left side of the old Edmonton highway ... There Mrs Moberly died. There was much sorrow in the valley all the native people gathered there and said prayers for her. There being no priest available, they were led by Adam Joachim, who had studied for the priesthood in St. Albert and Montreal. Albert's stepfather Mr Lewis Swift split boards by hand and planed them down and made the coffin for her.[29]

Her remains were taken across the Athabasca to the house of her son

Evan and buried nearby in a grave that is still cared for. Her first grave marker was a cross with the name Suzanne Cardinal engraved on it, suggesting that she might have had a relationship with a man called Cardinal later in her life. Her old friend Adam Joachim told George Camp that this was her name. However, recently some of her descendents have disputed this and a new grave marker has restored her maiden name: "Suzanne Karakonti."

Suzanne Karakonti's grave in 1965. JYMA, PA 20-21

Henry John Moberly, father of a Jasper Métis family, lived to a ripe old age. In 1926 he published a book looking back on his fur trade days, portraying a world that had already disappeared. No mention was made of his first wife and family. While Henry John was a relic of the past, his brother Walter symbolized the future. In that fateful year of 1871–1872 he was also in the Athabasca Valley working for Fleming and it is possible that he met his former sister-in-law living near the old fur trade post. Walter was one of British Columbia's leading surveyors, having been involved in the creation of the famous Dewdney Trunk Road, as well as other important colonial public works. He had been hired by Fleming to be his chief surveyor in the mountains and he and his crew had spent several months exploring the mountain passes of the region.

Walter Moberly set up a base camp in advance of the Fleming-Grant visit on the banks of the Athabasca River near the present bridge crossing to the Maligne Lake road. This camp also served as a cache for supplies packed in from Edmonton. Known as Athabasca Depot, it consisted of a bunkhouse, storage buildings, and a barn. Later, the ruins of the cache were confused with the ruins of David Thompson's base camp, Henry House, creating a misunderstanding that persisted through the next century. This confusion was reinforced by the Grand Trunk Pacific, which named a station in that vicinity Henry House. The area is now known as Henry House flats.

Although the CPR was built farther south, the Athabasca route was well publicized in Fleming's later writing. In 1877 he wrote of his investigation of a number of possible mountain routes: "These examinations, together with the surveys and explorations which have been made throughout the contiguous districts, show that beyond question the advantages of the Yellowhead Pass . . . outweigh those of any other passes."[30] The publicity that Fleming provided for the area resulted in two rival railway lines being located along the Yellowhead Pass route in the first decade of the twentieth century. Before this, the publicity that Fleming had given to the route led to some speculative settlement, because, when the railways came through, agricultural business became possible.

In the early 1890s, Lewis Swift and his wife established a homestead in the Athabasca Valley where the Palisades Training Centre is today, just off the Snaring road. Swift was an American who had sold lightning rods in New York and had driven a stagecoach in Deadwood, South Dakota. Born in 1854, Swift spent almost his entire life on the frontier, first in the United States and then in Canada. He drifted into Canada around 1890, seeking his fortune in the goldfields of British Columbia. In about 1890, he met his wife, Suzette Chalifoux, who was living in Edmonton at the time. Suzette was originally from a Métis community in St. Albert, but her name betrays her Iroquois freemen origins. When Lewis and Suzette met, she already had a son, Albert Norris, and the three moved to the upper Athabasca area around 1891, at first squatting in the ruins of Jasper House. In fact, it may have been Suzette who suggested the remote location for their future homestead on the upper Athabasca where some of her kinsmen still resided.

They spent the first two years at the old Jasper House. Then, a couple of years before the two were formally married in 1897, they moved to a piece of land farther up the Athabasca near the mouth of the Snaring River, in an area of meadow near Athabasca Depot called Henry House Flats. South-facing, it lay under the shadow of a distinctive cliff formation called "The Palisades." Swift cleared some fields, built a farmhouse, and managed to get a patent from the government to become the first landowner in the area. He was attracted by the challenge of pioneering life and seemed to enjoy being self-sufficient, growing or making the things he needed to live. He may have had another motive for settling where he did. He would have known that his property was on the original 1870s CPR survey line and would have surmised that any other railway coming through the area would have to cross his land.

By 1899 the Swifts had cultivated sixteen acres and begun to raise a family of their own. They grew barley and vegetables and raised cattle and chickens there until they retired to the town of Jasper in 1935, where Suzette had a well-regarded sideline making beadwork and moccasins. In 1939, one year before he died, the *Edmonton Journal* printed an article on Lewis Swift under the headline, "Jasper Park's First Settler Celebrates 85th Birthday."[31]

Swift's homestead became the focal point for the region during the first decade of the twentieth century. In 1908 American traveller Mary T. Schäffer arrived on the banks of the Athabasca after completing her epic journey from Banff. Swift's place was described as an oasis in the wilderness:

> Thirteen years previously Swift, and his wife had penetrated
> here to make a home. By degrees, he had brought in his stock
> from Edmonton over three hundred miles of as bad a trail as can
> well be imagined,—cows, horses and chickens. His wheat-field
> was yellowing, the oats were still green and waving in the soft
> warm wind. By a mountain stream he had built a mill for grind-
> ing his flour, and a large potato-patch was close by. His buildings
> were of logs, sound and solid, made entirely by himself, his
> residence composed of one large room.[32]

Mary Schäffer also remarked on Suzette's abilities as a homemaker and seamstress.

While the Swifts were the most prominent homesteaders in the area, some of the old Iroquois families had also begun to settle on the land

Lewis and Suzette Swift. PABC, 11087

during the 1890s. The patriarch of this community was the eldest son of Henry and Suzanne Moberly, Evan Henry Moberly. Born near the McLeod River in 1859, Evan, or Ewan as he was sometimes known, had shifted his home farther east, to Lac Ste. Anne or St. Albert. His usual hunting grounds would have ranged up the tributaries of the Athabasca River in the mountains, especially the Snake Indian and Smoky river systems into the southern Peace River area where game had remained relatively plentiful. He had taken Half-Breed land scrip, a government program that aimed to liquidate Métis land claims, in 1892 but around 1897 returned to his old haunts on the Athabasca to establish a homestead.

Evan Moberly built a substantial log house by 1899 and ploughed twelve acres to raise hay. Here he raised ten children and kept sixty horses and eight head of cattle.[33] In about 1899 his brother John established a homestead across the river from the present Jasper airstrip. It was not well used and Mary Schäffer remarked on its almost abandoned look when she visited the place in 1908. In addition to these places, two of Evan's sons also established neighbouring homesteads in the area. In 1891 Evan built a cabin on another quarter section downriver that he gave to his son Adolphus. "Dolphus," as he was known, moved onto the land in 1906. He spent three weeks each year, and kept sixteen horses.[34] Similarly, Dolphus's brother William also occupied land that had been set aside by their father. He lived

The Evan Moberly homestead, 1960s. JYMA, 37-12

32

in a cabin acquired from Donald McDonald and he claimed to have resided there since 1906. Joining this community was Adam Joachim, Evan Moberly's son-in-law. He claimed a quarter section near Spring Creek where he had lived since 1899. He had twelve horses and three cattle.[35] A sixth family was that of Isidore Finlay, who was also related to the Moberly's through marriage and shared their fur-trading heritage. Although Finlay's land had not been surveyed, he also presented himself as a settler who had made improvements on the land and who kept livestock near John Moberly's homestead.

The Arrival of the Iron Horse

When rival railway companies looked to a more northerly route across the Canadian prairies than the CPR, they sought a more northerly passage through the Rocky Mountains. Fleming's boosting of the Yellowhead route was still fresh in men's minds, so in the later 1890s, survey crews were again taking readings and driving stakes in the upper Athabasca valley. Two railways, the Grand Trunk Pacific (GTP) and the Canadian Northern (CNo), planned to use the Yellowhead route at the beginning of the new century. Both planned lines running across the northern prairies from Winnipeg, joining Saskatoon and Edmonton and then pushing west to the Yellowhead Pass. It was at this point that the two railway lines had different plans. The GTP's route would head straight west along a series of river valleys until it finally followed the Skeena River to the Pacific. Here the railway would establish a new port town that it would name Prince Rupert. Meanwhile, the CNo planned to turn its route south at Tete Jaune Cache, following the North Thompson River down to Kamloops and from there heading to its terminus at Vancouver.

While the two railway companies followed quite separate paths in British Columbia, their routes between Winnipeg and the Rocky Mountains were often ridiculously close together. This was especially true in the Yellowhead Pass where the two lines were within spitting distance. Although both railway companies were privately run, they received a lot of support from the Wilfrid Laurier Liberals who formed the federal government between 1896 and 1911. The Laurier government aggressively promoted the settlement of the West and such was its optimism that it encouraged the building of the two western lines, giving out land grants and rich subsidies to railway developers. GTP especially seemed to get preferential treatment from the Laurier government, since the new park of Jasper was established in 1907 largely for its benefit. GTP had a dynamic president named Samuel Hays and prided itself both in the quality of its track and rolling stock. This was in comparison to CNo, which tended to cut corners on costs and was much more conscious of the bottom line.

GTP got to the mountains first and therefore had its pick of the best route. It rejected Fleming's proposed route along Jasper House or the northwest side of Jasper Lake and instead opted to go around Disaster Point and then thread a route between Jasper and Talbot lakes, crossing to the other side at Moberly Flats near the mouth of the Snaring River, following the route that the highway now follows. This meant blasting thousands of tons of rock from the steep banks off the end of the Miette Range. Much of this rock was then used to fill a rail bed along the shore of the Athabasca River.

A construction road was built in advance of GTP's rail line. Particularly challenging was getting around Disaster Point where there was not much room between the Miette Range and the water in which to build a road. Although the railway right-of-way had been located on the east side of the lake, the contractors decided to build the wagon road along the other

Completed Grand Trunk Pacific railway line running between the Athabasca River and Talbot Lake, the present route of Highway 16. GLENBOW, NA 915-21

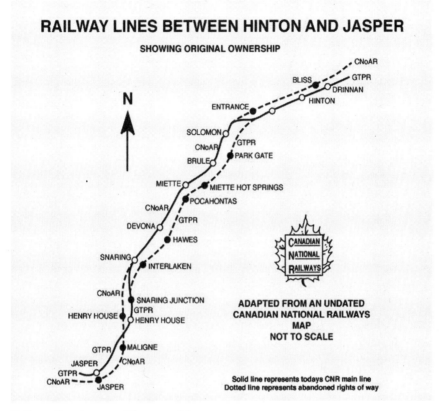

Railway lines between Hinton and Jasper. HEATHER WALL, PARKS CANADA, CALGARY

side. There were two reasons for this. First, the existing pack trail was too steep and treacherous for the wagons, and, second, to build a new road along the water's edge beside the right-of-way would have required considerable new construction. So instead, a cable ferry was established near the site of the old ford crossing over to Jasper House. From there the road followed an old trail along the other side of the Athabasca River, near where the present Celestine Lake road is located, toward the site of the present town of Jasper.

Camps were established at regular intervals along this wagon road, perhaps as close as every two miles. The camps contained bunkhouses, dining halls, barns, and storehouses. Most of the buildings had walls of chinked logs, although there were occasional frame buildings with milled lumber. Roofs were often canvas, denoting the temporary aspect of these camps, although rolled roofing was also used, as well as the occasional sod roof.

The camps were named after mileage points along the track west of Wolf Creek. Some of these camps assumed greater significance than others. Camp 111, for example, very near the present town of Jasper, was used as the headquarters of the railway's construction contractor during the winter of 1910–1911. This camp had a hospital with a resident doctor and a restaurant and temporary lodging for transients. Camp 109, on the other hand, was the base for the teamsters that winter, with space for eighty teams of horses. GTP engineers maintained a headquarters at Mile 113 that consisted of a group of substantial log and wood frame buildings.

Much of the work to the summit of the Yellowhead Pass was completed in 1911 and GTP opened the line the year after that. The CNo line was completed in 1912. Its route followed along the opposite shore of Jasper Lake and came close to Lewis Swift's place. Legend has it that he held the survey crews off with a rifle.

Despite the sparse settlement in the Rockies, both railways established stations at regular twenty-mile intervals along their tracks. GTP built a station at the eastern entrance to Jasper Park, named eponymously, "Parkgate." From there, station sites were surveyed at place names along GTP's line through the park at Miette Hot Springs, Pocahontas, Hawes, Henry House, the Jasper townsite, and at Geikie on the western boundary of the park. Stations were only built at Parkgate, Pocahontas, Hawes, Henry House, and near Swift's place. GTP's main station in the area was named Fitzhugh, after one of the company's vice-presidents. Fitzhugh evolved from the Mile 111 construction camp (1911–1912), but aside from the station building itself, there was little to distinguish it from a camp in the early years. Most of the first railway passengers were construction workers headed to and from the end of the line.

The Land of Open Doors

One of the more respectable passengers on the new GTP line was a young lay missionary named Burgon Bickersteth, an Englishman of course. He was a recent Oxford graduate who had decided to take what would now be called a "gap year" before carrying on with a career. After joining the Anglican mission in Edmonton, he was sent to the mountain construction camps to minister to labourers, many of whom did not speak English and showed little inclination toward his brand of religion. He bore up very patiently for such an unworldly

Locomotive 6013 (sister to 6015 that now stands in front of the Jasper station) hauling a freight train through Jasper in 1952. CSTM, CN 002774

man and his letters home were published as a series of advertisements for the opportunities being opened up along the new rail lines. The series was titled the *Land of Open Doors*. Bickersteth had great hopes for the West himself and in 1913 began teaching at Edmonton's University of Alberta. However, the outbreak of World War I dashed these hopes as young Bickersteth enlisted in the army. Bickersteth survived the war and returned to teach at the University of Alberta. But on returning to campus, he found that the pre-war optimism of the university was gone, so in 1921 he became principal of Hart House at the University of Toronto, a position he kept until 1947.

The building of the railways created a new transportation route, supplanting the ancient river routes of the past, and opened the mountain regions to the new Dominion of Canada. In addition, and perhaps just as important for this small part of the world, the railways brought about the creation of Jasper National Park. However, the optimism brought by the railways and the new park was short-lived as Alberta's economy nose-dived with the outbreak of war in 1914. Immigration dried up, the economy turned sour, and the two railways, which had struggled financially from the beginning, went belly up. World War I forced upon the companies a financial stringency that should have been taken in the beginning. The two railway lines were merged into one, which meant that much of the GTP line between Park Gate and Henry House Station was abandoned. Likewise, the CNo line from Henry House to the western boundary was also let go. These abandoned rail beds eventually formed the basis of the Yellowhead Highway through the park. The Government of Canada nationalized both railways and merged them into the Canadian National Railways in 1923. Coupled with its war debt, this kept the federal government in tough financial straits through much of the 1920s. Alberta took some time to recover as well, and it was a long time before the region recovered its sense of optimism.

Jasper's Railway Legacy

Jasper began as a railway town, and trains are still very much in evidence today. One reminder of the town's colourful railway history stands in front of the station, itself an historic railway building. Steam locomotive number 6015 was built for the CNR at its Kingston, Ontario, works in 1923. It was the first generation of locomotives specially designed for the CNR to work the steep mountain section of the line. Made obsolete by the diesel-electric locomotives of the 1950s, it was placed on display in Jasper in 1972.

Locomotive 6015 and some local Jasper steam enthusiasts. JYMA, 001.59.04

CHAPTER THREE

The Making of a National Park: 1907–1930

No one now knows who first suggested the idea of creating a national park in the upper Athabasca region of the newly created province of Alberta in 1907. Most likely, a principal proponent was the Grand Trunk Pacific Railway (GTP), which was then building its line through the Rocky Mountains in this vicinity and could see the advantage of having a mountain national park as a tourist destination, just as the Canadian Pacific Railway (CPR) was reaping the benefit of having a resort at Banff in Rocky Mountains Park to the south. Another likely promoter of the park was the Department of the Interior. As the federal government department directly involved in the administration of Crown lands in Alberta, the mighty Department of the Interior was also deeply involved in the park's creation. It prepared the drafts of the Cabinet memos that reserved the area from settlement, it defined the objectives of the park, and it sponsored the early surveys. If the park had a champion, it was likely an individual or group from one or both of these two organizations. Perhaps it was Samuel Hays, the dynamic and imaginative president of GTP. Or it could have been Frank Oliver, the federal minister of the Interior at the time. Oliver came from Edmonton and as a powerful western politician at the time of Alberta's birth, helped shape the fortunes of that part of the province. He had influenced the choice of Edmonton as the provincial capital and was closely identified with boosting the Grand Trunk as a northern alternative to the Canadian Pacific. Oliver was quick to see the potential of the northern Rockies as a significant asset, not only for Edmonton but also for its railway connections.

Many nineteenth-century visitors to the Jasper area raved about its charm. In 1872 George Grant compared it to the Yosemite Valley:

> There is a wonderful combination of beauty about these mountains. Great masses of boldly defined base rock are united to all the beauty that variety of form, colour, and vegetation give. A noble river with many tributaries each defining a distinct range, and a beautiful lake ten miles long, embosomed three thousand three

hundred feet above the sea, among mountains twice as high, offer innumerable scenes, seldom to be found within the same compass, for the artist to depict and for every traveler to delight in.[36]

Subsequent visitors agreed with this assessment: the area seemed a natural choice for a national park along the lines of Banff, Yellowstone, or Yosemite.

In 1907 the idea of a national park meant different things to different people. At the beginning of the twentieth century the idea of a national park was in transition and there were competing perspectives on what it should be. To some, such as American author John Muir, a national park represented a pristine wilderness protected from human development. To others, a national park was a developed spa resort. Some saw national parks as a romantic North American ideal, others saw them as resources that could be exploited for public and private benefit. These competing views are still being balanced in Canada's national parks. Nonetheless, there are some clear indications of what was intended when Jasper was first set aside as a park in 1907.

The idea of the national park in North America traces its origins to the mid-nineteenth century and first flowered with the establishment of Yellowstone National Park in 1874. Back then, Americans realized that the vanishing wilderness was also one of America's defining assets and a movement sprung up to preserve outstanding examples of original American landscape. The objectives of the conservationists coincided with big railway interests that saw the tourist potential of the spectacular mountain scenery of the West. Similar attitudes in Canada led to the reservation of the hot springs and mountain scenery around the railway town of Banff in 1887. This was Canada's first national park, originally known as Rocky Mountains Park, renamed Banff National Park in 1930. Subsequently, the Yoho and Glacier forest reserves were proclaimed as parks-in-waiting along the CPR line on the western side of the mountains. Lake Louise was reserved in 1892 and Waterton Lakes in 1895. Aside from these scenic parks, the Government of Canada also created a series of wildlife preserves, such as Elk Island near Edmonton and Buffalo in eastern Alberta. Called parks, they were established in 1906 primarily as wildlife sanctuaries. Buffalo National Park was decommissioned in 1940 and the area near Wainwright was taken over as a military training area. Elk Island remains as a fully fledged national park.

Jasper Park was established by an Order-in-Council to protect the lands along either side of the proposed GTP railway in the Rocky Mountains. An early version of the draft Order, prepared by the Department of the Interior in March 1907, deliberately adopted the language of the 1887 *Rocky Mountains Park Act*. It said in part:

> Whereas it is expedient in the public interest that a national
> park should be set apart and established along the line of the
> Transcontinental Railway in the Rocky Mountains in the
> Province of Alberta for the purpose of preserving the beauty of
> the scenery, of protecting the forests and maintaining conditions
> favourable to a continuous water supply, and of protecting, as
> far as the Parliament of Canada has jurisdiction, the animals,
> fish and birds within the park:
>
> . . .
>
> The said tract of land is hereby reserved and set apart as a
> public park and pleasure ground for the benefit advantage
> and enjoyment of the people of Canada.[37]

A difficulty with copying the *Rocky Mountains Park Act* was that with the creation of the Province of Alberta two years previously, the political circumstances had changed since the passage of that Act. Now, the province had jurisdiction over land administration, although, for the time being at least, the federal government continued to administer natural resources such as water, timber, and minerals. The closest mandate that the federal government had on hand was through the *Dominion Forest Reserve Act*, so the Order-in-Council was reworded slightly to call the reserve Jasper Forest Park. This was the first official application of the name "Jasper" to the area since the Hudson's Bay Company had named its post on the Athabasca after postmaster Jasper Hawes. The railway town that would take on the same name was, at this early date, called Fitzhugh, after one of the GTP's vice-presidents. For the first couple of years after its establishment, not a lot went on in the park other than railway construction. It was not until 1910 that steps were finally taken to manage the area as a park.

Jasper Park was initially run by the Dominion forestry branch of the Department of the Interior. Formed in 1906, the branch developed a comprehensive strategy for protecting the forests and watershed of the eastern slopes of the Rockies. It created a chain of forest reserves, bolstered by the Rocky Mountains, Jasper, and Waterton parks, that protected a watershed and timber berths comprising over 14,000 square miles. The water and timber were seen as vital resources for the new settlers flooding into the prairies to the east. That the parks also protected the natural scenery was considered a bonus in this scheme of conservation.

Clearing the Land

The creation of parks and forest reserves was part of a tremendous scheme of rationalizing land use in western Canada that had been underway since the 1880s and which was the principal business of the Department of the Interior. Various components of this vast organization used an array of legislated mandates, such as the *Dominion Lands Act*, to survey the empty lands into townships and lots, develop transportation routes, and encourage immigration and colonization. It was recognized that these lands were not completely empty—Aboriginals and wildlife had been occupying the land for millennia—but these were both being swept aside with the inevitable westward march of settlement and development. Through its Indian affairs branch, the Department of the Interior endeavoured to organize and transfer these First Peoples onto a network of numbered Indian reserves. Similarly, as has been mentioned, reserves were also set aside for certain species of wild game and for forests. Essentially, nature was meant to conform to these tidy units: wild animals, forests, and Aboriginal peoples were to keep to the reserves, while settlers settled on surveyed lots. In this bureaucratic scheme of things, there was little opportunity for mixing categories.

Access into Jasper Forest Park was delayed pending the completion of the GTP line, and the federal government seemed reluctant to curtail the railway's construction gangs despoiling the forests and game in the area. Pressure on the area's natural resources was doubled with the construction of a second railway line through the mountains and the Yellowhead Pass by Canadian Northern (CNo). Token administration of the park came from Edmonton, but through 1908 nothing happened save for the inauguration of land surveys. In 1909 Ranger J. W. McLaggan was appointed acting superintendent with the specific task of making sure there were no unauthorized residents living within the park. During these days of transition, there were many transients about the area; remnants of Aboriginal groups, pioneers, drifters, and pretenders. It was McLaggan's job to sort these people out, find out who was who, and make arrangements to have them move on.

Through 1909 and 1910, McLaggan visited the various homesteads in the area and found that some were more imaginary than real. Malcolm Groat claimed squatter's rights on a quarter section of land at the mouth of Fiddle Creek, but when McLaggan visited the place he found that Groat, a road builder for GTP, had not lived there for any appreciable time and that his home was really a shack put up by a railway survey party.[38] Similarly, at least three other former employees of GTP attempted to make belated claims to land in the area. None of these were taken very seriously by either McLaggan or the department.

Consideration was given to some of the former freemen families who had maintained ties to the area even after the closure of Jasper House. There were many families like this living near the old fur-trading centres and the federal government struggled with how to deal with them. It offered them three options: they could claim treaty rights and settle on a number of Cree-speaking Indian reserves; they could take a cash payment for their land as something called "Half-Breed scrip," a payout for extinguishment of Aboriginal title; or they could become settlers like the many immigrants flooding into the North-West Territories at the turn of the century. To allow these people to claim vaguely defined hunting rights in an area now set aside as a park was not seen as a viable option in the eyes of the federal government. Conservationists at the time blamed unrestricted Aboriginal hunting for the scarcity of game in the area and blamed the "half-breeds," as they were called, for rampant trapping. Nonetheless, despite considerable prejudice against Aboriginal people at this time, some were able to play the game and make the most of a situation that, for traditional people, seemed to be getting worse. Such was the case with the Moberly family and their relations.

McLaggan began negotiations with the bona fide homesteaders to get them to move. He offered them money, as well as vague promises to provide land elsewhere. The Moberlys, Isadore Finlay, and Adam Joachim all agreed to a price for their improvements, such as buildings and fences, and by the following year had gone. Lewis Swift, however, dug in his heels and refused to budge. He insisted that he had a legitimate land claim, made before the park was proclaimed, and demanded a patent. This was eventually agreed to by the department, although details were kept secret from the other families pending their move.[39] Today, this seems like blatant discrimination, and there may have been aspects of racism in the case. But there were other factors that influenced the decision to move among the Cree-speaking families. With the exception of Evan Moberly, they did not seem to be serious farmers and likely depended on hunting and trapping for much of their livelihood. This would not have been possible in the new park and it was therefore in their interest to find land elsewhere, where they could homestead adjacent to good hunting territory. They took their money without apparent complaint, hoping to get land elsewhere. The surprising thing is not that the other families were pushed out—this was standard procedure in establishing new parks well into the 1970s—but that Swift was allowed to stay. It may be that the government saw some use in a farm that grew useful provisions and, as we have previously seen from Mary Schäffer's commentary, Swift's farm was a well-regarded local landmark.

The Métis left in two groups. The largest group followed Evan Moberly along the old Iroquois hunting trail up the Snake Indian River into the Grande Cache area, where they joined with a larger Métis community. Historian J. G. MacGregor recounted a description of this exodus that he heard from old-timer James Shand-Harvey:

> Ewan Moberly and his group took their machinery and over
> 200 head of stock, mostly horses, over a road which they cleared
> out along older hunting trails. Up Solomon Creek they went,
> up the Wildhay River, past Rock Lake and on over the pass to the
> Sulphur River. Ever since, this way has been called the Moberly
> Road.[40]

Evan Moberly died in the flu epidemic of 1919. His brother John settled east of the park near the present town of Hinton, Alberta. John's sons Dave, Frank, and Ed did some trapping and hunting and would also work as packers in the park.[41]

The Palisades

Lewis Swift's farm became an enclave comprising the only freehold land within the park boundary. All other lands occupied by private individuals were held either by lease or license of occupation at the pleasure of the federal government. As such, Swift's place upset the park administrators, who wanted it kept under park regulations.

They offered to buy Swift out, but he refused. Then, when he finally did decide to move in 1935, the government hesitated, since it was the middle of the Great Depression. Swift had made up his mind to go, however, and so sold to the first buyer with the requisite cash, who turned out to be Englishman A. C. Wilby. The new owner converted the place into a dude ranch, building several new buildings in the process. Another opportunity to buy the land was squandered by the government following Wilby's death in 1947, when the place was sold to G. F. Bried who further developed it as a tourist facility. It was Bried who gave it the name "The Palisades." It was not until 1962 that the government was finally able to acquire the land and erase the freehold occupation. Since the mid-1960s, the Palisades Centre, as it is now known, has been used as a training centre for park wardens and other national park employees.

While the national parks discouraged agricultural holdings within their boundaries, in the early stages of their history other forms of industrial development were tolerated. Coal mining was especially important to the railways and significant mines were developed both in Rocky Mountains and Jasper parks. Even before McLaggan had arrived to deal with the squatters, coal mines were being staked in the Fiddle River-Moosehorn Creek area of the park. These claims were acquired by an American-backed firm especially to develop this area. Jasper Park Collieries began shipping coal soon after the completion of the GTP line in 1911. The company named the mine Pocahontas, after a Virginia coal mine. GTP established a station near the development with the same name. A large facility was developed beside the mine that included an electrically-driven tipple, a mechanism for separating the coal from the rock and then sorting the coal according to size and grade. A sizeable village grew up near the mine, housing 250 employees and their families at its peak.

By 1912 Pocahontas comprised a lower town for the mill operation, offices, businesses, and a bunkhouse, as well as an upper town that had fifty four-room houses, twenty three-room houses, and a school.[42] Soon after, a second mine opened at Brule along the CNo line and a community sprang up there as well. The park allowed limited agricultural leases to service these communities and milk cows grazed on nearby meadows. For a while, Pocahontas was the largest community in the park, but various problems following World War I led to the mine's closure in 1921. The place was soon

Jasper Park Collieries, Pocahontas. JYMA, PA 39-20

deserted and many of its buildings were either torn down or moved else-where. Farther down the GTP line near the town of Jasper, a limestone quarry was opened in 1916. The company operated a rock crusher and built bunkhouses, a cookhouse, and a dining car for its men. The quarry sent up to forty boxcar-loads of crushed rock a week but closed in 1929.[43] The Brule Mine, meanwhile, was excluded from the park when the east boundary was redrawn in 1930.

During these early years there was a minimal park organization, and that which did exist was initially preoccupied with the practical details of managing the land that it had: dealing with coal leases, surveying town lots, and figuring out just where the park boundaries lay. In 1910 Minister Frank Oliver moved the superintendent of Rocky Mountains Park, Howard Douglas, from Banff to Edmonton to serve as chief superintendent of national parks. There, explained Oliver, he would be able to focus on Jasper development.[44] But there was no money for development and Douglas was unhappy with the move, so the arrangement did not last. In 1910 Lewis Swift was appointed an acting game guardian for the park, but he found little game to protect; most of the animals had been hunted out during the railway-building boom. He spent some time patrolling the Athabasca Valley, evicting squatters who remained in the area. Some small efforts were made to initiate scenic trails and bridle paths—a trail was built to Maligne Lake, for example—but on the whole, very little was undertaken in the way of tourist development until after World War I. In the meantime, legislation was passed that gave the national parks a legal mandate and provided a central organization for their management.

Boundary Disputes

The passage of the *Dominion Forest Reserves and Parks Act of 1911* was meant to rationalize the parallel activities of national forests and parks. At first, this gave dominion parks an extremely limited identity as developments within national forests. As Minister Oliver explained when speaking to the Bill in Parliament: "Any portion of the area included in a forest reserve may be placed under the additional restrictions or provisions which would enable that particular area to be used as a park or pleasure resort."[45] The main difference between forest reserves and parks, according to Oliver, was that the former were intended to exclude people while the latter "look to the enjoyment by the people of the natural advantages and beauties of these particular sections of the reserves."[46] As developed tourist areas within the forest reserves, national parks did not need to be as large as they were before, and so the new Act drastically reduced the area of the mountain parks. Rocky Mountains Park was reduced in size from 4,500 to 1,800 square miles. Jasper was cut down in size even more drastically, to a ten-mile strip on either side of the GTP-line. Restoring these boundaries would be just one of many issues facing the new Commissioner of National Parks.

James Bernard Harkin (1875–1955) worked as a newspaperman in Ottawa before joining the Department of the Interior in 1905. In 1911 he was asked to head the newly formed national parks branch as the first commissioner. For the next twenty-five years he was an energetic and imaginative promoter of national parks. He sold them as preserving pieces of the original Canadian landscape, for being important places for outdoor recreation, benefiting the mental and physical well-being of Canadians, and as tourist magnets, boosting the national economy. He won a reputation as one of Canada's leading conservationists in the first half of the twentieth century, not only for his work with parks but for his work in the area of wildlife conservation and the North.

The national parks service initially concentrated on development; overseeing projects to build tourist infrastructure and regulating the various tourist services such as outfitters, livery services, and hotels. As a

J. B. Harkin, the first commissioner of Canadian national parks. LAC, 22781

former newspaperman, Harkin was an ideal candidate to publicize the developing tourist spots in the mountains. In addition, as a former special assistant to the minister, Frank Oliver, he was adept at dealing with the larger machinations of the department. His assistant, Frank Williamson, was an engineer, ideally qualified to oversee the building projects that would consume much of the parks' budgets. Conservation at this early stage was still considered to rest with the forest branch, as forest and game protection were seen to be closely linked. One of its foresters, H. N. Millar, was a nationally renowned expert on game in the Rockies. He presented a paper to the Canadian Conservation Commission in 1915 entitled "The Big Game of the Canadian Rockies: A Practical Method for its Preservation" that stressed the importance of conservation areas on the eastern slopes to encourage the recovery of threatened species such as bighorn sheep, elk, caribou, and bears.[47] It was not until the 1920s that Harkin established his branch as the principal authority on conservation.

As it happened, J. B. Harkin had other ideas for his program. He had no intention of playing second fiddle to the forest branch and immediately set out to disentangle the two programs. Consequently, under Harkin's leadership, the parks branch achieved three important goals over the next decade: it separated its activities from those of the forest branch; it expanded the network of parks across the country; and it took over authority for conservation in the national parks. In the process, the parks branch became the leading conservation agency in the country. These ends were achieved through landmark legislation in the conservation movement. A 1914 amendment to the *Dominion Forest Reserves and Parks Act* allowed parks to be created independently from forest reserves. The *Migratory Birds Convention Act* and the *Northwest Game Act of 1917* gave responsibility for wildlife on all federal land to the national parks branch. Its wildlife division became the basis for the future Canadian Wildlife Service. The branch developed an organization of park wardens to protect the assets of the parks from fire, poachers, and predators. It established new parks in Saskatchewan, Manitoba, Ontario, and Nova Scotia, creating the beginnings of a truly national system of national parks. Harkin's crowning achievement was the passage of the *National Parks Act* in 1930 that enshrined the principle of inviolability, protecting the parks from outside industrial development, including forestry and mining.

J. B. Harkin's Legacy:
National Parks Created between 1914 and 1930

The national parks branch inherited six national parks in 1911: Rocky Mountains (Banff), Waterton, Glacier, Jasper, and Elk Island. Under the dynamic leadership of J. B. Harkin, the branch acquired ten more over the next twenty-five years:

Mt. Revelstoke, BC (1914)
St. Lawrence Islands, ON (1914)
Pt. Pelee, ON (1917)
Kootenay, BC (1920)
Wood Buffalo, AB and NWT (1922)
Prince Albert, SK (1927)
Riding Mountain, MB (1929)
Georgian Bay Islands, ON (1929)
Cape Breton Highlands, NS (1936)
Prince Edward Island, PE (1937)

Throughout this period of expansion, Harkin and his branch struggled to define just what a national park was or should be; a process culminating in the passage of the *National Parks Act* that established the character and purpose of national parks for many years after. But first, a number of conflicting issues had to be resolved. On the one hand, Harkin aggressively sold parks for their usefulness to the nation. "Nothing attracts tourists like national parks," Harkin wrote in his annual report for 1913–1914. He added: "The most important service which the parks render is in the matter of helping to make Canadian people physically fit, mentally efficient, and morally elevated."[48] On the other hand, the branch recognized the national parks' mission of preserving unspoiled examples of Canadian landscapes. "In future years," Harkin wrote in 1915, "the parks should be the natural history schools of Canada, and the parks will probably be the only places where the native fauna and flora will be found in a natural state."[49]

Reconciling these two aims of national parks—use and preservation—was and continues to be a problem for national park policy and practice. However, Harkin's immediate aim was to wrest control conservation from the forest branch, and to create a wildlife division to be managed alongside his engineering programs. It is this background to the parks branch's larger mission that shaped some of the important issues that would play out in

Jasper National Park during the 1910s and 1920s. At the same time, discussions over Jasper's park boundaries led officials to consider what a national park should be.

Pressure for the restitution of the original boundaries of Jasper Park began soon after the enactment of the *Dominion Forest Reserves and Parks Act* in 1911. Both GTP and the Alpine Club of Canada (ACC) petitioned the minister of the Interior in 1912 and 1913. The following year Harkin prepared an extensive briefing note to advise the new minister on the issue. Based on information supplied by park officials, it included cogent reasons for extending the park boundaries. Harkin argued that the requested land was important for wildlife protection and for attracting tourists to the park. Regarding a requested extension of the northern park boundary, for instance, Harkin wrote: "This will give us the control of the old established trails up the Soloman, Moose and Stoney Rivers to Mount Robson and control of an excellent game breeding ground and fishing lakes." Of the requested southern extension, he wrote further in the briefing note, it "will save the splendid game country at the head of the Brazeau River."[50] By connecting to Rocky Mountains Park, the southern extension would also permit the construction of a scenic highway to link both parks. He also argued that Maligne Lake, Athabasca Falls, and the Whirlpool River were required for tourist attractions. Lobbying and staff work were rewarded by an amendment to the *Dominion Forest Reserves and Parks Act* in 1914 that restored Jasper to most of its 1907 dimensions.

The Jasper boundary issue resurfaced in the 1920s over the question of provincial control of natural resources. Throughout the 1920s, the federal and Alberta provincial governments negotiated the transfer of jurisdiction of Alberta's natural resources. At the same time, Harkin was refining his idea of national parks to exclude the possibility of industrial development. While the province saw the value of national parks as tourist attractions, it did not wish to alienate significant natural resources such as water, forests, and minerals from potential lucrative development. Harkin was pressed to compromise on this issue and allow for the development of water and mineral resources within the parks.

But the commissioner would not budge from his principle of inviolability, saying that he would prefer smaller parks that preserved their integrity to larger parks that did not. The result was the creation of a joint federal committee that was tasked with resurveying the eastern boundaries of the Rocky Mountains and Jasper parks. It was agreed that areas lacking in outstanding scenery but containing valuable resources would be excluded from the parks in the upcoming national park legislation. In Rocky Mountains Park, the coal mining town of Canmore and the Spray River, with its hydroelectric potential, were therefore excluded from the new Banff National Park. In Jasper, only the Brule mine area was proposed for exclusion. The Pocahontas area was not considered a valuable coal resource since the closure of the mine there and it also conflicted with the valuable tourist resource of the Miette Hot Springs. The water resources of the park had been surveyed for their hydroelectric potential but were thought to be too remote from urban centres to be considered viable natural resources capable of development.

Compared to Banff, which lost a significant amount of land along its eastern boundary, Jasper got off relatively unscathed. True, the northeast corner was lopped off to cede the Brule area to the province, but this was balanced by a boundary extension on the northwest corner. Moreover, the park managed to grab back part of the Brule land following the protest in 1927 by Jasper warden Dick Langford, who argued that the Moosehorn Valley should be kept because "it is one of the best winter sheep ranges and breeding grounds we have."[51] Although the province was insistent that the Moosehorn Valley should be included in the transferred coal lands, Alberta did not have strong public support for its claim. R. W. Cautley, the surveyor working on establishing the new boundary, agreed with Langford and pointed out that coal resources in this valley were of an uncertain quantity.[52]

Langford's proposed compromise provided a more visually obvious boundary for the park through the portal of the surrounding mountains. Added to this, the province did not enjoy a good reputation as a protector of game. This last argument was presented in a letter to the minister of the Interior from the Game and Fish Protection League based in Edmonton. Acknowledging that the disputed area would be a game preserve if transferred to the province, the league countered that the province lacked the resources to effectively enforce hunting regulations. This, it argued, would leave the area open to the depredations of the Brule miners, who, in the words of the letter writer, "are mostly foreigners, unamenable to most laws, let alone game laws, [and] will slaughter these animals in short order, as has happened in several very similar circumstances in Alberta."[53] The earlier efforts of the parks branch to keep on the good side of the hunting lobby were now paying dividends, for even though hunting was not allowed inside the park's boundaries, the notion that surplus game would move onto neighbouring hunting areas was widely accepted.

The restitution and protection of the park's boundaries was a major concern of the branch officials in Ottawa and in Jasper during the period from 1911 to 1930. Once defined, regulations had to be enforced for the protection of forests, fish, and game, and for the development of tourist facilities. From the beginning, tourist development was a primary concern for park officials, since, as the 1911 Act stipulated, parks were created and maintained "as public parks and pleasure grounds, for the benefit, advantage and enjoyment of the people of Canada."[54]

When the boundaries of Jasper were put right in 1914 there was not much opportunity to open the place up to tourists, as the outbreak of World War I disrupted the burgeoning tourist industry. Efforts to sell the park only began in earnest at the beginning of the 1920s, and were encouraged by the new Canadian National Railways (CNR) with whom the parks service made common cause. Sold as a wilderness destination, both the federal government and the CNR went to great efforts to present Jasper as a fashionable destination. In this endeavour they were helped by the Governor General, who at the time was the Duke of Devonshire. The duke and duchess visited the park in 1919 and their climbing and other wilderness sightseeing were accorded considerable publicity. This visit was surpassed by that of the duke's successor, Lord Byng, in 1922, who, along with his wife and entourage, spent three weeks in the park. During this visit, Byng made an adventurous horse trip to the north boundary of the park, an area now commemorated by the name of Byng Pass. The image of the park as a wilderness Eden was promoted in an ambitious advertising campaign. At the Ottawa winter carnival in 1922, for example, the parks branch installed an exhibit in the Union train station that pictured Mount Edith Cavell on a painted backdrop, along with a display of a miniature forest, tipi, and campfire "which by an ingenious arrangement of chemicals appeared to give off real smoke."[55] Smaller versions of this exhibit were later shown down the American Pacific coast.

Fountain of Life

Much was made in the early twentieth century of the curative properties of nature, of its ability to bring out the best in people. This grew from the earlier romantic notions espoused by writers such as Henry

David Thoreau and Ralph Waldo Emerson. But these earlier writers looked to a gentler, cultivated natural landscape. American John Muir, in his 1901 book, *Our National Parks*, wrote of the importance of a *wilderness* landscape. For Muir, a wilderness experience in a national park was a perfect antidote to urban life. Muir talked about being "overcivilized," a condition leading to bad nerves, disease, and general unhappiness. His words were cited in many sources including in the Annual Report of the Commissioner of Dominion Parks in 1912–1913: "Thousands of tired, nerve-shaken, over-civilized people are beginning to find out that going to the mountains is going home; that wilderness is a necessity and that mountain parks and reservations are useful, not only as fountains of timber, and irrigating rivers, but as fountains of life."[56] The curative properties of wilderness were especially important to veterans of World War I. One of the most illustrious of these veterans, Lord Byng of Vimy, Governor General of Canada, took a much-needed vacation in Jasper in the mid-1920s. Lawrence Burpee described Lord Byng's behaviour while on his Jasper camping trip using these terms: "The great general of the World War, who sometimes seemed rather shy and reserved at formal functions in Ottawa, proved himself to be a rare companion on the trail or around the camp-fire, friendly, utterly unassuming, and able and willing at all times to tell a good story, grave or gay, drawn from his own abundant experience."[57]

During the first half of the twentieth century, national parks like Jasper were as much creations of man as they were natural beauty spots. Legislation and government polices defined their boundaries and governed how nature and people could or could not interact. But in Jasper the park was also defined by the men and women who lived and worked there and who merged the developing park culture with that of earlier traditions. Jasper, in the years between the wars, was a world unto itself, a tight little community with four strands: the railway, the shopkeepers and hoteliers, the guides and outfitters, and the parks service. By 1930 the park staff had formed a distinct entity within the town. There was a superintendent, resident engineer, ten clerical staff, and eighteen wardens.

In the first decades of the twentieth century, the administration of Jasper National Park had a distinctly military flavour through Colonel S. Maynard Rogers, who was the park superintendent, with a few intermissions from 1913 until 1934. Rogers was from Ottawa, where he had developed some important social connections through his early service with the Governor General's Foot Guards. Although he was not a regular army officer (there were few of these around at the time), he was almost one in practice: he had served as a company commander in the first contingent of the Canadian forces to serve in South Africa and from 1905 to 1907 he was chief staff officer at the Rockliffe Camps near Ottawa.[58] He was a marksman, a hunter, and had been a member of the Dominion Rifle Team. During World War I, he took a leave of absence from Jasper to serve as commanding officer of the Ottawa Military District. In Jasper he assumed the role of a Scottish laird and had one of the most prominent houses in the town built at the government's expense. He had a reputation for being a bit of a martinet in the town of Jasper and pursued wayward cats and automobiles with equal vigour.

Rogers had three principal lieutenants that helped administer specific areas of the park: a principal clerk who oversaw records and finances and kept track of the land leases, a supervising warden who looked after resource protection, and a resident engineer who looked after the development of

Colonel and Mrs. S. M. Rogers at home in Jasper, 1914. JYMA, ACC. NO. 991.113.05

roads, bridges, and trails. The position of principal clerk may have been held by a succession of individuals and there is no single personality that emerges in the early period, but resource conservation and engineering were closely identified with two individuals. During the 1920s, supervising warden, Dick Langford, had a staff of sixteen wardens who were dispersed through the parks. Langford was an Englishman who had come to Canada as a young man in the first decade of the twentieth century. He had worked as a forest ranger before joining the Canadian Expeditionary Force in 1914, rising to the rank of sergeant major. He came to Jasper following the war and would have impressed Colonel Rogers with his military record. He left the park in 1935 to become chief park warden at Yoho National Park. John Snape, resident engineer between the wars, was an English-born civil engineer. He supervised a collection of surveyors, draftsmen, and construction workers who influenced the early physical development of the park. Snape took over a residence left over from the engineers' camp beside the town. Today, this area is known as Snape's Hill.

Many others left their mark in more subtle ways. Around 1920 the Rogers house engaged a young Métis woman, Marie Perrault, to act as maid. Despite being a domestic, and under the kindly but strict supervision of the Rogers, Marie had her own identity as one of only five single girls in the town. She would sneak out in the evening to attend dances and meet boys. She married George Camp in 1924, who became a warden in 1939, and was the mother of Frank Camp, who also became a Jasper warden and who would later entitle his memoirs "Roots in the Rockies."[59]

CHAPTER FOUR

Backwoodsmen

Jasper National Park was not simply created by legislators, surveyors, engineers, architects, and administrators. It was an idea, or perhaps an ideal, held in the minds of those men and women who helped define it during those early years. Certainly, the views of Commissioner J. B. Harkin, Superintendent Maynard Rogers, or William Thornton of Canadian National Railways (CNR) did much to foster an image of the place that was becoming a park. Yet, there were also individuals who themselves were closely associated with the image of the park and became emblematic of its character.

If there is one figure who epitomized the park during its early years it was the backwoodsman. Early writers often alluded to the romantic association that the Athabasca Valley had with the explorers and fur traders of the previous century, and the park's surveyors and engineers were conscious of selecting their routes along "old Indian Trails." In the 1920s, backwoodsmen like Curly Phillips and Fred Brewster were thought to embody some of the attributes of these early heroes. And so too were the park wardens who, in their own way, were thought to represent many of the ideals, and even personify the wilderness ideals, of the park.

When historian Lawrence Burpee visited Jasper as part of the ACC's summer camp in the Tonquin Valley in 1926, he was inspired to return and write two books about the park.[60] At the time, he was one of Canada's leading men of letters, a prolific writer, a member of the Royal Society, and one of the founders of the Canadian Historical Association. His Jasper books evoke a strong sense of place that lays heavy emphasis on its wilderness setting and historical associations. A linchpin in the several vignettes that make up these books is a warden who guides the narrator along the various backcountry routes. Quiet but capable, he is the quintessential backwoodsman, able to discourse on philosophy as well as horses:

"Don't you find it lonely out here at times?" I asked the Warden.

"Lonely? Why, no. I have my work to do, and in the evenings, if I happen to be here in the cabin, there is usually something to

Percy Goodair's grave in the Tonquin Valley. Goodair had let it be known that when he died he wanted to be buried in the mountains rather than back in town. He was given a funeral beside his cabin and his grave is still tended in the Maccarib Pass overlooking the valley. COURTESY THE AUTHOR read. I wouldn't exchange the peace of this Tonquin Valley for all the luxuries of your noisy cities."[61]

The Warden's character was based on a real warden, Percy Goodair, an Englishman who had travelled extensively before settling down in Jasper. Goodair was renowned for his solitary nature and before the publication of Burpee's second Jasper book, he was killed by a bear at his Tonquin cabin.

The tradition of horse use, both for riding and for packing, is closely associated with Jasper's backcountry culture. Horses were an important part of the Jasper House operation as the fur-trading post supported crossings over the mountain passes. Horses were also crucial in the railway construction era, bringing men and equipment to build the rights-of-way along the Athabasca and up the Miette rivers. Horses continued to be important during the first decades of the park's history. Horses carried the surveyors along the park boundaries and, before the advent of roads, brought tourists to see the sights. In the first decades of the twentieth century, a small group of men put down roots in Jasper and made their living by supplying horses and guides to the tourists. Names like Curly Phillips, Fred Brewster, and the Otto Brothers became closely identified with the park during its early years. These men were wise in the ways of horses and backwoods travel. Equally tied to horse culture in the backcountry were the park wardens, the men hired to patrol the park and protects its assets against poachers and fire. As we shall see, the backgrounds of both of these groups of men varied—some had been raised in the backwoods, while others were graduates of English public schools—but many of their attitudes and values were the same and they developed closer ties through family and friendship.

The Packsaddle

Mountain travellers perfected the packsaddle with its system of hooks, ropes, and knots in the nineteenth century. The old outfitters used the sawbuck packsaddle, which resembled a wooden sawhorse. Variations of this saddle had been around since the time of Genghis Khan. Meanwhile, the wardens used a British army packsaddle with a wooden frame, metal hooks, and leather padding, which they acquired as war surplus in 1918. There is still one hanging in the Jasper tack shed that has the British Army broad arrow on it and the year 1917. Regardless of the saddle, both the outfitters and the wardens have been packing their horse the same way for over one hundred years. Large wooden boxes are attached to each side of the saddle, packs or equipment are arranged on top, and the whole pack is lashed together with a five-metre length of rope in an arrangement known as the famous diamond hitch. The diamond hitch is thrown, not tied.

There was a small Métis community living outside of the park that provided links to the accumulated lore of previous generations. Adam Joachim, Albert Norris, Adolphus Moberly, and Dave Moberly worked as guides and packers for the new generation of park outfitters, showing them the old routes and the intricacies of leading pack horses in the mountains. For instance, when Curly Phillips guided mountaineer A. P. Coleman into the Mount Robson area in 1908, he followed a route that had been shown to him by Adolphus Moberly. Some of these men continued to work in the park through to the middle of the century. E. J. Hart noted in his history of mountain park outfitters that Curly Phillips turned over much of his horse-guiding to Adam Joachim and Dave Moberly following his marriage in 1923.[62] Phillips married a Métis woman, as did park warden George Camp.

Curly Phillips (left) with packers Dick Dickinson, Albert Norris, and Dave Moberly.
JYMA, PA 38183

The Métis epitomized the frontier; the life on the margins of civilization that many of the newcomers came to Jasper to seek. At the beginning of the twentieth century, most people agreed that North America south of the 60th parallel was finally becoming civilized: the empty places were filling up and new technology was changing the way the pioneers had lived. Jasper represented one of the last accessible North American frontiers and men were drawn here to experience the wild outdoors, and hunting and trapping if possible, but otherwise just to be "out there." Guiding or warden work offered the opportunity to live the life in a sustainable way.

The Otto brothers, Jack, Bruce, and Closson, had come to the Banff area from Ontario in 1904 and began working as wranglers and packers for Tom Wilson, the famous Banff guide. They struck out on their own in Field, BC, working in Yoho National Park and then around 1910 moved up to Athabasca country to work as teamsters for the railway construction camps.[63] The following year they were hired by the park to clear a trail to Maligne Lake in anticipation of it becoming a popular tourist attraction. They were among the first to see the possibilities of leading horse tours in the park and soon established a livery service and stables. When Conan Doyle visited Jasper in 1914, it was the Otto brothers who led him to the various sights.[64]

Otto brothers: guides, outfitters, and car rental. JYMA, 997.07.294.18

Donald "Curly" Phillips was another Ontario native who had come west seeking opportunities on the frontier. He, too, worked as a teamster for the railways, but he soon found work guiding gentlemen explorers to the newly discovered mountain peaks in the area. In 1909 he helped the Reverend George T. Kinney almost reach the summit of Mount Robson, the highest peak in the Rockies. Although Phillips had little previous experience either with horses or in the mountains, he learned on the job and established a reputation for his calm competence. A. O. Wheeler, government surveyor, member of the interprovincial boundary commission, and one of the founding members of the ACC, invited him to work for the ACC expedition to Mount Robson in 1911. Phillips also helped Wheeler's survey parties around that same time and then participated in the larger ACC camp held at Mount Robson in 1913.[65] For that ACC expedition, Phillips enlisted the help of Jim Shand-Harvey, a young Eton graduate who had been working as a packer in the area since 1905.[66] This experience allowed Phillips to become extremely knowledgeable of the Mount Robson area, and he developed trails and bridges to make access to the summit easier. He soon established a reputation that helped him build up a loyal clientele of mountaineers. His business centre was located at the back of the town of Jasper, on what is now called Pyramid Drive, near the stables of the Otto brothers. Business was so brisk that he was joined by his father and brother, and his sister's husband, Bert Wilkins.

Although brought up as a backwoodsman in Ontario, much of Phillips's knowledge of horses and mountaineering had been learned in the Rockies. He did have considerable experience as a canoeist, however, and found an outlet for this talent on Maligne Lake, where he also guided tourists and rented out canoes. He built a boathouse on the shore of the lake as the centre of his Maligne operation that still stands today as a local landmark. By the 1930s, Phillips had also become a proficient skier and began developing routes in the Rockies to lead guided ski tours. It was while exploring new ski routes that he and a companion were killed by an avalanche in Elysium Pass in 1938.

As prominent as Curly Phillips had been, he was overshadowed in the world of Jasper outfitters by the entrepreneurial Fred Brewster, who had become the leading Jasper outfitter during the interwar years, building a full-service offering of trails, camps, and activities.

Fred Brewster came from a prominent Banff family where his father and uncle had successful livery and outfitting businesses. Young Fred was sent away to school and graduated from Queen's University with a degree in mining engineering, but like so many others he was drawn back to the frontier and by 1912 had established a business in partnership with his younger brother Jack and brother-in-law Phil Moore. Like the Otto brothers and "Curly" Phillips, Brewster and his partners had begun by freighting for the railway construction camps, but by 1912 they were guiding wealthy American sportsmen like S. P. Fay.[67] Seeing the need for accommodation in the park if they were going to attract more customers, the Brewsters and Moore established Tent City on the shore of Lac Beauvert. However, the onset of World War I put a dent in the tourist trade and diverted Fred Brewster into the army. He joined the engineers and commanded a company of miners, sappers who specialized in tunnelling under the battlefields to blow up enemy gun emplacements. He was promoted to major and won the Military Cross and Bar for bravery at Vimy Ridge. After the war, Brewster returned to Jasper to become one of its leading citizens. He built up a business that, for its size and complexity, greatly surpassed that of his competitors. He had lodges at Maligne and Amethyst lakes for riding, boating, and fishing. He established camps at Little and Big Shovel passes and Tekarra basin for the Trail Riders of the Canadian Rockies, an organization in which he played a leading part. He was also an original member of the Jasper Ski Club, which was formed in 1926, and pioneered ski tourism in the park. His enterprise was helped by his alliance with the CNR, which emerged after World War I as Jasper's leading tourist agency, not only holding a virtual monopoly on transportation to the park but developing its premier resort at Jasper Park Lodge. Brewster got the rights for the horse concession at the lodge and began running tours from there as well. His most popular tour was to Maligne Lake and he developed a complex system for giving people an enjoyable visitor experience. Tourists were coached to Medicine Lake, then carried by motorboat to a lodge on the far shore where they were given lunch. From there, they proceeded by horse to Maligne Lake where Brewster had a larger lodge and camp. Guests could stay one or two nights before returning to Jasper Park Lodge. Brewster also took horse trips into the Tonquin Valley, where guests stayed at his fishing camp on Amethyst Lake, and along the Skyline Trail to Maligne. He built a log shelter and dining room at his Tonquin camp in 1940, primarily to support his winter operation there. His longest excursion was the week-long ride to the Columbia Icefields. As the Icefields Parkway was nearing completion in 1939, Brewster built a chalet there on the site of the present visitor centre, and it became a centre for visitor activities at the south end of the park. He also became interested in ski touring and his summer camps did double duty as ski destinations. He retired in 1961.

A sideline pursued by many of the outfitters was guiding hunting parties. This autumn activity dovetailed nicely with guiding sightseers and anglers in the summer months and attracted some wealthy clients. Although hunting was prohibited within the park boundary, there were good hunting areas just beyond it, especially to the north in the Smokey River area and to the east in the Coal District bordering the foothills. Fred Brewster established his Black Cat Ranch just beyond the 1930 eastern boundary of the park as a base for his hunting safaris. The most popular big game was the bighorn sheep, valued for the rams' trophy heads. This

Fred Brewster at home in Jasper. JYMA, 994.45.82.1

species had already been largely exterminated in the United States and so big game hunters turned to the Canadian Rockies. Elk and caribou were also prized trophies. Although the caribou were never around in large numbers outside of the park boundary, the number of elk grew by leaps and bounds following their reintroduction to the park in 1920, and by the 1930s, they were grazing outside the park. Bears were also hunted, although these solitary animals were hard to find outside of the park. The Otto brothers asked that they be allowed to shoot grizzly bears in Jasper, arguing that they were a danger to the public, but Commissioner J. B. Harkin turned down their request.[68] However, the brothers were allowed to keep captive bears at their place in town, something the park superintendent hoped would become a tourist attraction.[69]

The Jasper guides and outfitters had the respect, and support of, Canadian parks service but they could not be relied upon to look after the park resources that they benignly exploited. To protect its assets, the park hired wardens to guard against forest fires and look after the animals. The warden service traced its origins to Howard Sibbald, who had been hired in Banff in 1909. He set about building an organization for Rocky Mountains Park that would be the model for all national parks for the next half-century. Each park was divided into districts, each with a warden headquarters in the form of a simple log cabin. Trails were built through the districts and lesser patrol cabins were established at regular intervals. Cabins were equipped with crank telephones that connected the wardens to park headquarters. The wardens were expected to live out in their districts for weeks, often months, at a time, with little or no human contact save the daily telephone call to HQ. Sibbald sought special qualities in his wardens: integrity, an ability for wilderness travel, a thorough knowledge of horses and how to pack them, and an affinity for living alone. The pay was not very good; what the job offered was the romance of living on the frontier. Although wardens were supposed to have the prerequisite experience before being hired, they, like the outfitters, often learned on the job.

Warden Telephones

The working life of the Jasper park warden was one of isolation. Throughout the era of the district system, which lasted until 1970, the typical warden spent much of the year working alone in the backcountry. There was no mail service to these isolated posts and the chief warden made infrequent visits, often just during his annual inspection. To counter this isolation and to provide regular contact between the wardens and headquarters, a crude telephone system was established. A single strand of heavy gauge wire was strung between trees through the forest, or attached to makeshift posts across alpine and swamps, extending to each district headquarters. Each cabin was equipped with a crank telephone, the kind with the mouthpiece attached to the wooden box and a separate candlestick earpiece. Former Jasper warden Mike Schintz describes wardens using equipment like this until the mid-1950s and it was not until the 1960s that radios replaced the cumbersome system of wires. The wardens checked in at scheduled times, using a designated ring to raise a specific telephone. As Mike Schintz explains: "Thus to raise the Jasper switchboard one might use one long ring, about four revolutions of the crank handle, and to call the Maligne Lake Station, three short rings, about one crank of the handle each."[70] While immensely useful,

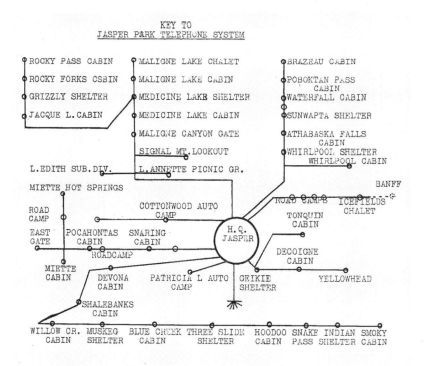

Jasper's warden telephone system. JNP

the telephone system required a lot of maintenance because the lines were constantly being cut by falling trees. The wardens on patrol would therefore carry climbing spurs and belts, as well as tools, for repairing the line.

The first Jasper warden was Lewis Swift who worked out of his home near the Snaring River between 1910 and 1914. He enjoyed a considerable reputation for knowing the country as he had lived there longer than almost anyone else. It was not until after World War I that Jasper began to organize itself along the Sibbald model. District headquarters were established at Yellowhead to cover the west, at Blue Creek to cover the north boundary, at Pocahontas to cover the east gate, and at Rocky River and Sunwapta to cover the south boundary, as well as at other stations at strategic locations such as Maligne Lake, Athabasca Falls, and Whirlpool. As the district system was developed after the war, most of the wardens were centred well out of town. To complete the north boundary patrol, the responsibility of the Blue Creek warden, still takes two weeks' riding in one direction by today's wardens and may have taken even longer back then. The other boundary patrols were equally as arduous.

As the organization of the park began to take shape after the war, the warden service found it lacked the necessary credibility to assert its authority over Jasper's community of backwoodsmen. Part of the blame lay with the chief warden, J. James, who seemed indecisive and earned the ridicule of the outfitters. During the boundary disputes of the 1920s, Commissioner Harkin had sought James's advice as an informed backwoodsman, but his reports did not inspire confidence and his reputation was further undermined when Curly Phillips's opinions were leaked back to national park headquarters in Ottawa. In a letter to Banff big game guide Jimmy Simpson, Phillips wrote: "James would not know a sheep range from a quill-pig and is so damn scared of his job that he would be afraid to make any suggestions."[71] James's assistants' reports were also marked by ambiguity and so, in an effort to get credible advice, Harkin dispatched a trusted Waterton warden and Howard Sibbald himself to investigate and report on the Jasper boundary situation.

Sibbald devised a system of operation that would define warden work for many years after. Each park was divided into a number of districts. Each of the districts had a large cabin that served as headquarters for the warden and a series of patrol cabins spread a day's riding distance along the routes that they were to patrol. The horse was central to this system. It was how the warden and his family, along with their supplies, packed into the districts each spring and out again in the fall. From spring into the fall the warden patrolled on horseback and so the width and grade of the trails and the spacing of the patrol cabins were determined by the requirements of a horse.

The wardens' horses were all owned and managed by the park and bore the distinctive ram's head brand on their left shoulder. Each warden was usually assigned three animals, one to be used as a saddle horse and two as pack horses. Until 1960, the Jasper horses wintered in the park, in meadows along the western boundary on the Colin Range, and then up around Willow Creek. A report in 1952 said there were fifty-six government horses there at that time.[72] The job of caring for the horses—training, shoeing, checking on their health, and organizing the spring and fall roundups— was taken on by the barn boss who, as he still is today, was based at the stables near Jasper Park Lodge. Since 1961, Jasper horses have wintered at the regional horse ranch, called the Ya Ha Tinda, located on the Red Deer River just beyond the eastern boundary of Banff National Park. There is still a small pasturage and barn kept for the seasonal horse in the park, and the Jasper barn boss still looks after the park horses in the summer season.

Over the years the Jasper wardens have developed their own distinctive style. They tie their packs in a variation of the diamond hitch that still gets disapproving comments from the Banff barn boss. They lead their pack horses differently from Banff wardens. They even, as Mike Schintz has explained, tie their rain slickers in a particular way:

Tied behind the cantle, in a compact roll no more than 16 inches log, was the traditional yellow slicker. This method of rolling and tying the slicker was a hallmark of the park wardens of Jasper National Park at the time, as was the very neat, tied-off-at-the-top method of throwing the diamond hitch. The whole aspect of a good park warden trail outfit was one of neatness and utilitarianism—nothing flapping, nothing dragging, no loose ends.[73]

One of the reasons for the distinctive character of the Jasper wardens was the personality of the chief warden who oversaw their development during the 1920s. Following the replacement of J. James by Dick Langford as supervising warden in 1922, the Jasper wardens began to emerge as one of the best outfits in the national park organization. He had joined the Jasper warden service after the war and, as a former army non-commissioned officer, was a natural to succeed James. He knew the park, was confident, and knew how to lead men. Moreover, he established a tradition of combining local bush smarts with military spit and polish.

Through the 1920s, Langford developed a stable group of wardens who came to know the park like no others. Some of the first wardens had come from farms and ranches and benefitted from having rural backgrounds, while others found themselves thrown into the deep end. Percy Goodair, for many years the Athabasca warden, was an Englishman like Langford and had knocked around Africa and tried mining in British Columbia before joining the warden service after the war. He was a recluse and far preferred being by himself in the district than mixing with people in town. He was featured in many of the stories written by historian Lawrence Burpee, who had travelled with him in the 1920s. By this time Goodair was the epitome of the experienced backwoodsman. However, this experience did

Wardens Charlie Matheson and Frank Wells, and Chief Park Warden Dick Langford and unknown person in front of Brazeau cabin, c. 1930. JNP, H3660

not save him from a fatal encounter with a grizzly one day in 1929 when he stepped out of his cabin at Maccarib Pass, probably to jingle his horses. Other wardens who joined up after the war came from rural Canadian backgrounds. Men like Charlie Matheson and Ed McDonald seemed to have personalities akin to that of Goodair, and preferred to be out in their districts rather than enjoy civilization in town. Legendary wardens like Frank Bryant, the town warden; Alex Nelles at Snaring; Charlie Matheson at Sunwapta; Frank Wells, who succeeded Percy Goodair at Athabasca; and Ed McDonald at Rocky River helped earn the Jasper wardens a reputation for toughness and backcountry smarts.

Jingling Horses

When the warden arrived at his cabin at the end of the day, he would tie up his horses, unsaddle them, and feed them their oats. They were then turned out for the night, free to forage as best as they could. The warden cabins were selected partly with an eye to decent grazing and water. Although a good idea in theory, the horses would often take advantage of the liberty granted to them to wander as they pleased. Some horses were naturally inclined to head back down the trail toward home come morning; others just lit out for the hills. Wardens countered these tricks by building crude fences across the trail or hobbling the horses at night. Still, when the warden got up in the morning he faced the uncertain task of jingling the horses—in other words, walking out with a halter trying to find where his horses had gotten to during the night. Sometimes they were right there, other mornings he could face a walk of a few kilometres.

Many stories are told of the wardens' grit. When Ed McDonald's horse was spooked by a grizzly, McDonald was thrown and fractured his pelvis. It took six days for him to crawl back to his cabin and then he had to wait another day for help to arrive to pack him the fifty kilometres back to town. He was reported to have said of grizzly bears: "Hell, you can't tell me that they will slap you down and eat you up. They had an opportunity on four successive nights and . . . they turned me down!"[74] Still, he lived to return to his duties, although the story has it that he had the telephone moved lower down on the wall in his cabin, just in case he was similarly afflicted again.[75]

Frank Bryant was another one of the early generation of Jasper wardens. He was one of the first wardens on the scene to search for the bodies of Curly Phillips and Reginald Pugh after they had been buried by an avalanche in Elysium Pass in 1938. He trekked for many hours and then stuck there until the bodies were recovered.

The phrase, "men for the mountains" connotes images of manly courage and hardiness; a romantic ideal that feminist authors have enjoyed poking fun at.[76] But in Jasper, at least, women have had a long association with the backcountry, beginning with women like Suzanne Moberly, Suzette Swift, and Mary Schäffer, and continuing to present-day women wardens and horse packers. And then there are the Harragin sisters. Mona and Agnes Harragin started working as camp cooks for the Fred Brewster outfit at Medicine Lake in 1927 at about the time that the first tourists were driven up the road from Jasper Park Lodge to Medicine Lake. They were ferried by motorboat across the lake and then fed at the camp. From there, tourists went by horse to Maligne Lake or started on a couple of backcountry tours, one of the more popular being the Circle Tour to Shovel Pass and then on to Jasper along what is now known as the Skyline Trail. At the end of the 1927 season, the girls were invited to a wedding at Maligne Lake. Charlie Matheson, the area warden, lent them some horses. The string of horses was short one saddle and Agnes opted to use a wooden packsaddle, padding it with a folding blanket. She could have ridden bareback, but she thought that this would be more of a challenge.

The following year, the sisters were invited back by Fred Brewster to cook, but they insisted that they would only return if they could work as guides, conducting backcountry horse tours. They were accepted into this select group of horsemen and became the first women to work as guides in the park. They were tough, these women, and had to endure many pranks, as well as getting up at four in the morning to wrangle horses and suffer long days with complaining customers and more than their share of "knot heads and rangy ponies." They learned on the job how to pack horses, practicing the two-man and triple diamonds, as well as the barrel hitch. But their love affair with horses continued and they returned for two more summers. Mona stayed at Maligne when she married warden Charlie Matheson. As extraordinary as their story is, the Harragin sisters pull together a number of interesting threads in the early history of the park. They worked for some of the first guides and outfitters in the park—Fred Brewster and Curly Phillips—and they were friends with another family of original outfitters, the Otto brothers. They were introduced to the area by Adam Joachim, and Mona went on to marry the warden Charlie Matheson.

Before 1970, many wardens' wives lived out in the districts with their husbands, where they raised their children and assisted as unpaid helpers. If a warden ran into difficulty, especially while fighting fires, his wife was often the nearest adult that he could ask for assistance and was therefore often drawn into the fray, providing communication, cooking, or other support. These women were what Ann Dixon has described as being "silent partners." Herself the wife of a former park warden, Dixon began soliciting stories from and about other warden wives, both past and present.[77]

The stories Dixon gathered about the wardens' wives relate many tales of unsung heroism. One story tells of Beatrice Bryant, who was accompanying her husband, Frank Bryant, on a patrol in 1925. It was hot summer weather and she had brought their two children, aged four and nine, on the three-day ride. Along the way, Frank came upon a potentially serious forest fire and without hesitation stopped to fight it. Beatrice parked her children and the horses under some trees and instructed nine-year-old Kathleen to take charge. She then returned to work beside her husband on the fire line, taking only occasional breaks, for thirty-six hours.[78] Another story tells of Mona Matheson, who lived with her husband, Charlie, in a district cabin. She relates how, one day, Chief Warden Langford called her when her husband was out on patrol: A fire had broken out and the crew needed supplies. On her own she rounded up a string of horses, packed them, and led them to the firefighting crew.[79] This way of life for the spouses of the wardens continued into the 1960s. Another woman, Julie Winkler, tells the story of taking her baby to Brazeau cabin in 1960 and filling her time by making elaborate wooden carvings while her husband, Max, went on his twenty-day horse patrols. This was not the sort of life for the inexperienced or faint of heart.

Guides and outfitters, wardens, and their families constituted Jasper's horsey set. Of course, the biggest users of horses in the interwar period were the tourists. They were the raison d'être for all those guides, packers, and horses in the park. Many guests at Jasper Park Lodge or in the town rented horses for day trips. But many others went on longer excursions. Travel writer Eleanor Broadhead went on a twelve-day Brewster pack trip in 1941, following this up with a week's stay at the Rocky Mountain Ranch.

Mona Harragin packing a horse in Jasper. GLENBOW, NA 2677-1

The horse outfitters continued their business after World War I and thrived into the 1960s. But their area of operation tended to be increasingly curtailed by highway development and the imposition of park wilderness restrictions. The Skyline Trail to Maligne Lake is now a world-famous hiking trail, but horses are not permitted. Yet, throughout the backcountry there are still many of the old outfitters camps with their hitching rails and tent poles neatly standing, waiting for the next riders to camp. And though the wardens have not been stationed in their districts since 1970, they still occasionally go out on patrol. Horses are still trained at the government stable and many of the old district cabins still stand. The past lives on in the trails, campsites, and cabins of these old backwoodsmen.

The past also lives on in the traditions of the horsemen. Although not as many wardens regularly travel in the backcountry on horse as they used to, those that do are taught the old ways of saddling and packing their horses. No plastic or Velcro straps allowed here. Young wardens are still taught how to throw the diamond hitch using packsaddles that are considerably older than they are. And horses are still named at the Ya Ha Tinda Ranch just as they were during the 1920s, using the first letter of their names to denote a particular year. Thus, all of the horses born in a particular year are given a name beginning with the same letter. In this way, the names of the horses are repeated down through the years: Amos, Buck, Charley ("a bit of a character"), Dallas ("real nice disposition"), Echo, Friar . . .

Memory and nostalgia play a part in defining the present-day Jasper as well and much of this is tied to the backwoods tradition. Nostalgia has always been about old-timers telling the younger generation that things are not what they used to be. For example, Peggy Fowlie describes setting up her home at Devona cabin in 1928 or 1929. Her husband George was a young district warden and had left her alone while he went out on patrol. During this time she was visited by old Mr. Busby, a warden who lived in the neighbouring district, twelve miles distant. This is how Peggy remembers their conversation:

One of the things he said to me very distinctly was he certainly felt that the wardens of today (and that was including my husband who was just a new warden) were being pampered by the parks. He had all of the north boundary from Miette on the east to Little Smokey River to the northwest, the whole north end of Jasper Park. He told me that he patrolled this whole area on foot as all he was supplied with were two pack horses. He pointed out to me that now the warden, as well as every member of the family, was supplied with a saddle horse as well as the pack horses.[80]

Today, in one of the Jasper bars, where the wardens like to go occasionally after work to have a glass of beer and some conversation, some of the old-timers will still tell versions of Busby's tale. It is in the bar and at other gatherings of old wardens that memory sometimes works its magic. Tales of the wardens, outfitters, and horses of long ago are retold and passed on to the younger men and women who join the particular culture that is Jasper.

CHAPTER FIVE

Jasper Builds

The twin mandates of protecting scenery and wildlife while promoting visitor access and enjoyment created a need for a variety of development within the Jasper Park. The creation of a park called for the building of infrastructure such as trails, roads, and buildings, as well as a host of necessities to keep people healthy, safe, and happy in its environment. At first the railways undertook much of this development, but by the 1920s the park's own engineering service, supported by head office professionals, was engaged in the bulk of the road building and planning. By the 1950s and 1960s private enterprise was undertaking much of the new construction. Together, the railway, the national park, and private entrepreneurs created a distinct environment for Jasper National Park. This environment forms part of the scenery for travellers, while it provides shelter, food, and other services important to the modern tourist.

In Jasper, which was modelled on Rocky Mountains Park (now Banff National Park) to the south, the creation of a townsite was seen as an early priority. In the first years of the park's history, townsite development was left to the railway that located the different townsites beside its principal stations. The Grand Trunk Pacific's (GTP's) situation was further strengthened by the special position it enjoyed with the Wilfrid Laurier government, which actively supported the second transcontinental railway until the government's defeat in the general election of 1911. GTP therefore took advantage of the situation to make independent decisions about what would go where. It had two objectives: to optimize its position in the park, and to deny any advantage to its rival, Canadian Northern (CNo). It sought to make the park a GTP enterprise, just as Rocky Mountains Park was the domain of the Canadian Pacific Railway (CPR).

GTP initially identified two possible townsites that it proposed to develop in the park: one near the mouth of the Fiddle River at the eastern gate of the park, which it designated as a tourist resort, and a second near Mile 112, which it intended as a railway divisional point. A large hotel was planned for the Fiddle River site, which would have had water piped into it from the hot springs above it—just as it was at the CPR's Banff Springs

Hotel. GTP went as far as having architect Francis Rattenbury prepare preliminary plans, but the site was never developed, possibly because of its proximity to the coal town of Pocahontas and because the company was having to economize to concentrate on building the railway line. The second site was named Fitzhugh after one of the railway's vice-presidents and this site began to absorb the activities of the neighbouring work camps. The earliest construction program in Fitzhugh concentrated on establishing facilities for the considerable railway yards that GTP planned to build at the town. A series of parallel tracks was constructed to allow for the formation of trains. A twelve-stall brick roundhouse, complete with turntable and maintenance shop, was completed in 1911. A substantial railway station with space for passengers, goods, and staff quarters was completed the following year.

The station was the most substantial one in the vicinity and was intended as a tourist portal to the park. The problem was that in 1912 there were no other tourist facilities in the town, as Rocky Mountains area superintendent Howard Douglas noted to national park headquarters that July: "The GTP are now running two passenger trains daily to Fitzhugh,

Fitzhugh, 1913. The streets have not been laid out and many of the buildings are temporary structures associated with the railway construction camp. LAC, PA 020485

and at present there is only one tent accommodation at the station, all the others are over a mile east, and it is a hardship on the public that stores and temporary stopping places are not nearer the station."[81] There were no defined streets and few frame buildings. Most buildings were temporary structures. Outside of the station, the most substantial building was a one-storey false-fronted frame building that housed the Fitzhugh Pool Room and Barber Shop. Fitzhugh remained largely a construction camp. The park superintendent wrote toward the end of 1912: "There is a floating population being daily fed at one canvas stopping place, by actual count from myself at one meal, of 135 men . . . These men are travelling back and forwards to and from the railway construction camps, as also a number of business men."[82]

Getting Fitzhugh surveyed into streets and lots so that a proper town could be established was a serious concern for both the railway and the parks branch. Preliminary plans for the town of Fitzhugh had been drawn up by the federal Department of the Interior's surveyor general's branch in 1911. The earliest drawings depicted a substantial town with a scenic drive bordering the Athabasca and Miette rivers. The GTP station grounds bisected the town as the community was the exclusive domain of the railway. By the end of 1911, however, the government realized that the rival CNo line would have to be accommodated, and so the original plan was scrapped.

A new plan was prepared at the end of 1912 that placed the town of Fitzhugh west of the GTP line. Surveying the streets and lots began in 1913. The bench above the river was reserved for the CNo line and the intervening space largely allocated for GTP railway yards. But though space was allocated alongside of the town for the CNo line, the presence of the GTP yards in town prevented the CNo from establishing a station there. Consequently, the CNo station was established a kilometre to the west and Fitzhugh remained a GTP town. The GTP station was made the focal point of the town by situating it at the intersection of three prominent streets, subsequently named Connaught, Miette, and Patricia. The park's new superintendent, S. Maynard Rogers, had named the main street in front of the station Connaught, after the country's Governor General at the time, the Duke of Connaught, Patricia Street was named after the Governor General's daughter, Princess Patricia of Connaught and Strathearn. She also gave her name to a nearby lake and to a famous Canadian regiment formed at the beginning of World War I.

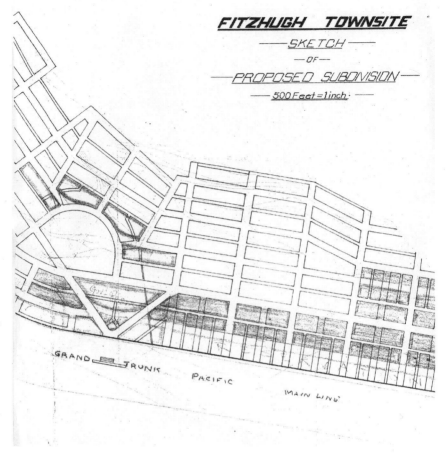

Fitzhugh town plan, 1912. LAC, RG 84, VOL. 523 J-19, PT. 1

With the lots surveyed, Fitzhugh began to take on a more permanent character. The impressive park superintendent's residence and administration building (now the park's Information Centre) was built across from the railway station in 1913. Designed by Edmonton architect Alfred Calderon, it was an early example of the rustic building tradition characterized by the use of logs, local stone, and a picturesque setting that became the hallmark of the national park building programs in the first half of the twentieth century. By 1914 there was a school, two churches, shops, and a permanent population of 125 people. That same year the town's name was changed to Jasper. Although the name change reflected the town's growing importance as the centre of the park, it was still very much a railway town as the railway supported the majority of the permanent residents. There were few tourist facilities at this time and the onset of the war delayed development for some years to come. Although there was little development, there were some initial assumptions made about activity zones that guided what little building did take place. Connaught was designated the commercial street and efforts were made to place stores and businesses along the one-sided strip facing the railway line. The noisy and dirty activities of the stables were placed along the back of the town, along Pyramid Street.

One of the few attempts to create a tourist facility during the 1910s was the Tent City at Lac Beauvert. The facility rented wooden-floored tents to tourists and erected a large marquee as a dining hall. Tent City hosted 260 guests during the 1915 season but then closed for the duration of the war.

Park superintendent's residence/park administration office, Jasper, mid-1930s. Designed by Edmonton architect A. M. Calderon and built between 1913 and 1914, his building established the benchmark for fine architectural standards in the town. It is one of the earliest and best examples of rustic design in the national parks and was consequently designated a national historic site. CSTM, CN 005557

The Brewster brothers took it over in 1919, building a log dining hall and a dance pavilion over the lake. It was taken over by the newly formed Canadian National Railways (CNR) in 1921.[83]

Beginning in 1922, a new force emerged to develop tourist facilities in the park. During World War I, both GTP and CNo lurched into bankruptcy. At first they sought to cut costs by co-operating instead of competing. They merged their line through the park, for instance. They then sought government loans, but with the escalating costs of the war, money for westward expansion had all but dried up. Finally, both lines were taken over by the Dominion government, which merged them into an enterprise that became known as CNR. Born out of financial calamity and political controversy, the publicly owned CNR sought to erase the stigma associated with its predecessors by adopting a bold expansionist program. In 1922 the federal government hired American-born Sir Henry Thornton as the railway's first president. The best way to make CNR viable, Thornton believed, was to be innovative. Among Thornton's many initiatives during his ten-year tenure was the expansion of the railway's hotel chain. This included the revival of a resort hotel scheme for Jasper National Park. Under Thornton's direction, CNR spent over two and a half million dollars on the development of this resort, which it called Jasper Park Lodge, on the former site of the Tent City at Lac Beauvert. Through the 1920s and into the 1930s the tourist centre of the park was CNR's Jasper Park Lodge.

When Jasper Park Lodge first opened for business on 19 June 1922, it consisted of nine small cabins built during the preceding months, along with two cabins inherited from the previous Tent City operation. Under Thornton's direction, this modest bungalow camp was transformed into a luxury resort containing approximately fifty log buildings during the next three years. The CNR's architectural department, headed by J. S. Schofield, turned the bungalow into a dramatic and impressive example of rustic architecture. The centrepiece of the resort complex was the main lodge, which opened for business in the summer of 1923. In its original configuration, the lodge consisted of a central rotunda from which three wings radiated. Although it contained a small number of guest rooms, the central rotunda and wings functioned primarily as a dining, social, and administrative centre. The rotunda was the visual centre for the resort: its interior was highlighted by a vaulted ceiling supported by an exposed log truss system replete with burled columns and bent-stick brackets. CNR boasted that it was the largest single-storey log structure in the world. The main lodge

Jasper Park Lodge c. 1925. The concept for a rustic cottage community offering luxury service was the notion of Sir Henry Thornton, the American-born president of Canadian National Railways. The first cottages were simple but exhibited fine rustic detail. PAA, 69.165/14

The interior of the original Jasper Park Lodge main building. The log cabin structural motif was carried into the large central building. Designed by Canadian National Railway's chief architect, John Schofield, it exemplifies the theme of luxury in the wilderness. CSTM, CN 005576

had massive log and stone walls and wicker-like verandah supports, taking the park's rustic tradition to new heights. The surrounding cottages and service buildings were designed to harmonize with this rustic theme.

The lodge resort was a huge success and filled to capacity during the summer season. This success inspired an expansion program between 1927 and 1931 that increased the number of buildings at the lodge from fifty to seventy. The new buildings, also designed by Schofield's architectural department, included new guest bungalows, staff dormitories, a new garage for the lodge's fleet of limousines, a golf clubhouse, and a golfers' bungalow. The golf facilities were part of the equally successful golf course that had recently opened. It was a redevelopment of a nine-hole course that had been built adjacent to the lodge by the parks service in 1924. This course was scarcely opened before the government leased the three hundred acres of land to CNR and, again under Thornton's direction, a much more ambitious project was undertaken. CNR hired leading Canadian golf course architect Stanley Thompson to design a sophisticated eighteen-hole course that was completed in 1925. Thompson's design called for the blasting of stone outcroppings and the transportation of forty freight car loads of new topsoil to develop new bunkers, fairways, and greens on eighty-five acres of the site. Many of the golf holes were lined up with surrounding mountain peaks, giving golfers distinctive landmarks to "aim" at. Opened in 1925, the course became one of Jasper Park Lodge's most celebrated attractions, and influenced subsequent development at the resort.

At the same time that Jasper was being developed as an important tourist destination, CNR was also building an important operational centre in the town. CNo's divisional point for the mountains had been in Lucerne, on the British Columbia side of the Yellowhead Pass, but in 1924 this operation was transferred to Jasper, essentially doubling the population of the town to 250. As a result of this transfer, the railway facilities were expanded. The roundhouse for repairing locomotives was enlarged to include six new stalls that could accommodate the larger locomotives then in use. A one-hundred-foot turntable replaced the original one in 1930.[84] To accommodate the larger passenger service, another track was added between the existing tracks and the town.

In 1924 fire destroyed the old GTP station, providing an opportunity for CNR to replace it with a stylish new facility. CNR's new Jasper station, designed by the railway's building department in Winnipeg, was built to accommodate the burgeoning tourist traffic. It was one of the railway's first

Canadian National Railways train station, Jasper. Built in 1925 to replace an earlier station that had been destroyed by fire, the new station reflected the building's status as the focal point of the town. While the stone work echoes the nearby park administration building, it expands on the traditions of the English Arts and Crafts movement. JYMA, 89.36.09

large stations. The size and stylishness of the station reflected the growing optimism about Jasper as a tourist destination and emphasized the importance of the station as a portal for arriving visitors. Prior to building the new station, CNR announced that the building's style would be "in keeping with that of the park administration."[85] Indeed, the station does echo some of the features of the former administration building with its dormer windows, steeply pitched roof, and cobblestone trim, although it differs from the park building in several respects: it lacks the rustic details such as the park building's log construction and its hipped irregular roofline. Rather, the station's prominent stepped chimney, projecting bays, and rough stucco finish give it a more English appearance, showing the influence of the English Arts and Crafts movement. It also differs in scale. Where the park building resembles a rustic cottage, the station resembles a large English country home.

Initially services in the town of Jasper were provided by the railway.

The chief water main ran from Cabin Creek to the CNR shops located across from the station. Nearby houses tapped into this line for their own use. Similarly, the principal source of electricity was the CNR generator located at the roundhouse. Sometime in the 1920s, the federal government ran a line from this generator into the town so that residences could operate electric lights.

Through the 1920s, the parks service undertook several engineering projects aimed at facilitating its operations, such as warden patrol, fire protection, and enhancing tourist travel in the park. In 1921 J. B. Snape was sent from Ottawa to act as Jasper's resident engineer and most of these early projects were carried out under his direction. A series of first-class ten-foot-wide pack trails, often with bridge crossings, was built to open up the Snake Indian, Southesk, and Brazeau districts. Later trails were built into the scenic Tonquin Valley. In addition, although the park was still only accessible by rail through the 1920s, the construction of a road system was begun that would convey autos and motor buses to popular sightseeing destinations in the park.

Mount Edith Cavell received considerable attention when in 1916 it was named after a British nurse who had been shot by the Germans during World War I. It was a nearby destination that attracted visitors for its outstanding views and impressive glaciers. Construction of a mountain access road was commenced in 1916, but the work was carried out slowly until the 1920s. By 1924, however, the park had completed 16.5 miles of road to allow motor access to within a mile of one of Cavell's glaciers; a footpath continued the rest of the way. Then, in 1927, the road was extended over the last mile to the glacier and finished with a car park. A log tea house was built to provide refreshment at the end of the road and the park's engineering service developed trails to scenic viewpoints above the glacier. Originally named Ghost Glacier, in 1925–1926 the Geographic Names Board of Canada changed its name to Angel to allude to the winged figure its shape seemed to resemble and perhaps to allude to a spiritual association with the martyred nurse.[86] Church memorial services are still held at this site.

Another early highway project was the construction of an auto road toward the eastern boundary of the park. Construction was made easier by the use of abandoned rail beds. In 1923, the old CNo grade from Jasper to Snaring was turned into a road. After 1924, when the closure of Pocahontas allowed for the removal of the old GTP spur line of the CNR, road construction proceeded along that right-of-way. By 1928 the province had commenced building a highway west from Edmonton to Jasper and the park pushed to extend the Pocahontas road east to the park boundary by the end of the decade.

This road east to the park boundary opened up the scenery of the northeast Athabasca valley and made the hot springs at Miette slightly more accessible. The trail from the road up to the hot springs was improved in 1925, although it was still an arduous journey by horseback. In the 1920s development at the hot springs was rudimentary. According to engineer Snape's recollection, "The only work done on the springs had originally been done by Indians who went there in the early days and with logs built a small bathing pool, and a few sweat houses where you could go in and 'sweat' in the heat and steam of the hot water."[87] Snape forgot to mention the government-built facilities that had gone up before World War I. In 1913 a crude bathhouse and sleeping shelter were built there. These were soon followed by several changing rooms. Just after the war, this motley collection of buildings was in a very dilapidated state and the whole arrangement was described as being very unsavoury.[88] The change rooms were dilapidated shacks, there were no washroom facilities, and the grounds were strewn with garbage.[89] Part of the problem stemmed from the heavy use that the miners made of the place. Respectable tourists would have stayed away, not wishing to get close to the uncouth workers.

While Jasper Park Lodge remained the tourist centre of the park, parks engineers made the improvement of road links between the railway station and the lodge a priority. A first-class steel girder bridge was constructed in 1920 crossing the Athabasca River near Old Fort Point. In 1927 and 1928, the road from the bridge to the lodge was paved using tar sand from Fort McMurray. This was an experimental project and proved to be very successful. The park also worked to improve the system of trails leading from the lodge toward Maligne Lake. Although the tours themselves were managed by outfitters such as Fred Brewster and Curly Phillips, the trail system and eventual road connection to Medicine Lake were built by park construction crews. The park also developed a system of scenic trails along the Maligne Canyon portion of this route that had become a popular day trip for park visitors. The construction of a footbridge across Maligne Canyon in 1925 allowed for a circular walk to be opened up on both sides of the canyon. The Maligne Canyon trail system was upgraded during the 1930s by unemployment relief workers.

Another area of interest for the park engineering service was the town of Jasper. By 1914, a cluster of town buildings had gone up that included, aside from the park headquarters, two churches, a post office, fire hall, general store, and several dwellings. Some log buildings were still left at the former GTP engineers' camp at the west end of town. A few park employees found accommodation there, including the supervising warden and the resident engineer, J. B. Snape, who bestowed his name on this neighbourhood that was afterward known as Snape's Hill.

As the town grew in the 1920s, the park engineering service was called on both to enlarge the number of town lots and expand the available services. The original water supply from Cabin Creek was improved by the construction of a dam in 1927–1928 that raised the level of the lake by three feet. New water mains were also laid at this time. Following the creation of the town as a railway divisional point, the park engineers laid out four new residential blocks to provide housing for the people who had moved to Jasper from Lucerne. Later in the 1920s, efforts were being made to improve the appearance of the town, to make it seem more of a tourist resort than a functional railway town. Sidewalks were built and indigenous shrubs and trees were planted along the boulevard that ran down the middle of Connaught Drive.

The 1920s was a time of considerable growth for the town of Jasper. Not only did the railway expand its divisional point there, but new tourist facilities sprang up to cater to the growing number of tourists. The annual number of visitors climbed from seven thousand in 1920 to over fifteen thousand in 1929, leading to an increased demand for hotels, restaurants, shops, and livery services. A banner year was 1928, when the annual report of the Commissioner of national parks announced: "Building operations in Jasper included 14 new residences, 8 stores and business premises, 1 new bank, 1 new church and a number of garages and small buildings."[90] These new buildings generally reflected a quality of design and materials that contrasted sharply with the usual boom towns of the time. This high standard of design was largely due to the strict planning and design guidelines that were imposed by the national parks branch through its recently established architecture and town planning division.

Commissioner J. B. Harkin had realized even before the war that national park towns would have to be carefully planned if they were to compete with European tourist centres. He had previously invited English town planner Thomas Mawson to devise preliminary plans for Banff in 1914. After the war, he turned to Thomas Adams for advice. Adams was a pioneer town planner in Britain with experience in planning garden city communities for industrial residential areas before he came to Canada in 1914 to join the Commission of Conservation, an extraordinary federal agency established in 1909 to advise the government on the latest ideas relating to managing natural resources. Later it came to include social issues such as town planning and sanitation in its mandate. From his Ottawa base, Adams was involved in the planning of a number of Canadian communities, including the company town of Témiscamingue, Quebec; the part of Halifax that was devastated by the 1917 explosion; and the Ottawa suburb of Lindenlea.[91]

Close but informal relations were continued between Adams and Harkin's office until 1921 when he joined the parks branch as part of its new town planning division. That year, Adams prepared a comprehensive plan for the new Jasper townsite, integrating new building with the park setting. Park subdivisions were Adams's specialty. His biographer, Michael Simpson, described the Jasper project as one of his more successful efforts: "Adams retained the wooded nature of the location, drawing roads in gentle curves alongside the railway which had a pleasant railway approach surrounded by a business centre. Garden suburb housing for residents was complemented by abundant camping and recreational grounds."[92] Unfortunately, Adams's complete plan was never realized and Jasper is still characterized by the grid street plan, a concept to which Adams was resolutely opposed.

Adams's involvement in the town planning division meant that Ottawa assumed greater control over new park planning, for Adams argued that individual initiatives had to be co-ordinated for the larger good. "The towns and villages that grow up in these parks need also to be planned in such a way as to serve their main purpose as recreational centres and tourist resorts," Adams wrote in 1923. "A proper feature of which is to make them attractive by conservation of natural beauty and erection of agreeable buildings with good sanitary conditions."[93] There was a degree of elitism in Adams's thinking, since he believed only his office could properly decide what was or was not suitable. By 1922, therefore, the commissioner stipulated that all plans for new buildings in Jasper National Park be submitted to the town planning office for review and approval. Of the plans submitted during the fiscal year 1922–1923, the annual report of the commissioner claimed that "in the majority of cases improvements were suggested and in many cases entirely new drawings prepared with a view to establishing more suitable and effective architecture in the various social settlements."[94] Adams gradually drifted away from the parks branch after 1923, but his work in supervising park building was assumed by his very capable associate, W. D. Cromarty. As an architect, Cromarty restructured the division to place more emphasis on architecture and it was soon re-named the architecture and town planning division. Nonetheless, along with the engineering division, Cromarty's group continued to play an important role in defining national park development through the 1930s. Later, in the 1950s, architecture would be merged with engineering and planning would re-emerge as a distinct unit but in the interwar period the two disciplines were joined under Cromarty's direction.

Like Adams, Cromarty had been trained in England and had some experience in that country, as well as in Sudan, before immigrating to Canada in 1912. He taught briefly at a few Canadian universities, including a brief stint at the University of Alberta School of Architecture where he likely was associated with architect Alfred Calderon. Cromarty's influence on national park architecture was profound, especially in Waterton, where he spent time as a seasonal superintendent in the 1920s, and in Riding Mountain National Park in Manitoba, and Prince Albert National Park in Saskatchewan, where he greatly influenced the appearance of the new towns of Wasagaming and Waskesiu, respectively, that were built there in the 1930s.

Cromarty's work incorporated elements of North American rustic style with those of traditional English architecture then being revived by the Arts and Crafts movement. A typical Cromarty building might combine log walls, large stone chimneys with a steeply pitched roof, and irregular eave lines. Characteristic features of his buildings are the half-timber effect on smooth plaster walls and cobblestone foundation walls and pillars. In Jasper, however, Cromarty's rustic Tudor work has been overshadowed by the CN station and the many fine buildings of Calderon, many of which also demonstrate the influence of the English Arts and Crafts movement. In some ways, these earlier buildings may even have influenced Cromarty's own work. His 1926 design for the sub-detachment building for the Royal Canadian Mounted Police (today, the municipal library), for example, while typical of his work, also shows the influence of the CN train station. Cromarty's more original contributions can be seen on some of the commercial buildings along Connaught Drive. His Chaba Theatre (1926) and the new front for the Jeffery Store at 410 Connaught (1927) both incorporate second-storey awnings and parapet fronts typical of imperial architecture in warmer climes like Australia and Africa.

*Jasper's RCMP building. Built in 1926 after a design of the national parks'
architectural division's W. D. Cromarty, it is in the style of the English Arts and
Crafts movement and reflects the influence of the recently completed CNR station.
This building in turn influenced many national park buildings built in the 1920s
and 1930s. The RCMP building was converted into the town library in 1975.*
JYMA, PA 20755

In its vision for park accommodation, the early national parks branch designated an intermediate development between permanent residences in townsites and rental accommodations such as hotels and lodges. Seasonal cottages were becoming popular with residents of nearby urban areas. Most of the branch's western parks also had provisions for seasonal cottage developments. Often organized along lakefronts as at Waterton and Wasagaming, these developments catered to a more local clientele who wished to spend their summers at a particular park location. These were usually in proximity to the main townsites, yet formed separate suburban entities. This was a concept that Adams was very familiar with and he soon got into the spirit of designing new villa lot developments in Jasper. Summer cottage subdivisions had been surveyed at Patricia and Pyramid lakes in 1913. No cottages were built at Patricia Lake, however, and only eight cottage lots were let at Pyramid Lake between 1922 and 1928 when the last lease was issued.[95]

Jeffery Store, c. 1930. The present front was added on to an earlier building in 1927. Designed by the national parks' architectural division, it shows the influence of colonial architecture with its built-in awnings and decorative brick work. The camera store on the left was designed by A. M. Calderon and built in 1925. Its use of stone, half-timbering, and gabled roofing shows an affinity to commercial buildings designed by the architectural division's W. D. Cromarty. JNP, H5143

Lake Edith was not one of the original cottage subdivisions laid out by the park, but it was the only cottage area that was developed. It was the site of a YMCA camp that had been located on the south shore since 1915 and it was beside the Lac Beauvert Tent City that would shortly become Jasper Park Lodge, so the area was already the focus of summer occupation. The notion for a cottage subdivision here grew out of a proposal for a writers and artists' colony approved for the north shore of the lake in 1920. According to Ferg Lothian, who based his history on the departmental record in Ottawa, the prototypes for this colony were an artists' colony in Mt. Carmel, California, and a writers' colony in Santa Fe, New Mexico. The proponent of the colony was a Canadian, then living in New York, named Agnes Laut (1871–1936). She was an author, well known in Canada and the United States for her romantic novels, histories of the fur trade and exploration, and travel accounts. She contributed three volumes to the then prestigious

Makers of Canada series, including *The Adventurers of England on Hudson Bay*.[96] Much of Laut's writing is set against the backdrop of the Canadian wilds. It was fitting, then, that she sought a rustic setting for a summer retreat.

According to the annual report of the Commissioner of Dominion Parks for the fiscal year 1921–1922, "Miss Laut, the well-known writer and publicist, and Miss Julia E. Follett, of New York, have erected four attractive bungalows, the first of the proposed colony of authors, artists and university professors which Miss Laut hopes to establish in the park."[97] The area was surveyed in 1921 and again in 1923 when the formal subdivision was laid out. The layout for the Lake Edith subdivision, as it was called by 1923, was considerably larger than the proposed artists and writers' colony approved in 1920, as it also included cottage lots that were to be open for general leasehold. In some respects, the cottage subdivision was similar to large private developments of the 1920s, such as Seba Beach on Wabamun Lake west of Edmonton and Victoria Beach on Lake Winnipeg. These developments shared a number of characteristics: they were summer villages with a large number of relatively small cottage lots arranged on blocks set back from a common waterfront.

Despite the grandiose schemes of Agnes Laut and the Ottawa planners, the subsequent Lake Edith cottage development did not turn out as predicted. There does not seem to have been the level of interest indicated by the initial enthusiasm shown for the project. First, transportation to and around the park was a problem. There were few vehicles in Jasper in the 1920s and park visitors relied on the train to get them to the park and livery outfits to get them around. These circumstances favoured resorts like Jasper Park Lodge where the visitors could be completely catered to during their stays rather than the more rugged back country cabins of Lake Edith where guests had to fend for themselves.

A second reason why the proposed artist colony did not get off the ground may have been Agnes Laut's own inertia. As a New Yorker, she was a long way from the scene and had increasing difficulty keeping in touch. For these and other reasons, the artist colony was stillborn. Only six cabins were built in the Laut reserve before 1930 and these were rented out indiscriminately. For a while it seems as if Miss Laut used a local handyman named Jim Cunningham to look after the cabins. Cunningham probably built most, if not all, of the cabins on the reserve. At times, Miss Laut would use the park superintendent, the always sympathetic Maynard Rogers, to help rent the places. Miss Laut also let cabins to the YMCA, which ran a camp on the south shore of Lake Edith.

However, by the 1930s the few buildings of the Laut colony that had been built were becoming run down and were catering to less respectable guests than the park had been promised in 1920. Colonel Rogers's attempts to keep up appearances took on an increasingly pathetic tone as his efforts to attract decent clientele were thwarted by the unwashed denizens of the place. Writing to Laut in 1933, Rogers told of finding a respectable mother and daughter who were looking for a summer place. "Feeling that likely you might not come out here this year," he wrote, "I thought the Byng Bungalow would just fit the bill if you wished to rent it. I took them over there and found the door open and the cabin in a very filthy state ... Evidently Jim's [Cunningham's] man, a bohunk, is living there."[98] In 1935, Rogers, who seems to have acted as Miss Laut's advocate, was replaced as park superintendent by A. C. Wright who was less sympathetic to the aging writer and her dreams of a socially upscale retreat. The new superintendent wrote to Ottawa in 1935 saying, "There is no reason to continue any reservation for Miss Laut as she has displayed no active interest in this area for at least ten years and it is my understanding that she has now disposed of her properties on Lot 4 Block 6 and Lot 3 Block 9, to the YMCA of Edmonton."[99] The following year, Laut died and the idea of an artists' colony died with her. Well before this time, Blocks 8 and 9 were being managed like the other cottage lots on Lake Edith. Meanwhile, during the 1930s and 1940s, a group of largely well-to-do Edmontonians began to build on the Lake Edith cottage lots, developing a cottage colony of a different order that still flourishes today.

A new spate of building commenced in the mid-1930s, driven by the need to accommodate the growing number of automobile tourists and funded by Depression-relief spending. In the summer of 1936, for example, over one thousand motor vehicles entered the park through its east gate. New facilities were needed to accommodate this new visitor influx—less formal and expensive than the railway facilities like Jasper Park Lodge. Auto-campgrounds had been introduced in the mountain parks to the south in the 1920s. They were favoured by the parks administration because they appealed to a broad spectrum of visitors, including those of limited means, and they promoted healthy outdoor activity associated with the national park mission. They were closely identified with highways—first, because the campers arrived by vehicles and, second, they were often built beside the highways that served the parks. The range of motor vehicles that existed in this era was much less broad than today, roads were slower, and vehicles did not go as fast, so campgrounds provided a chain of simple flexible accommodation that offered safe havens along the park highways.

Jasper Park and the Ottawa office both wanted to develop the Miette Hot Springs as a major tourist destination and yet the anticipated costs and difficulty of the task caused the project to be delayed. Relief workers began improving the road access to the springs in the early 1930s, but development of the springs themselves was beyond the means of the relief projects. Meanwhile, the facilities at the springs were primitive at best and rapidly getting worse as they became overused. In 1933, the assistant parks commissioner, F. H. H. Williamson, wrote Jasper superintendent Rogers to express his concern: "I shudder to think of what would happen if any person should take some pictures or send out to the newspapers reports of the conditions of the Hot Springs." He added that "if these places cannot be maintained in a thoroughly clean, orderly and sanitary condition, then we must immediately close them."[100] The hot springs development was high on the list of projects submitted for funding through the 1934 *Public Works Construction Act.* That year the parks branch's architectural

Miette Hot Springs bathhouse (demolished in the 1980s). Built in 1937 using Depression relief funding, the building employed the Tudor Rustic style favoured by the national parks' architectural division for its larger buildings during the interwar period. JNP, H2246

division designed a large rustic Tudor revival building at the springs to house change rooms, showers, and related facilities, along with a 40x16-metre pool and a laundry and caretaker's residence. Still, it was not until 1936 that actual construction was funded and the facility formally opened in the summer of 1938.

The opening of such an important tourist destination as Miette Hot Springs created a need for other tourist facilities. A campground and picnic facility was built there by the park, but the federal government also planned for a related privately run bungalow camp. A license to establish a bungalow camp near the Miette Hot Springs was granted to W. Fay Becker in 1937, who began construction the following year. The general plans and cabin specifications were drawn up by the architecture and town planning division in Ottawa. The actual designs were produced by Addison Scratch, who designed Becker's other bungalows in Banff. The main dining room and store building was constructed in 1939 and by 1940 there were about ten cabins situated around the central building. The cabins and lodge are still in use today.

Park development was curtailed during World War II, followed by the brief lull of post-war recovery. Tourist numbers also declined during this period. But following this hiatus, tourists returned to the park in ever-increasing numbers. The post-war tourist boom in Jasper also brought a post-war building boom. The new buildings reflected the growing prosperity of the park, as well as the revolutionary new approaches that were being applied to construction and design that form part of modern architecture.

This new modern look for Jasper is exemplified in a number of key buildings, the earliest being the new central building of Jasper Park Lodge. In 1952, the old main lodge building was destroyed by fire and a new lodge quickly put up in its place. The second lodge building was a worthy successor to the first, giving a corresponding majesty and presence to the facility. However, unlike the mainly log construction of the original, the second lodge introduced a modern reworking of the old rustic tradition. It skilfully fused reinforced concrete and steel construction and contemporary post-war architectural forms to the historical traditions embodied in the older log buildings on the site. Broad low-pitched gable roofs convey an appearance reminiscent of Frank Lloyd Wright's Prairie style. Gable ends angle outwards, accentuating the horizontality and shading the soaring glass-panelled wall surfaces below. Exterior surfaces are clad with cut fieldstone or slab log siding. The new/old look set the tone for subsequent

The new Jasper Park Lodge main building, built in 1952–1953. The new building blended elements of the original rustic style, such as stone pillars and timber beams, with elements of modern architectural design. It is a fitting successor to the original building. CSTM, CN 006876

development at Jasper Park Lodge through the 1950s and 1960s. The lodge began to replace many of its more dilapidated log cabins with newer, more densely placed cabins designed along the new motif.

The town was transformed in the 1960s and 1970s and modern buildings brought greater density and efficiency to the tourist infrastructure. During this period, there were virtually no imposed architectural and planning guidelines as there had been in the pre-war era and it is fortunate that the streetscapes have preserved the amount of distinctive atmosphere that they do. In part, the attractiveness of the new architecture reflected the wealth that the town's business community was experiencing. The development of Jasper as a year-round resort further encouraged the creation of more substantial-looking buildings. Curiously, during this period of expansion, there was very little administrative park-building. Most of Parks Canada's building programs were centred on highway construction, with very few public buildings going up. Exceptions were the Icefields Information Building, and the new campground buildings that appeared at Wapiti campground, both erected in 1962. New public buildings began to appear again later in the 1990s, most notably a new bathing facility at Miette Hot Springs and a large visitor centre replacing the old Brewster lodge at the Columbia Icefields.

Much of the new building in Jasper townsite has, like the new building at Jasper Park Lodge, attempted a modern reinterpretation of the rustic building tradition with the use of river rock, clear stained wood, and pitched gable roofs. This tradition has been continued outside of the town in the Icefields Interpretive Centre, a large building whose massing and materials evoke an earlier time. While government buildings of the 1960s occasionally attempted the blending of modern and rustic (the Wapiti kitchen shelters discussed in the next chapter being an excellent example) or, alternatively, tried bold modern designs, as in the former Icefields Information Building, more recent buildings have reflected government austerity programs and tend to be plain and utilitarian in appearance. Despite

The Columbia Icefields Information Building, demolished in the 1990s. Built in 1962, the building shows the modern international style favoured by the national parks' architectural division in the 1960s.
JYMA, JASPER NATIONAL PARK COLLECTION

these recent aberrations, Jasper National Park has a valuable and interesting collection of buildings, from early representations of the rustic tradition, such as the Infocentre and Jasper Park Lodge bungalows, to later examples of English vernacular styles, such as St. George's Church and the Jasper station, all complemented by many sensitively designed newer buildings. Nor is the rich architectural tradition of the park confined to a few isolated monuments. The streetscapes and building clusters of the residential developments and commercial areas intermingle with carefully planned and well-maintained green spaces to create a unique ambience.[101]

CHAPTER SIX

Campers

Although some might feel nature is just a scenic backdrop to Jasper's tourist facilities, others believe the essence of the park is in its natural environment. And like enthusiasts from the beginning of the twentieth century, many still believe the best way to experience nature is to camp out in it. Mary Schäffer, along with two guides and three other companions, travelled to Jasper by way of Lake Louise and Maligne Lake in 1908. They were among the first real tourists to visit the park and they were campers. After all, there was nowhere else to stay. They camped along the shores of Maligne Lake and the Athabasca River, picking the most convenient spots to pitch their tents and build their fires, and cutting spruce boughs for their beds. Camping was an integral part of Schäffer's experience of the wilderness park and it began a strong tradition in Jasper that continues to this day, although the practice has become much more organized and more lavishly equipped than in Schäffer's time.

Camping was first organized in Jasper by the horse outfitters who initiated set tours into the backcountry. Gradually, like at Maligne Lake or the Tonquin Valley, permanent camps were established with tipis and log dining shelters. With the advent of auto tourism in the 1920s, national parks introduced more formal camping spots along the highways that followed the idyllic tradition of the horse camps. The campgrounds had kitchen shelters and were situated beside streams for water, and left the tourist to park his car, pitch his tent, and build his fire more or less at random on the grassy meadows provided. Pioneer auto-campers brought their own specialized equipment, such as air mattresses, sleeping bags, gas stoves, and umbrella tents. Gradually, as increased use began to affect both the physical and social environments of the park, park engineers designed campgrounds with designated spots for parking, tents or trailers, toilets, and fires. Yet, the elements of the early idyllic tradition persist: camping remains non-commercial in the park, although a fee is charged; the campfire remains an integral part of the camping experience and; until recently at least, the kitchen shelter remained a quaint throwback to the horse camp dining shelters.

The Jasper outfitters, who generally organized tourism in the park during the 1920s and 1930s, were campers. Outside of the town and Jasper Park Lodge, tents were the only accommodation in the park until bungalow camps began to appear in the late 1930s. And even bungalow camps, one could argue, are a development of the campground model. In the backcountry, camping was, as it still is today, an important part of the overall experience. The outfitters took care to make their camps as pleasant as possible. They were usually located in open meadows, beside streams or lakes. Outfitter Fred Brewster had more or less permanent camps set up at Medicine, Maligne, and Amethyst lakes and in Shovel Pass on the Skyline Trail. Wooden floors were built for the tents, fire pits and benches for the evening bonfire, and hitching rails for the horses. Eventually, some of the camps offered log chalets to provide more secure food storage and cleaner and drier environments for the cooks. Outside of the town and these proprietary camps, people were allowed to camp wherever they liked in the park, although there were well-known regularly used stopping places along the main backcountry routes.

Magic in a Camp-fire

Since John Muir first wrote about the virtues of national parks to overcivilized Americans at the beginning of the twentieth century, there was the growing belief that camping out was an ideal way to enjoy nature. Early in the twentieth century, a romantic ideal of the backcountry camp emerged. Horace Klephart wrote in his handbook, *Camping and Woodcraft*, in 1917: "If one would realize in its perfection his dream of peace and freedom from every worldly care, let him keep away from summer resorts and even from farms; let him camp out; and let it be the real thing."[102] Lawrence Burpee's books written in the 1920s relate experiencing this ideal in the backcountry of Jasper. Of one camp he wrote: "In the evening in the open tent with everything snug for the night and a camp-fire burning cheerily before us, we made ourselves as comfortable as the mosquitoes would permit, and the warden, being once more in a reminiscent mood, spun some of his yarns." Elsewhere Burpee wrote: "There is magic in a camp-fire, and very special magic in a camp-fire in the mountains."[103] Camping out in Jasper also helped Burpee to make imaginative

Early campers, Jasper, c. 1914. JYMA, PA 7-112

contact with historical travellers, such as the early fur traders, missionaries, and surveyors who would later grace the pages of his books.

Campground, Jasper, 1919. This may actually be part of the Brewsters' Tent City establishment, but it illustrates the sense of community that existed in many of the parks' campgrounds in the first half of the twentieth century. PAA, B1.277/3

When auto-tourists began coming to Jasper in the early 1930s, many of these people also camped. In those days, camping reinforced the sense of the freedom of the open road. Where cars allowed people to travel without timetables on flexible routes, camping allowed the travellers to stop wherever and whenever they pleased. As highway routes were developed across North America, it was common to find small lay-bys where an auto-camper could park his car, pitch his tent, and brew up a cup of tea. The curious thing about auto-camping as it gained in popularity in the 1920s was that it was socially acceptable. No longer associated with gypsies, vagabonds, or the poorer classes, automobile tourists gave camping middle-class respectability. It was this tradition that automobile tourists brought to Jasper in the 1930s, fusing it to the earlier ideal of backcountry camping in national parks.

In the tradition of the time, the first auto-campers pitched their tents wherever they pleased outside of the town. A favourite early camping place was Lake Annette but, as there were no facilities, it soon became unpleasant. Jack Brewster, who opened one of the first gas stations in town, reported in 1932 that people were complaining about the lack of more formal camping facilities. "Why don't the Parks establish a regular camp ground here like they have at Banff?" was the common refrain.[104]

Depression relief work ended up providing the means to create just this sort of thing. The first formal campground to be opened in the park was Cottonwood Creek, completed in 1934 and situated on the Athabasca River in front of the town of Jasper. A more deluxe campground opened at Patricia Lake on the slopes behind the town the following year. As more highways were built later in the decade, the park built campgrounds at Miette Hot Springs and Medicine Lake. With the exception of the small Medicine Lake site, which was of a simpler design, the 1930s campgrounds had washrooms with flush toilets and cold water sinks, kitchen shelters equipped with wood-burning stoves, and picnic tables. The camping areas were open grassy fields, criss-crossed by access roads. There were no allocated sites and cars and tents were randomly scattered across the area. Occasionally, groups would cluster together while individuals or couples would search for more seclusion. The kitchen shelters, which were meant to be communal, brought strangers and family members together in the shared experience of camping, and people recounted stories of the road and other camping spots along the way, forming a culture of modern-day travelling people.

The Patricia Lake campground, located a few kilometres from the town, was by contrast more carefully landscaped. The work was carried out by relief workers who occupied a nearby camp. The annual report for the national parks service described the work being done on the grounds in 1933. The main street was graded for a length of 2,500 feet. Four blocks were surveyed and staked, and five cross streets were laid out. Five kitchen shelters of standard park design were constructed. Five hundred conifers were planted along the west side of the entrance road and on the bench near Patricia Lake to enhance the natural beauty of the campsite. Patricia Lake seems to have been intended to be the premier campground of the park for its building received more attention than elsewhere. Although the washroom buildings were of the same plan as Cottonwood Creek, they were built of log. The kitchen shelters were similar, being open and supported on eight log posts but had a medium pitched gable end roof. The old Patricia Lake campground was closed and given to Patricia Lakes Bungalows in

1954. The new owners cleverly recycled some of the well-built campground buildings. Three of the four former washroom buildings have been converted into staff accommodation, the fourth has been converted into rental accommodation. One of the kitchen shelters exists virtually unchanged as a barbeque area, the other has been converted into a storage building.

Although the campgrounds met a growing demand from the automobile tourists, none of them was ideal. Cottonwood Creek campground had problems because it was immediately downstream from the main sewer outfall from the town. This made bathing in the area unappealing, if not dangerous to health, and although the drinking water was taken from the nearby creek, this source was laden with sediment. Patricia Lake, although equipped with deluxe service buildings and landscaped with imported trees, had a reputation for being cold, windy, and uncomfortable. Miette Hot Springs was a long way up a dead-end road and Medicine Lake was small and equipped with only pit privies. For these reasons, Jim Wood, the new superintendent of Jasper, recommended in 1938 that the parks service abandon both the Cottonwood and Patricia Lake campgrounds and establish a major new campground near the town on the Athabasca River. However, the parks service had invested too heavily in the different campgrounds to change its mind so soon, and so they spent several years trying to improve them before they were both disposed of later in the 1950s.

After the end of World War II, tourism soon regained its pre-war peaks and began to soar with the terrific growth in Jasper tourism driven in part by the new highway construction. The pre-war tourist-count high had been fifteen thousand. In 1946, almost thirty thousand people came to the park, in 1951 almost 100,000. In 1955, over 150,000 visitors came, two years later the number had risen to 330,000. Through this period, Cottonwood remained the premier campground in the park, and park staff struggled to keep up with both demand and rising expectations for campground quality. In 1950, they built new kitchen shelters and washroom buildings and added a ten-unit trailer facility and an outdoor theatre to Cottonwood. Further expansion followed and by 1954, its 225 tent and forty-four trailer sites made it the second largest campground in the national parks system after Tunnel Mountain in Banff.

Meanwhile, park camping capacity was improved by developing satellite campgrounds. Although the Patricia and Medicine lake facilities were closed down, new simple small-capacity campgrounds were built at Pocahontas near the east gate at the foot of the Miette Hot Springs road, at

The Miette campground, early 1980s. COURTESY, MIKE DILLON, JNP.

Snaring River, and along the Icefields Parkway. The norm at this time was for each national park to have one fully serviced campground with hot running water, showers, and sometimes even laundry facilities. Cottonwood was earmarked to receive these upgrades. With Cottonwood's facilities quickly reaching maximum capacity, park planners began scouting out possibilities for another large campground.

At first the planners proceeded with the idea that the park should create a second fully serviced campground south of town on the old Banff–Jasper Highway (now Highway 93A). Wabasso campground, as it was named, opened in 1959. Two years later, a second campground was planned closer to town and with more convenient access to the rebuilt Icefields Parkway that opened in 1961. The resulting Wapiti campground, which opened in 1962, originally had 180 sites. Both new campgrounds had individual sites, screened by trees and shrubs with separate spaces for tents, trailers, and vehicles. Wapiti campground introduced some of the new ideas for campground design introduced by the national park architects in Ottawa in the 1960s. Called a "semi-serviced" campground, it was intended to fill a niche between the small unserviced campgrounds like Snaring and the

The Wapiti campground, 1964. The girl is crouched in front of the authorized wooden tent platform. PAA, PA 3371/2

Wapiti kitchen shelter. COURTESY THE AUTHOR

large suburban fully serviced campgrounds like Cottonwood. Simply put, Wapiti tried for a natural rustic setting but with flush toilets. Wapiti was also distinguished for introducing a new architectural style. Earlier shelters and washrooms were traditionally built in a rustic style, with log and stone finishes. In contrast, the Wapiti shelters and washroom buildings had a distinctly modern look with post and beam construction, brightly coloured plywood panels, and low-pitched roofs.

Through the 1950s, the national parks branch had the policy of establishing two classes of campgrounds in each park. The first, called a serviced campground, would be located near the townsites and would provide modern conveniences such as flush toilets and hot and cold running water in the washrooms. The second type, located away from park centres, would be much smaller and equipped with minimal facilities, often only having a pit privy and a single cold water tap. While each park took responsibility for building the unserviced or primitive campgrounds, building the large serviced campgrounds was the responsibility of the Ottawa-based engineering services division.

At the end of the 1950s, the division was planning to initiate a large building program that would put a new fully serviced campground in almost every national park in the system. While design work was underway, a discussion took place at headquarters about whether the new campground design was compatible with the national park experience. The chief of planning, Lloyd Brooks, asked, "Are we not gradually destroying the whole concept of camping through introducing automatic washers, electric stoves etc?"[105] As a result of this criticism, the planners began promoting the idea of a "semi-serviced" campground that sought to redefine the concept of a larger national park camping facility. This new campground would have flush toilets and running water, but it would not have hot water and certainly no showers or laundry facilities. Wapiti campground in Jasper was the first of four semi-serviced campgrounds also built in Waterton Lakes, Kootenay and Yoho national parks between 1961 and 1964.

Wabasso and Wapiti introduced a new way of camping in Jasper Park in the 1960s. At Cottonwood, people had registered and then found a place to camp on the open field, which sometimes led to overcrowding. A complaint submitted in 1960 about Banff's Tunnel Mountain campground on a bad night could just as easily been applied to Cottonwood on the August long weekend: "Owing to the late hour we camped our tent side by side with others jam-packed into a filthy, dusty area over which autos could proceed without any traffic control."[106] At Wabasso and Wapiti there were numbered sites; visitors would first register and then be assigned a particular site by the campground attendant. At first this led to some confusion as some people ignored their assigned site and instead chose another more to their liking.

The new campgrounds benefitted from being more carefully landscaped than the earlier generation of largely open fields. Influenced in part by the popular new British Columbia provincial campgrounds, and encouraged by the newly hired landscape architect at headquarters, the new campgrounds were more heavily vegetated than before. Shrubs and trees screened the individual campsites, and although the original forest was brushed out to make way for the new campgrounds, many of the original trees were maintained. Boulder and log boundaries protected vegetation from the devastation of random traffic patterns. This design had the advantage of providing a more natural setting because the campsites were organized in small groupings, and the roadway entrances to the various nodes were kept short and curvilinear to preserve the atmosphere of the forested setting. The forest floor at the various sites was protected by the introduction of wooden tent platforms that saved the earth from compacting around tree roots. The platforms never really caught on with campers, however, and they were later replaced with gravel pads. The 1960s campgrounds also introduced standard concrete fireplaces, and heavy wooden picnic tables of the sort that had become popular in British Columbia's provincial parks.

Wapiti and Wabasso helped, but did not stem, the rising numbers of campground users. Wabasso, campground users felt, was too far from the town, so to meet these needs a third site was planned near Wapiti campground. At first, Whistlers was planned to supplement Cottonwood as the park's premier campground. Plans for the construction of an east-west highway south of the Jasper townsite rendered Cottonwood untenable, however, and by 1964 plans for Whistlers campground were accordingly expanded. The strategic importance of Whistlers grew with the opening of the Yellowhead Highway to Prince George in the mid-1960s. Although planned as a fully serviced campground, Whistlers was more utilitarian than its predecessors, with plain and functional service buildings and only one shower building. Its layout followed the lead of Wapiti, having a circular access road with stem roads leading to pinwheel clusters of camping sites on the inside of this circle. It too retained a natural treed setting.

Eventually, Whistlers came to include 781 sites, making it the second largest campground in the national park system after Banff's Tunnel Mountain. The venerable Cottonwood Creek campground was closed. All traces of it were later obliterated by a highway bypass and a sewage treatment facility.

Whistlers campground offered an efficient, no-frills approach to national park campgrounds that reflected the view of the chief parks planner, Lloyd Brooks, toward such developments: "So long as they are convenient to attractions and are in themselves attractively developed, this is about all we can be expected to do in future large scale campground and trailer park development."[107] The emphasis on functionality caused some complaints. One camper wrote to say, "Whistler's [sic] Campground in Jasper National Park shocked us with its numerous streetlights which destroyed the undisturbed pleasures of campground living."[108] But for people travelling with young children wanting cheap accommodation close to town, or people in large self-contained motorhomes or trailers, Whistlers was just perfect. And many found that being camped under the stars and sitting around the fire at night evoked a satisfactory sense of the old camping ideal.

Whistlers campground was the last major campground to be built in the park, although park officials did continue to expand it and Wapiti. Even though Whistlers and the other campgrounds were soon filled to capacity, by the early 1970s park staff were beginning to reconsider further expansion. For one thing, there was the question of money as federal government spending was cut back to redress fiscal imbalance. But there were local practicalities to consider as well. There were only a few weekends during the summer when the park was strained to capacity and for a time overflow campgrounds were used as a cheap quick fix. Overflow facilities were established along the parkway at the old rodeo grounds south of town and in an old gravel pit near the Snaring campground. As the regional director, George Raby, explained in 1973: "They were a response to the situation whereby camping increased at a rate far in excess of our capability to construct additional campsites. This problem was accentuated by our own concern that we could not afford to build campgrounds indefinitely to keep pace with the ever rising demand."[109]

In 1973 Jasper visitor services manager, Doug Welleck, advanced a more radical solution, suggesting that eventually visitors would have to reserve campsites on busy weekends and when the campgrounds filled, people would be turned away. Welleck represented the bright new generation of specialists coming into the park. A graduate of the University of British Columbia, he had held visitor service positions in Ottawa and Calgary before coming to the park the year before. "We don't want to do it," he was cited as saying by a reporter from the *Toronto Star*, "but we can't have people coming here for relative solitude and finding themselves in the middle of a Bay-Day (western slang for sale day at a big store) . . . Also the animals need protection from too many people."[110] Eventually, Welleck's idea took root and the Rodeo overflow campground was phased out, leaving Snaring overflow for the occasional capacity long weekend.

While Whistlers was the last of the auto-campgrounds, there were some new forms of campgrounds introduced to Jasper in the 1970s. In 1971, the park established a transient youth camp, also known as the "free camp" or, in the words of Chief Park Warden Mickey McGuire, "Hippy, Yippy Haven."[111] It operated through the decade in a series of locations until it closed in the early 1980s. It was first located near Old Fort Point on the site of the World War I internment camp.

The free camp was a response to the growing numbers of young people who were free-camping around the park, upsetting the town folk, and damaging the environment. Jasper superintendent Jim Christakos figured that a camp specifically targeted at young travellers, within walking distance of

The Free Camp, c. 1980. COURTESY KIM FORSTER, JNP

the town, would contain many of the problems associated with this new type of traveller. Despite the many cultural differences between the young inhabitants of the camp and the park authorities, the park tried to take an enlightened approach to the problem. As long as the campers stayed within the perimeter of their ghetto, the wardens and police tended to ignore the string of misdemeanours and infractions that took place there: smoking marijuana, drinking in public, nudity, and dogs running off-leash. This bothered some of the old-timers, but generally they let it go. The superintendent drew the line, however, when the campers tried to organize politically and he refused to deal with community representatives. Instead, Visitor Services Manager Doug Welleck hired one of the more mature denizens of the free camp and made him campground caretaker. He reported directly to Welleck and some of the more dangerous tendencies, such as untended fires and the presence of criminal types, were taken care of before they or their actions mushroomed into larger problems.

Hippy Yippy Haven

There was a deep gulf between the outlook of the post-war urban kids and the largely rural conservative mindset of the wardens. Chief Warden McGuire, especially, did not like denizens of the camp and wrote in a memo on the transient youth camp under the subject "Hippy, Yippy Haven:" "I think the day is fast approaching when society is going to demand these punks to either 'cut bait or fish,' and the idea of being able to convert [i.e. close] this campground is not too far out."[112] Even with this prejudice, the wardens generally adopted a laid back approach. Still, they could occasionally be provoked. Warden Mike Schintz describes in his memoirs how he came across five sleeping youths who had lit a fire in a fallen Douglas fir. Getting a lot of lip, he called in the police and the young men were taken into custody. The problem was that the park was not capable of dealing with the offenders locally so, much to the amusement of the offenders, they were flown to Edmonton for trial. They were quickly let go by a sympathetic judge. According to Schintz, "Just in case we might ever forget them, this one guy, whose old man was an MP down east some place, writes to the park shortly before Christmas and thanks us ever so much for the nice plane ride across the Rockies and all the amenities so kindly provided, at taxpayers' expense, while he and his buddies were on their summer vacation."[113]

Backcountry camping also changed in the 1970s as a result of increasing tourist numbers. Beginning in the late 1960s, a new era of backcountry use was ushered in with the growing popularity of the self-contained hiker. Jasper, served by an excellent trail system built by earlier generations of wardens and outfitters, became a popular destination. But the new hikers, with their Norwegian hiking boots and lightweight tents and other gear, sought a different experience from the horse campers who travelled with heavier and more equipment carried on pack horses. Typically, the backpackers found their own camping spots near to the horse camps and gradually an informal system of regular camping spots was established. But the new campers had difficulty following the standards set by the horse campers. The practice back then was to dig and bury garbage and human waste, but the lightly equipped backpackers found this practice challenging because they usually did not pack shovels or large axes. This disinclination to follow existing practices, combined with the sheer numbers of hikers out on the trails, soon meant that the more popular destinations had become fouled and smelly.

In 1973 a young district warden named Bob Haney began looking at the camping situation in the Tonquin Valley, a favourite destination for hikers and horse riders alike. He saw there was a problem with overuse and began reading up on the literature from the US Parks Service that examined solutions for similar situations in national parks south of the border. Talking it over with his colleagues, he considered for the first time the issue of carrying capacity, just like Doug Welleck had done with front country campgrounds that same year. He prepared a report that recommended establishing authorized camping areas in the Tonquin Valley, each with designated numbered sites and a pit privy.[114] Working with the visitor service people, the wardens devised a permit system that was tied to the allocation of particular sites. Backpackers would have to use reserved campsites as a condition of backcountry use. This effectively set limits on the people allowed into the area and had the additional advantage of giving wardens a more accurate idea of the itinerary of backcountry travellers should an emergency ever occur. The Tonquin model was soon adopted for the rest of the park and by 1976–1977 designated sites were built on the Skyline Trail, the other popular backpacking destination in the park. There was some resistance initially, especially in the little travelled areas of the park where people argued for the continued freedom of random camping. In addition, according to Haney, "the outfitters were tough to deal with at first."[115] However, gradually the new system became the accepted norm and people appreciated the limited impact of regulated campgrounds in the backcountry.

Backcountry campsites at Jonas Cutoff. COURTESY JIM SUTTILL, JNP

CHAPTER SEVEN

Game in the Garden

Through the first half of the twentieth century, two often competing views toward wildlife management guided the superintendent and wardens of Jasper. The first, and, for a while the exclusive view, was that the park was a utopian sanctuary, a Garden of Eden where good animals—classified as game—were protected from the evils of the corrupt modern world, including humans (both settlers and hunters) and predators such as wolves. In contrast to this perspective, there began to emerge in the 1930s an awareness that predators were an important part of the natural world as well, and that without them, the health of the larger environment, including game animals, suffered. This awareness was championed by wildlife biologists who began working in Jasper in the 1940s. They promoted the view of the park as a flawed but nonetheless viable ecosystem and valued the interrelationship between all living things, not just a few select species.

By the 1960s, this view had completely supplanted the old view of the park as a game sanctuary, but in the years between 1930 and 1960 there was considerable overlap of these competing views. Both sides tended to refer to "the balance of nature" when arguing for either the eradication or the protection of predators. As well, there was not a perfect distinction between scientists being on the side of predators and wardens being opposed to them: occasionally the old-school wardens could appreciate that perhaps some wolves and coyotes were a good thing, and there were instances, during the 1950s especially, when the scientists approved the culling of predators, often by brutal methods such as strychnine traps. Historian Alan MacEachern wrote that "as late as 1950 the victory of science was far from complete," adding with delicious turn of phrase: "when pressed, the park staff continued to bow to the barstool biology of livestock owners and hunting groups."[116] In Jasper, this view that predators were bad prevailed much later than that—to 1960 at least—and through this period the park attempted to accommodate both views, admitting the viability of all species while continuing to practice limited culling of predators.

Despite the overlap, the two schools of thought stemmed from two quite different traditions, the one steeped in old-world agrarian consciousness, the other in new-world scientific rationalism. Each has its own background and history. For this reason, we will examine each of them in turn, beginning with the "park as sanctuary" idea or, as historian George Colpitts phrased it, the "game in the garden."[117] The scientists and their views are the topics of the following chapter. While these views toward managing wildlife are central to the history of Jasper, they are also typical of other national parks in their corresponding times. The history of wildlife management in Banff National Park, for instance, closely parallels that of Jasper.

When Jasper Forest Park was established in 1907 there were not many animals in its five thousand square miles. There were not many more when Jasper Dominion Park was created by authority of the *Dominion Forest Reserves and Parks Act* in 1911. The herds of bison and elk had never been numerous in the nineteenth century and by the turn of the new century they had been extirpated in the area. A small herd of elk in the Brazeau Valley, beyond what was then the southern boundary of the park, was the only known remnant of a once plentiful species on the eastern slopes of the Rockies.[118] Moose, too, had virtually been wiped out and there were few deer or bears to be seen. Only on the higher slopes were there scattered herds of bighorn sheep and mountain goats and, deep in the recesses of the alpine meadows, at least one small herd of mountain caribou. But there was hope and high expectations that, with the protection afforded by the park, the game would return and, along with the spectacular mountain scenery, become an attraction for tourists.

Early federal legislation reflected the idea of national parks as game sanctuaries. The 1911 *Dominion Forest Reserves and Parks Act* outlawed poaching and authorized park staff to prevent forest fires and kill predatory animals. From the outset, national park wardens were almost as intolerant of predators as poachers, and wolves and coyotes were relentlessly pursued so that by 1918 the acting superintendent reported that "the number of predatory animals in the park has been considerably decreased."[119] The wardens used guns and traps to cull the numbers of predators. In 1918 Jasper Superintendent Maynard Rogers acquired two Russian wolfhounds that were added to the wardens' arsenal. In his report for the fiscal year 1921–1922, he reported that "the warden service has continued an active campaign against all forms of predatory life."[120] That winter, the Jasper wardens eliminated one wolf, twenty-one coyotes, three wolverines, five weasels, one lynx, and one eagle. Still, parks Commissioner Harkin urged greater vigilance, writing to Superintendent Rogers: "I desire to emphasize the necessity of vigorous steps being taken to destroy in particular wolves and mountain lions is an essential part of your parks' work."[121] That there were virtually no wolves or cougars in Jasper when this was written points to the almost mythical significance of the predators at this time.

From the perspective of the park as a game sanctuary, the park super-intendent's success was measured by how much game had multiplied, how tame it had become, and how many predators had been destroyed.[122] Rog-ers devoted much of his reports to citing his triumphs in this regard while seeking new ways to improve his counts. When he returned to his job after serving in World War I, Rogers reported some increase in the numbers of bighorn sheep—he estimated that there were around five thousand in the winter of 1919–1920.[123] Deer were reported to be frequenting the townsite and golf course in the 1920s and this was seen as being good for tourism. Yet, during the 1910s there were still no large ungulates such as moose or elk evident in the park, and Rogers requested that numbers of these species be reintroduced. A response was postponed until after the war, but in the winter of 1920 Jasper received eighty-five elk from Yellowstone National Park in the United States. When the elk arrived in February 1920, Rog-ers placed them in a grassy meadow just south of town at the mouth of Cottonwood Creek. This was an area where the fur traders had customar-ily pastured their horses in winter because the bunchgrass was nutritious

Yellowstone elk in Jasper, c. 1920–1921. JYMA, 84.32.279

and the Chinook winds kept the snow from getting too deep. But Rogers was not going to take any chances with his precious herd and the following winter he reported that he was feeding the elk between two and three hundred pounds of hay a day. Feeding the elk of course made them more domesticated, kept them close to town, and kept them in one spot, characteristics that made them ideal tourist attractions and something that Commissioner Harkin encouraged.[124]

By 1925, Rogers was reporting huge increases to the Jasper game populations. Elk were numbered at nine hundred. He also estimated there were 1,000 caribou, 2,000 mule deer, 500 moose, and 150 bears. The elk numbers were increasing especially fast and in 1931 the superintendent suggested that their numbers might be problematic. "These animals are driving other game from ranges in the Athabasca Valley where previously deer and moose ranged." But the big game were seen as good and therefore could rarely do any wrong. Rogers referred to elk as "these interesting and beautiful animals."[125]

Game Counts

Throughout the history of Jasper National Park, efforts have been made to count the numbers of various animal species in order to report on the overall health of the park. At best, this is an imperfect science. Even today, with helicopter surveys and the co-ordinated efforts of scientists, the park finds it difficult to calculate precise numbers of migratory herds like elk. In Colonel Rogers's era, the subject was particularly important because showing an increase of "good" animals and a decrease of "bad" animals reflected his own efficiency as a park administrator. For these reasons (the imprecise nature of counting animals and Rogers's desire to prove his success), Jasper game counts in the 1920s and 1930s seem especially suspect. Animal census data from the time claim that between 1924 and 1932 the moose population rose from 170 to 14,000; elk from 650 to 5,000; and sheep from 8,000 to 26,000. These figures are incredible in light of what is known about the park's ecosystem today. Such huge numbers could not have survived on the natural vegetation of the park. A 2005 elk census, by comparison, gave the number between three and four hundred.

That the deer and elk invaded the gardens of the townsfolk was considered a small price to pay for the pleasure of seeing these attractive animals close at hand. The town residents learned to build fences to keep them out. However, increasing numbers of game meant correspondingly larger numbers of predators, and these the locals could not tolerate. The war on predators was complicated by a new policy from park headquarters in Ottawa that banned wardens from using traps. For some years, Commissioner Harkin had been concerned that the wardens were in a possible conflict of interest by being allowed to keep the pelts of the animals they trapped, because they were in a position to sell the skins and earn a small bonus on their admittedly small salaries. In 1924, he moved to curtail the wardens' fur trade by limiting the species of animals that could be legitimately trapped to wolves, lynx, and coyotes, and prohibiting the trapping of the more lucrative marten and otter. But traps, as everybody knew, were indiscriminate hunters and the commissioner suspected that other animals were still being trapped. Besides, it would have grated his Ottawa sensibilities to condone public servants making money from a sideline. So, in 1928 he instituted a total ban on trapping and proclaimed in an accompanying edict that all predators killed by wardens had to be turned in to the park superintendent. At this time, the notion that killing predators might in itself be wrong did not form part of the commissioner's argument. Indirectly, though, the commissioner's edict contributed to the notion of a predator problem.

Game as Pets

The tendency to want to domesticate the deer encouraged their overabundance in the town. Newspaper articles from the 1930s and 1940s identified several instances where deer had been adopted as mascots:

"Jasper Mourns 'Old Tubby.' Injured in Battle, Deer Shot.
All Jasper is in mourning, for the famous friendly deer . . .
photographed as often as the totem pole . . . the smallest child
was safe with the gentle old fellow, whose mild gaze held a
depth of wisdom."
—*Edmonton Journal*, 26 November 1936

"Have you ever met Billie? Dozens of pictures are taken of him
daily and he simply absorbs attention like a sponge. He struts

up and down and is a bit choosy of what he eats; his jaded taste being hard to please."
—*Edmonton Bulletin*, 15 February 1939

"Myrna Loy adopted Peter the Deer during her stay at Jasper Park Lodge in the Rockies."
—*Montreal Gazette*, 23 July 1941

A tourist getting close to nature. The driver of a Jasper Park Lodge touring car feeds a fawn. CSTM, CN X5555

The response from the Jasper wardens to the commissioner's edict banning the trapping of predators was both fierce and protracted, and bordered on outright mutiny. The wardens' immediate response was a work-to-rule campaign; predators would only be killed in exceptional circumstances. Where Jasper wardens had killed 102 coyotes in 1926 and forty-two in 1927, in 1928 this number fell to twelve and in 1930 only four coyotes were killed. At the same time, the wardens launched a campaign to create the sense that

MT.
ROBSON
PROV.
PARK

JASPER
NATIONAL
PARK

Hinton (80 km) and
Edmonton (370 km)

Roche
Ronde

Celestine
Lake

Roche
Miette

ALBERTA

BRITISH
COLUMBIA

Prince George
(363 km) and
Fort St. James
National
Historic Site
(536 km)

Snaring

Jasper
Lake

Talbot
Lake

Utopia

Snaring
River

Rocky
River

Fiddle
River

Kamloops (439 km)
and Vancouver
(791 km)

Bridgeland

Pyramid

Roche
Bonhomme

Pyramid
Lake

Miette
River

JASPER

Tekarra

Maligne

Medicine
Lake

The Whistlers

Wabasso
Lake

Maligne
River

Amethyst
Lakes

Astoria
River

Cavell
Lake

Moab
Lake

Athabasca
Falls

Kerkeslin

Maligne
Lake

Maligne

Edith
Cavell

Whirlpool
River

Geraldine
Lakes

Fryatt

Buck
Lake

Brazeau

Sunwapta
Falls

Sunwapta
River

Pobokton Creek

Poboktan

Jonas Creek

Brazeau
Lake

Brazeau
River

Wooley

Sunwapta

Stanley
Falls

Kitchener

Snow Dome

Lake Louise
(230 km from Jasper) and
Town of Banff
(288 km from Jasper)
BANFF NATIONAL PARK

COLUMBIA ICEFIELD

Kilometres 0   10   20   30
Miles   0   5   10   15

Jasper National Park

ROB STORESHAW, PARKS CANADA, CALGARY

Old Canadian Northern Railway Right of Way in the Yellowhead Pass. MIKE DILLON

Aerial view of Jasper House showing historic trail and Athabasca River.
ARCHAEOLOGY COLLECTION, PARKS CANADA, CALGARY

Sawbuck pack saddle. PARKS CANADA, WINNIPEG

IN THE TONQUIN VALLEY, JASPER NATIONAL PARK, ALBERTA   Jasper Series No. 30

In the Tonquin Valley, hand-coloured postcard ca. 1925. JYMA 2006.20.07.05

THE DEPOT, JASPER, ALBERTA.

Jasper Station, 1920s postcard. JYMA 001.56.07

Pyramid Mountain and Golf Course, 1920s postcard. JYMA 001.56.08

Swimming Pool, Jasper Park Lodge, 1920s postcard. JYMA 01.56.05

GOLF COURSE AND LAC BEAUVERT, JASPER, ALBERTA

Golf Course and Lac Beauvert, 1920s postcard. JYMA 001.56.04

GHOST GLACIER AND MOUNT EDITH CAVELL, JASPER, ALBERTA.

Ghost Glacier, Mount Edith Cavell, postcard ca. 1925. Originally called Ghost Glacier, in 1925-26 the Geographic Names Board of Canada changed its name to Angel to allude to the winged figure that its shape seemed to resemble. JYMA 001.56.02

Mary Schäffer camping in Jasper in 1911. WHYTE MUSEUM OF THE CANADIAN ROCKIES
V527, PS1-27

The town of Jasper ca. 1920. JYMA 999.20.1.25

Projectile points found in Jasper National Park. JNP

there was a predator crisis in the park. Park reports began referring to the predator problem. The *Annual Report* for 1930–1931, for example, noted:

> The increase of game for this year has not been as great as in previous years owing to the destruction of fawns, lambs and kids by coyote and lynx which are on the increase within the park, and prey on all young animals.[126]

No mention was made of wolf or cougar depredations, because at this time these animals were virtually extirpated in the park. Supervising Warden Dick Langford also reported that "[t]here is a tremendous increase of coyotes within the Park," and added: "[A]s these animals work mostly at night, it is impossible for the warden to shoot them and I would again strongly recommend that Wardens be instructed to trap them in order to protect game and bird life."[127]

That the Jasper wardens had the support of Superintendent Rogers was natural given the long association between the colonel and his men in the field. Rogers wrote numerous memos on the subject to the commissioner, making sure there was no doubt as to his views objecting to the policy. The wardens went beyond registering their objections through the superintendent; they mounted a widespread publicity campaign to have the policy overturned. They easily gained the support of the Jasper outfitters and guides who had long advocated tougher measures for predator control. A meeting in 1932 of the Athabasca Guides and Trailmen's Association passed a motion that was communicated to Ottawa: "Resolved that this Association recommend that the Wardens of Jasper National Park be allowed to trap and shoot all predatory animals and retain their skins."[128] Similar resolutions were sent to Ottawa by numerous Alberta fish and game societies; so many, in fact, that Commissioner Harkin and his Ottawa staff suspected collusion. In his brief to the Minister of the Interior, Thomas G. Murphy, Deputy Minister H. H. Rowatt said: "We are inclined to believe that the agitation is instigated by our own wardens."[129]

It did not stop there. The Alberta newspapers were glad to help out in defending local sentiment against Ottawa and lurid reports began circulating about roving bands of predators in the park:

> Last winter the coyotes took a heavy toll of the park deer, and are now hunting in packs. In driving along the park roads the

The chief warden's wife, Dolly Langford, shows off prime coyote pelts. JNP, H3644

absence of deer is apparent. Fifty to 100 would be seen a few years ago along a motor road. The coyotes are reported to have steadily increased in the park since the ban on trapping. Shooting of these beasts is difficult.[130]

Although it took a few years to gather momentum, the wardens' publicity campaign was effective in getting the minister of the Interior to question his staff. Requests for briefing notes were passed down the line to the deputy minister, assistant deputy minister, and the commissioner, finally ending up on the desk of Hoyes Lloyd, head of the wildlife division. Lloyd, one of the few scientists on staff of the parks service, provided a lengthy and cogent analysis of the situation for the commissioner. He went back over the history of the development of the policy, reiterating the argument that traps were indiscriminate killers and adding that their use was prohibited in national parks in the US. He noted that predatory animals played an important role in limiting the numbers of grazing animals in the park, using the story of the plight of the deer in Kaibab National Forest in Arizona near the Grand Canyon to illustrate his point. In a well-publicized account, American scientists had studied the depredations of deer on the vegetation of the Grand Canyon area, a situation that had led to their eventual starvation, and blamed it on the fact that predators had been eliminated from the national forest. Lloyd applied this argument to the Jasper environment and concluded:

> There is no need whatever to heed the cry of "wolf" from Jasper
> Park. We have there a superabundance of game animals, and
> if the reports of the Superintendent are even approximately
> correct, we will soon have to deal with the question of disposition
> of excess numbers of those animals.[131]

Lloyd then cited the steady growth of game animals in Jasper between 1924 and 1932. Even if the numbers of predators was being exaggerated, given that the park had claimed the numbers of game animals had skyrocketed, it was only natural that there would be a corresponding increase in predators. The relationship between predators and ungulates was not only natural, Lloyd and other scientists maintained, it was necessary to contain overpopulation. Lloyd therefore argued that given the trend of these numbers, it might be prudent to introduce more predators in the park rather than to cull them.

The amount of correspondence going up and down the line in Ottawa and back and forth from the park was also indicative of a fierce debate raging in the parks service at the time about the role of science in determining park policy. In an early draft of his briefing note to Commissioner Harkin, Lloyd questioned the ability of the wardens to properly understand the subject of wildlife management and recommended Banff and Jasper each hire a resident scientist. "We will not have an accurate picture of wild life conditions in these parks until we have resident naturalists to keep in touch with each area. This is specialized work on which the word of a warden or superintendent is not sufficient."[132] While there are no records of what the wardens thought of the idea of interfering scientists at this juncture, Rogers did not hide his views. Writing on the subject of coyotes in Jasper to Commissioner Harkin in 1932 he remarked, "In this connection I am more impressed every day that Ecologists and other 'gists' to the contrary, the policy of preventing Wardens from trapping coyote is causing a most serious, and in my opinion, shameful waste of our wildlife."[133]

Hoyes Lloyd believed that animals should be left free to kill and be killed and his memorandum to Harkin cited above reflects this attitude. He was the biggest exponent of the ecological philosophy at this time and likely influenced the drafting of the statement in the 1933–1934 *Annual Report* concerning predator policy. This said in part, "the weight of scientific opinion, based on the observation of eminent naturalists and biologists, tends to prove that the extermination of all predatory animals is actually inimical to the conservation of herbivorous animals."[134] Commissioner Harkin wanted to believe, but could not quite bring himself to support, his science advisor as he confessed in a memo to Assistant Deputy Minister Roy Gibson:

> Quite frankly, I have delayed reports and action on this
> subject because of the difficulties I find in definitely making up
> my mind as to the action that should be taken. I cannot say that
> I fully concur in the memorandum prepared by Mr. Lloyd for my
> signature though it is very largely correct. I do not concur fully in
> it because I am inclined to believe that it will probably be found
> necessary for us to take some further steps than we have yet
> taken in this matter of predator control.[135]

Ever the consummate publicist, the commissioner was aware that predators were bad for the park's image. Sensitive to public opinion, he was also aware of political direction. In the summer of 1933 the minister of the Interior had visited Jasper where there was some discussion of the issue of predators. The minister's views were communicated back to Mr. Harkin: "The Minister does not see why it should not be possible to direct our Wardens to take whatever steps are necessary to preserve the balance as between predatory and other animals, even to the extent of setting traps for predatories [sic]."[136] This use of the word "balance" to justify culling predators would be used regarding the park well into the 1950s.

The locals had got the minister's ear but only partially. There was no way that the commissioner would reverse his position on the wardens being prohibited from trapping. But he did agree that the number of predators in Jasper needed to be reduced. Again, he cracked the whip on the back of the Jasper wardens. Within the year, Supervising Warden Langford would be demoted to a position in Yoho Park. Meanwhile, he was instructed to devise quotas of predators that would be set for each warden, for as even the minister acknowledged: "Our wardens are not very active in this work."[137] Superintendent Rogers again stuck his neck out to protest but to no avail—the commissioner was adamant. Henceforth, monthly reports were submitted to the deputy minister on the numbers of predators killed in the park. Wardens' performances would be appraised on their ability to meet their quotas. They caved in. In November 1933, Langford said that he and his twelve wardens had set a park quota of seventy predators a year.[138] Despite their previous warnings that predators could not be successfully hunted without traps, they exceeded expectations. In the fiscal year 1935–1936, the wardens killed seventy-three coyotes and nineteen cougars.[139]

The hunting of predators in Jasper reached a new level of efficiency with the campaign to eliminate cougars. The cougar or mountain lion had been largely absent from the park in the 1920s but had reappeared in 1930. Its presence inspired a revulsion almost greater than that caused by wolves. They were depicted by Jasper locals as ruthless killers, more efficient than wolves, even though they hunted singly. They were accused of being wanton killers, slaughtering animals for mere pleasure. And, finally, they were accused of being outside interlopers, not indigenous to the area. Bert Wilkins, of the Athabasca Guides and Trailmen's Association, wrote that "[t]his species is acknowledged as the most wanton killer that roams the weeds and is a real scourge to our game life."[140]

So, when cougars were reported in the park there was a vigorous response on the part of the wardens. Commissioner Harkin authorized the purchase of four coon hounds from a breeder in Tennessee.[141] The dogs were bought as pups and trained by Warden Frank Wells, who became their handler. Two of the trained dogs were intended for Banff, but as one of the dogs subsequently died, Wells ended up having three dogs at his disposal. The method used to seek out the cougars involved driving along roads in the park, waiting for the hounds to pick up a scent. When they started to bark, the chase was on, leading to the inevitable treeing of the cat and the shooting of the cougar by the warden. The chases were often physically demanding; the supervising warden, C. V. Phillips, reported that he and Wells often returned from the hunt "with their clothing in rags and weary to the point of exhaustion."[142]

Not surprisingly, these tactics had a devastating effect on the cougar population. In 1935 thirteen cougars were killed; in 1936 the wardens destroyed nineteen cougars. By 1938 only two cougars were killed, not through want of trying but because they had virtually been eliminated from the park. The parks service considered the cougar issue so important

Warden Frank Bryant and a "good" cougar. JNP, H3648

that the tracking and killing of each animal was carefully reported to head-quarters during that first year of the hunt. Often these reports included comments about the badness of the animals. Writing of the killing of the fourth cougar in 1935, Phillips added: "This animal was a female and had recently killed two sheep about three miles east of Jasper."[143] Similarly, he commented on the sixth cougar, saying that "this animal was seen play-ing with a wounded deer."[144] The cougar campaign met with enthusiastic approval from Commissioner Harkin. He passed the reports upward to his superiors in the department and asked that the skin of a particularly large specimen be mounted as a rug and shipped to his office as a trophy.[145]

Through the 1950s, the parks service continued to overreact to any hint that predators were a problem in the park, while ignoring or minimiz-ing evidence that they were beneficial to the park's ecosystems. These views were supported by the outlook of the provincial authorities, who took the view that wolves and coyotes were detrimental to hunting and agriculture. Wolves and coyotes became even less tolerated following an outbreak of rabies in the northern part of the province in 1952. Coyotes were blamed for spreading rabies among the ten farm animals and four dogs that con-tracted the disease that year. As a result, the province of Alberta initiated a program aimed at virtually exterminating the wild canines. National park officials followed suit and in early 1953 the superintendent of Jasper was informed by the branch director that "in view of the spread of the rabies epizootic in Alberta, and the possible serious repercussions should it enter the national parks, it has been decided that control of canids by means of poison should be considered and necessary steps taken to permit rapid implementation of programs as required."[146]

As the rabies threat subsided in the mid-1950s, the park resorted to resurrecting the old fear of declining game counts to justify continued predator culls and use of poison traps. As a result of this pressure, Donald Flook, a biologist with the Canadian Wildlife Service, was sent to Jasper in 1955. His report, "Big Game Survey, south-east Jasper Park," was exten-sive and thorough, making many references to earlier reports to provide a larger overview of population trends in the area. He reiterated a previous colleague's theory that the sheep die-off was likely the result of a series of severe winters, and that the winter ranges had become degraded from overuse but that they were now making a slow recovery. He observed that "[a]ny great increase in game, especially elk would be undesirable," and concluded: "It is the opinion of this writer that the most practical method to manage this area is, to as much as possible, leave game and predator populations uncontrolled."[147]

However, the park superintendents did not agree with this approach and as late as 1959 Jasper superintendent John Pettis argued for predator control. Pettis advocated shooting as being preferable to poison and added that limited shooting now would mean that widespread use of poison would not be needed later:

> From conversations we have had with Mr. Flook on this subject it is evident that the procedure as described above does not conform to Mr. Flook's thinking on the control of predators in the Parks. We have given the matter considerable thought and in the opinion of the Chief Warden and myself, the present procedure seems to fit the immediate situation, insofar as this particular area is concerned.[148]

These views prevailed in the park into the 1960s. When change did occur, it was because the wardens themselves had begun to adopt ecological views about the territory they were charged to protect.

CHAPTER EIGHT

Scientists Visit the Park

Today, Jasper National Park is widely understood as a complex ecosystem, containing hundreds of species of birds, fish, and mammals living together in an interconnected web of co-dependence. Much of this understanding is based on the work of generations of scientific study and today scientists continue to examine the complexities of its ecosystems and advise on policies to better protect and manage its resources. This was not always the case. In the first half of the twentieth century, the park's management seemed indifferent to scientific investigation, and were inclined to dispute the findings and recommendations of the scientists. As late as the 1960s park development such as highway construction and resort expansion was carried out with innocent or wilful disregard of the effect it would have on the environment. But change was in the air, and the appearance of science-based park management in the 1990s was the culmination of a slow process of transformation that had begun in the 1940s.

The first scientists working for the national parks were based in Ottawa, where Maxwell Graham and later Hoyes Lloyd headed the wildlife division of the national parks service. Lloyd had become interested in Jasper in the mid-1930s when it seemed to be the epicentre of the controversy over predator control in the national parks. As an adherent of the new ecological ideas then sweeping the science office of the US National Parks Service, Lloyd opposed the slaughter of wolves and coyotes. However, the directors, Commissioner J. B. Harkin, and after 1936, F. H. H. Williamson and James Smart, were conscious of public opinion and sought limited culls while paying lip-service to ecological principles. Lloyd argued his theories, but needed to obtain accurate local information in order to support his case.

In the late 1930s Lloyd sent two distinguished scientists to investigate the conditions in Banff and Jasper parks. Both men pointed to problems of overgrazing by deer and elk. Dr. Rudolph Anderson, the last to report, ended his memo with a sneering comment on the "game in the garden" mentality of the parks: "It is time we get away from the idea that the National Parks are merely 'game farms' and fish hatcheries alone, producing stunted animals in quantity with insufficient winter range."[149] But the locals countered that *they* were the experts on local conditions. Until scientists could spend extended periods in the park, their views would always be suspect. This continued to be a theme of the park-science relations through to the 1960s. It was to address this criticism by locals that in 1942 the national parks service contracted Ian McTaggart-Cowan, a young professor of Biology at the University of British Columbia, to carry out extensive research and report on conditions in Jasper.

Ian McTaggart-Cowan was an apt choice to initiate wildlife research in the park. He had completed his Ph.D. at the University of California, Berkeley, where he was introduced to the teaching of Joseph Grinnell, an ecologist who was closely associated with Yosemite and Yellowstone national parks in the United States. McTaggart-Cowan joined the faculty at UBC in 1940, where he helped initiate the first university program on wildlife conservation in Canada.[150] One of the textbooks used in his classes was Aldo Leopold's *Game Management,* the new bible of the US Parks Service scientists, first published in 1942.[151] McTaggart-Cowan was therefore in a position to apply approaches to wildlife management that had been developed

Ian McTaggart Cowan. UBC LIBRARY

in the US national parks to their Canadian counterparts. He brought this considerable expertise to inform three consecutive summers of fieldwork in the mountain parks of Banff and Yoho, while at the same time paying particular attention to Jasper.

McTaggart-Cowan began his fieldwork in the summer of 1943. He was assisted by two students, James Hatter, an honours undergraduate, and Egbert Pfieffer, then completing his M. Sc. Hatter supplemented the summer fieldwork of the team with a research trip to Jasper in December 1944 to study the winter ranges of the sheep, elk, and deer. In his preliminary report written in 1943, McTaggart-Cowan confirmed the earlier scientific reports that predators were not a significant problem in the parks. Where game populations were so high, it was only natural and, indeed, even beneficial, he argued, to see increased numbers of predators. In McTaggart-Cowan's opinion, there was a much bigger problem in the increasing numbers of grazing animals adversely affecting their range. This was especially evident in the Athabasca Valley of Jasper and required urgent attention:

> It is estimated that the carrying capacity of these Athabasca
> Valley ranges has already been reduced from 50 to 60 per cent of
> normal. There is urgent and immediate need for a reduction of
> the pressure on these areas. Every additional year that the present
> condition is permitted to persist will further reduce the carrying
> capacity and protract the recovery period.[152]

Already elk were found to be starving in both Banff and Jasper parks and McTaggart-Cowan called for an immediate cull of the elk herds. His subsequent research would focus on understanding the relationship between range land, grazing herds, and predators. Jasper was given particular attention not only because of the dramatic deterioration of the Athabasca ranges described above but because, alone of the mountain parks, it still had wolf packs.

With Hatter as his assistant, McTaggart-Cowan spent much of the summer of 1944 following herds of deer, elk, and sheep and, where possible, noting their interaction with coyotes and wolves. They were assisted by the park wardens who provided vast experience of their particular patrol districts. Besides being an accomplished student who would later go on to earn his doctorate in wildlife management, Hatter was also an experienced hunter and his method was to stalk and shoot predators and then examine their stomach contents. He made a number of cogent observations that he recorded in his field book. He found, for instance, that coyotes did not hunt sheep, deer, or elk in packs. For the most part they fed on ground squirrels and hares. When they did eat sheep or deer it was usually as scavengers. Hatter cited several instances where sheep showed little signs of alarm when approached by lone coyotes, proving that they were not in the habit of being harassed.[153]

Among the examples given by Hatter is the following excerpt from his field notes. Here, he cites examples given to him by two Jasper wardens as well as his professor:

July 13, [1944] Devona
Frank Burstrom saw a coyote walk up to a sleeping ram and apparently believing it dead, nipped it in the abdomen. The ram jumped up and chased the coyote along the side hill. Bob Jones says he saw a coyote chase a small band of sheep. He also found where coyotes had killed a sheep in about 2ft. of snow.

Dr. Cowan saw a coyote among some sheep which were paying no attention to the coyote, continuing with their feeding.

Hatter concluded that there were not sufficient numbers of wolves in the park to cause significant depletion of the grazing herds, insufficient numbers to even cull the sick or starving animals that populated the ranges. He wrote facetiously: "Instead of killing wolves, I think they should raise them and teach them to kill elk."[154] Hatter's observations about the predator/prey relationship in the park being weighted in favour of the grazing animals was supported by McTaggart-Cowan, who drew more definitive conclusions in his 1945 report. After describing the ranges of the various wolf packs, and estimating that the total number of wolves in Jasper was between thirty-eight and fifty-five, he concluded: "Even so there are indications that predator pressure is not removing all the seriously weakened animals."[155] Among the most extreme examples of this were his encounters with "senile deer so weakened from parasite infestation that they were incapable of running."[156]

Although McTaggart-Cowan had been tasked with studying the predator/prey relationship in the mountain parks, he and his students came to realize that the most serious threat to the animals was overgrazing of the montane and subalpine meadows. Hatter in his field notes described watching the dust storms in the Athabasca Valley as soil, deprived of sufficient grass cover, simply blew away.[157] Bert Pfieffer, the other student working for McTaggart-Cowan, devoted his master's thesis to studying range conditions in the valley. He, like Hatter, went on to earn his doctorate and later taught ecology at universities in the US. Working under the supervision of his professor, Pfeiffer identified a series of study areas along the valley, and established exclosure plots, fenced areas intended to keep grazing animals off the grass. They then examined the cemetery, located just outside the town of Jasper, as a comparison area. The cemetery was of interest because it had been fenced off forty years previously and would show how the area would look if it had not been subjected to heavy grazing.

Pfieffer's principal observation from the study was that the vegetation in the park had been seriously impaired by overgrazing. The grasses had been largely depleted and the animals were proceeding to eat the shrubs, willows, and aspen in the area. The depletion of the aspen through browsing was in turn encouraging the growth of conifers in their place, making the area even less productive for grazing animals. Pfeiffer further concluded: "Unless present trends in the ecology of the area are reversed in the very near future, the health conditions of the ungulate herds of the area will be seriously menaced due to malnutrition."[158]

Pfeiffer's detailed conclusions were anticipated in McTaggart-Cowan's 1945 report to the national parks service.

It is apparent then that at the present stage of the investigation all evidence points to the wolf as being of lesser importance to the survival of game in the parks than the welfare factor of which the most important is food supply adequate in amount and composition.[159]

In other words, if there was a problem with animals in the park, it lay not with the wolves but with the elk, who were multiplying beyond the feeding capacity of the park, while destroying forage for other species in the process.

As a result of his analysis of the situation and the accompanying dire warnings about what would happen if drastic measures were not taken, McTaggart-Cowan recommended the immediate removal of seven hundred elk from the Athabasca Valley. The officials in Ottawa agreed with the recommendation, although practical difficulties involved in slaughtering

Elk slaughter, Jasper Park Lodge golf course, c. 1950. JYMA, 84.32.74

that many animals without an abattoir facility meant that only about 367 were actually culled.[160] Most of the meat was shipped to Indian reserves or burned.

The work of McTaggart-Cowan and his students introduced an ecological approach to examining Jasper's wildlife. Conducting more accurate wildlife counts, tracking the movements of wildlife through their seasonal cycles, sampling the health of individual animals, determining what they actually ate instead of what they were believed to have eaten, and studying the carrying capacity of the various grazing areas of the park led to a much greater understanding of the park's ecosystem. More importantly, McTaggart-Cowan introduced methods of research that are still used to this day.

The wildlife division of the national parks service followed up on the work of the UBC team by hiring a young mammalogist named Frank Banfield to carry out further research on the mountain parks. Although much of Banfield's career still lay ahead of him in 1946, he showed considerable promise. He quickly adopted McTaggart-Cowan's ecological approach and sought to ensure that his recommendations were implemented at the park level. From his Banff office he directed a series of memos aimed at the park management. His report on Jasper written in September of 1946 is typical for its profundity, and its acerbity. Like Pfeiffer, he focused on the problems of range use in the Athabasca Valley. While noting the problems caused by the overabundance of elk, he also argued that elk reduction alone would not fix the problem. He developed an idea that Pfieffer had only briefly touched upon; that forest fire prevention might not be an altogether good thing for the environment: "In Jasper National Park the fire prevention has been good, in fact too good. The Athabasca valley has had in the past, extensive grassy slopes which were used by the game animals as winter forage. But the fact is everywhere evident that the ranges are shrinking in size because of the encroaching climax spruce forests."[161]

A. W. F. (Frank) Banfield (1918–1996)

Frank Banfield studied at the University of Toronto before joining the wildlife division in 1946. Upon the formation of what became known as the Canadian Wildlife Service the following year, he became that organization's chief mammalogist. Besides working in Banff and Jasper, he did pioneering work on the barren land caribou, on which he wrote his Ph.D. thesis at the University of Michigan. He left the service in 1957 to become chief zoologist for the National Museum in Ottawa and later was the first director of the Museum of Natural History. He is best known today as the author of the monumental *Mammals of Canada* (1974). Although undoubtedly brilliant, he was hampered by a difficult personality. Reading between the lines of the Jasper correspondence, he was clearly not liked. He is remembered at the Canadian Wildlife Service for his arrogance and abrasiveness. The memoir of the first director of the service gives him only three sentences.[162]

Banfield had been in his post for less than a year when in 1947 the wildlife division was taken out of the parks service and reorganized as the Dominion (later the Canadian) Wildlife Service (CWS). The mandate of the CWS was huge, reporting on animals and fish in the national parks and in federally managed land in the Yukon and Northwest Territories. It opened an office in Edmonton that presided over research in the mountain parks, as well as wildlife in the western NWT. Banfield became increasingly preoccupied with studies of barren-ground caribou, a topic that concerned the federal government because of the caribou's importance to both sport hunters and local Aboriginal populations. While it was occupied with the caribou, the CWS hired two young biologists from UBC to carry out research in the mountain parks. One of these biologists, Dean Fisher, plunged right into the wildlife census work by going on an eighteen-day survey of Jasper's south boundary with Warden Frank Camp in 1948. The other biologist, J. P. Kelsall, began work the following year on a study of elk in the mountain parks. Inevitably, both young biologists were soon deeply immersed in the issue of predator control.

Fisher's initial findings were shocking. Not a single bighorn sheep was seen on the entire trip. While he could not speak with absolute authority, Fisher suspected that heavy winter snows had caused the herd to starve to death. The lack of food may have been worsened by heavy elk foraging, a situation noted by McTaggart-Cowan three years earlier. Wolves were not apparent in the area. Action was called for, and despite the conclusions of Fisher's report, the parks service thought it knew what to do. Director R. A. Gibson, who oversaw the activities of both the Canadian Parks Service and the CWS, wrote:

> It looks to be about time we did something about the wolves and coyotes in Jasper Park. I know Mr. Fisher has been investigating and he told me that he did not see much evidence and did not consider there was need for coyote measures, but everyone else in the park is keen about the coyotes and wolves.[163]

Despite the absence of supporting evidence, the parks service used the sheep die-off to justify killing more wolves. The director's directive forced the wildlife biologists to participate in the wolf reduction program as part of its professional service to the park. The justification to cull wolves from the park was complicated but, in its way, rational. In the case of the health of the bighorn sheep, it was realized that wolves were not directly to blame for their demise. Even without exhaustive research, the effect of large elk populations on the sheep habitat was well understood. And, in the case of the Cairn Pass sheep, everyone agreed that the previous two winters had been hard on the animals. The connection between elk numbers and wolves was also generally understood. Everyone agreed, too, that it would be beneficial to remove surplus elk. But, with elk numbers reduced, what would the wolves eat? And with the sheep numbers already threatened by the winter die-off, there was general agreement that a wolf cull would speed up the process of recovery.

What is difficult to understand is why the scientists recommended the use of poison traps for the cull. Fisher initiated the Jasper wolf control program by bringing in fifty cyanide guns "for wolf control in the areas where it is indicated that wolves have increased, such as Devona, Moberly Flats and Buffalo Prairie."[164] A quota was set for twenty wolves to be removed that winter. The cyanide guns were considered to be effective against predators. A trap was set so that when the animal took the bait, a poison projectile was fired into its mouth. Although these devices were commonly used in the province of Alberta, the arguments against the use of traps in the national parks were long-standing. Commissioner Harkin had pointed out that they were indiscriminate killers in 1928 and they had long been banned in the US national parks as well.

The use of poison on the wolves posed another ethical problem because it could easily get into the food chain when animals scavenged on the carcasses of the dead animals. Yet, the scientists were reluctant to countenance wardens shooting wolves, even though some were destroyed this way. Perhaps the scientists felt the impersonal killing by traps was more objective and fit in with notions of scientific management. The new head of the CWS, Winston Mair, agreed that shooting was preferable to poisoning but did not believe that predators needed to be culled at all. While acknowledging the decline in sheep numbers, he added, "There appears to be little biological evidence at present to support predator control." He was against poisoning but allowed that some shooting would be all right if it made the wardens feel better.[165]

While the hysteria over the bighorn sheep census led to a vendetta against wolves in the park, it also encouraged support for further research to examine the extent and duration of the sheep die-off. In February 1951, Frank Banfield returned to the park to carry out winter wildlife investigations. He counted only 287 sheep in the Athabasca Valley and compared the number to the 699 recorded by McTaggart-Cowan in 1943. Still, he was more sanguine about the situation than others and reported to Ottawa that, generally speaking, mammal populations were normal and there was no surplus of wolves, coyotes, or cougars.[166] Banfield emphasized the deteriorated range conditions as a serious problem and reminded the park that although horse grazing had been prohibited in the Athabasca Valley in 1947, there were still close to two hundred horses grazing in the area. The controversy over animal numbers also led to a greater effort to sustain an accurate census. To this end, the Jasper wardens were asked to fill out census cards while on patrol in their districts. The cards were regularly submitted to the CWS office in Edmonton, where their tallies were analyzed and used to create an informed and reasonably unbiased picture of the state of the wildlife in the park.

The Wildlife Division Becomes the Canadian Wildlife Service

A wildlife division was integral to J. B. Harkin's parks service almost from its inception in 1911 and its staff included some of the leading wildlife biologists of the day. It suffered a downturn in the 1930s, due to a combination of the Depression and the reorganization of the national park branch; then World War II delayed its revitalization, but following the war the parks service sought to strengthen the presence of its wildlife officers in the mountain parks. Frank Banfield was hired to be the first mammalogist based in Banff. This resurgence was short-lived, however, as the wildlife division was removed from the parks service in 1947 to form the nucleus of the new Canadian Wildlife Service (CWS). Although the CWS continued to supply professional services to the national parks, it lost some of its focus on park issues. Banfield was moved out of Banff, for instance, and the CWS biologists became increasingly preoccupied with studies in the Northwest Territories. A separate reporting relationship, where CWS biologists communicated to their superior in Ottawa and then had their findings communicated back down to the parks, further curtailed their effectiveness. This arrangement lasted until 1985 when Parks Canada began to hire its own wildlife professionals.

The wildlife biologists were routinely distracted by public hysteria over predators in the park. In 1951, Gertrude Webber, a young seasonal employee at Jasper Park Lodge, wrote the minister to complain about packs of coyotes that were attacking deer along the fence of the golf course. The minister's reply was drafted by Harrison Lewis and said in part: "The National Parks are, in effect, outdoor museums, in which the intent is that all kinds of wildlife native to the region shall be present in normal numbers and relations."[167] But the minister refused to sign the letter as worded and a revised version was prepared that said:

I have asked the Director of the National Parks Branch of this
Department to have the coyote problem of Jasper carefully
examined ... I share your interest in the deer and shall make sure
that our officers in the park do everything in their power
to prevent the numbers of the coyotes and their relationships
to the deer from becoming abnormal.[168]

Mammalogist Frank Banfield was dispatched to Jasper to carry out the promised investigation. He discovered a different reality than that reported by Miss Webber. He told of deer being fed by the lodge staff, of the animals becoming so tame that they could be enticed into the cabins. Some wore ribbons with bells around their necks and had been given names. The results were fatal. The semi-domesticated animals, elk as well as mule deer, had not moved on to greener pastures but had overgrazed the grounds of the area so that there was nothing left to eat, and now they were slowly starving to death. In the one case that Banfield found of a coyote feeding on an elk, he determined that it was actually a case of the coyote scavenging the carcass of an animal that had already died from starvation.

The CWS was, as its name implied, focused on animals. Moreover, the CWS animal studies were also often concerned with understanding particular problems. Thus, in Jasper at least, a lot of attention was given to elk, whose population boom was still an issue through the 1960s. From 1957 to 1967 biologist Don Flook undertook intensive studies of elk in the mountain parks. Meanwhile, bighorn sheep became the specialty of John Stelfox, who carried out a series of studies in the mountain parks in the 1960s and 1970s. And Ludwig Carbyn produced a series of reports on wolves in Jasper during the same time period.[169]

Eventually, the scientists and wardens learned to co-operate. After the warden reorganization of the 1960s (discussed in Chapter 12), increasing emphasis was placed on their training as conservation officers. As they had been guiding the scientists into the field since the 1940s, a long history of collaboration began to influence their outlook. The wardens began to internalize many of the attitudes of the scientists. By the 1970s wardens were carrying out their own vegetation studies and beginning to understand more about the complexities of the Jasper ecosystem. By the 1980s some of the Jasper wardens had university degrees in biology and related disciplines.

Science in the parks was affected by other organizational changes.

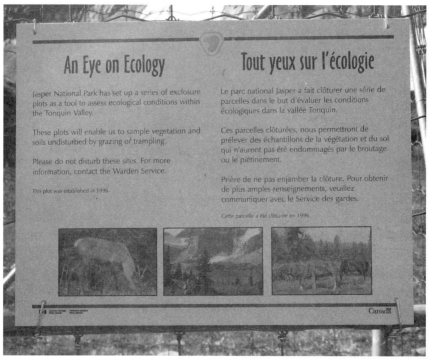

Tonquin Valley exclosure plot. COURTESY THE AUTHOR

Beginning in the mid-1960s, professional biologists were hired as park naturalists. Their duties were directed mainly at tourist education, but they also undertook limited inventory work. In 1966 Park Superintendent Bruce Mitchell reported: "One-third to one-half the time spent this summer was on inventory work, mainly phenological collections of plants, altitudinal distribution of small mammals and a survey of amphibians and reptiles of the park."[170] A major shift occurred in 1985 when Parks Canada took the responsibility for wildlife studies away from the CWS. Henceforth, resident scientists, either at the regional office in Calgary or in the park itself, directed scientific research in Jasper. This led to greater emphasis being placed on ecological issues, although the wildlife inventories of the earlier period continued to form the bread-and-butter of the different projects. One new direction was the revelation that Banfield had been right in 1946 about the encroaching forest, and so in the late 1980s a program of controlled burns was initiated in Jasper and the other mountain parks, intended to restore grassland that had disappeared over the previous eighty years of park protection.

One of the earliest of the warden scientists was Wes Bradford, who joined the Jasper warden service in 1975 and then in 1982 became a specialist in wildlife management. He represents the new science-based approach to wildlife management in the park. His studies of elk-wolf-human interactions in the park confirmed what the earlier scientists had argued—that wolves were beneficial in keeping elk numbers in check. However, he also discovered some new and disturbing trends. Between 1945 and 1970, elk numbers were kept in check by annual slaughters. Numbers were further reduced during 1973–1974 when the combination of a harsh winter and high numbers of wolves reduced the elk population to less than one thousand. But after this setback, the elk began to take refuge in the town. According to Bradford: "By the mid-1980s elk were starting to live year round in and around Jasper Townsite and large bulls began to rut in the townsite."[171] This caused a serious public safety hazard as rutting bulls could charge and injure bystanders. Eventually, the park introduced a policy of removing aggressive elk from the townsite and, as one warden remarked, "These elk were *not* relocated anywhere."[172]

Fish

Although Jasper's aquatic environments are closely associated with the larger ecosystem, the history of their management is quite a different story. For many years, fish management in Jasper National Park was in stark contrast to its wildlife management. Whereas hunting was strictly prohibited, to the extent that visitors could not even bring firearms into the park, angling was actively encouraged. And where, in other respects, scientists and wardens were often on opposite sides of the fence on matters of game management, in the realm of fish they were usually in more or less perfect accord in wanting to create an artificial reality. The principal native fish of the area was the whitefish, first netted in the fur-trading era at Talbot Lake. But anglers wanted trout and so from the 1920s through to the beginning of the 1970s, the park stocked its lakes with exotic species such as Eastern Brook, Rainbow, and Speckled trout, and even a hybrid called Splake. By the early 1930s there was a small hatchery in the basement of the administration building and in 1942 a large hatchery was built at Sixth Bridge near Maligne Canyon. The wardens were directly involved in the fish-stocking program, the hatchery attendant was part of the chief warden's staff, and the district wardens carried the young trout to remote lakes in specially designed panniers on their pack horses.

Government scientists had helped develop the fish-stocking program in the 1920s and 1930s. After the formation of CWS in 1947, scientists became even more directly involved in Jasper's fish enhancement program. In 1949 Jean-Paul Cuerrier was recruited from the Université de Montréal to become the agency's limnologist. Cuerrier focused much of his attention on improving the mountain park trout fishery. As the Jasper hatchery came to be regarded as the best of its kind, Cuerrier recommended the consolidation of all mountain park hatcheries at Jasper in 1954. With CWS support, the Jasper hatchery expanded through the 1960s and at its apex in 1966 was producing well over a million trout annually for stocking the waters of the western national parks. CWS promoted other methods to stimulate trout populations in Jasper even further. The park was directed to create artificial spawning beds by dumping gravel on the lake bottoms and to add weed control chemicals to Mildred Lake. Beginning in 1956, so-called coarse fish were poisoned before the trout fingerlings were introduced, removing all native species from the lakes.[173]

The trout enhancement program continued until 1972. That year, park resource conservation staff and regional fisheries specialists from CWS met to discuss the issue of fish stocking and agreed that "many of the small lakes in the remote areas of the Park not be stocked."[174] The following year, the hatchery was temporarily closed because of a viral disease that developed in its water, and in 1974 the park took the opportunity to close it down permanently. There seems to have been little public outcry for its retention. Greater awareness of ecological integrity of the park's aquatic environments seems to have led to another compact between the wardens and scientists. There has been no serious proposal, however, to remove any of the introduced species from the lakes. People still come to the park to fish and there has been no desire to upset that balance of nature, regardless of its dubious origins.

CHAPTER NINE

Jasper the Bear

As the symbol of Jasper, the bear deserves a chapter of its own. Bears are an interesting phenomenon in the mountain parks. On the one hand, they are large fascinating animals that thrill visitors. In the past, they were often pictured as friendly loveable beasts, "clowns of the forest," and the cartoon figure of Jasper the Bear created by James Simpkins came to symbolize the park. However, bears also have their dark side, and as a danger to humans, bears are without equal in the national parks. There is no record of anyone ever having even been attacked by wolves or cougars in Jasper National Park, but there have been many instances of bear maulings. Warden Percy Goodair was killed by a grizzly in 1929, young Barbara Coates was killed by a black bear in 1958, and a British tourist was killed by a grizzly in 1992. Besides these fatalities, bears have been responsible for several instances of injuries or close calls, and many instances of property damage.

Despite their obvious danger, the park was slow to enact effective policies to minimize unfortunate bear/human encounters. While individual "problem" bears were routinely shot by the wardens, bears as a species were not hunted down as were wolves, cougars, and coyotes. One reason was that people liked them. They were seen as "good" animals, sometimes bad "good" animals, but nonetheless viewed as an attractive species and symbolic of the wildness of the park. Their importance to the Jasper visitor experience also led park officials to tolerate practices that kept bears close to human use areas. This occurred despite the repeated warnings by wildlife biologists that human garbage was a serious hazard to the welfare of the bears, as well as to public safety.

Jasper the Bear

The cartoon "Jasper," depicting a resident bear in the park, first appeared in *Maclean's Magazine* in 1948 and was a regular feature of that magazine for the next twenty-four years. Created by James Simpkins, Jasper, like his counterpart Yogi Bear in Yellowstone, was a likeable and friendly observer of park life, happy to share the

"Where are all the tame bears this park is supposed to be full of?"

Jasper the Bear, created by James Simpkins. COURTESY THE ESTATE OF JAMES SIMPKINS

park with the tourist visitors while sometimes running afoul of the park ranger. The bear became the mascot of the community after which he was named, and a wooden statue stood near Athabasca Park for many years. After it was damaged by vandals, a new concrete replica was made to replace it in 2004. More recently a newer image has been picked up by the town, where it appears on signs and is even embossed in the crosswalks on Connaught Drive. But this new image is of a more realistic and fearsome grizzly.

In the early years of the park, bears were not seen as much of a problem at all. In 1916 Commissioner J. B. Harkin noted that grizzlies were sufficiently rare to be given absolute protection. Only if their numbers increased and they posed a threat to other wildlife, he added, would he sanction their destruction.[175] The more numerous black bears were also to be protected, although authority was given to shoot the "nuisance" bears that became too fond of raiding people's food. Maxwell Graham of the wildlife division went so far as to recommend that bears could also be removed from fishing areas so as not to interfere with anglers.[176] Yet, for the most part in these early years, park officials welcomed bears around the town where they could be seen more easily by tourists.

At the beginning of the 1920s, as Jasper tourism was just starting to grow, bear watching had already become a popular tourist activity. An *Edmonton Journal* article in 1921 described how visitors flocked to the town dump to see the bears feeding on the garbage: "One, a big cinnamon bear, a powerful looking beast with tremendous forearms, has become so tame that he allows himself to be fed by hand."[177] The large cinnamon grizzlies were especially popular and, far from discouraging this behaviour, the superintendent seemed to promote it as a good thing. In his interim report for 1924, Superintendent Maynard Rogers noted the growing numbers of grizzlies in the Snake-Indian, Smoky, and Rocky River valleys. He then added: "[A] few different ones have been reported up the Athabasca and it is hoped that this most interesting animal will gradually become accus-

Loretta Norris and an unnamed bear at Jasper Park Lodge, early 1930s. JYMA, PA 7313

tomed to man, as they are in the Yellowstone Park, and gradually work closer in where visitors may see them."[178] The superintendent got his wish and grizzly bears did move closer to town where they fed at the town dump and the dump used by Jasper Park Lodge. Few at the time saw this as a catastrophe in the making as humans learned to get close to bears, and the bears, addicted to human garbage, lost their shyness of people.

Park wardens of the 1930s recalled one incident in particular. A Toronto football team stopped over in the park on its way to a championship game in Vancouver. Visiting the dump to watch the bears, they spotted a brown-coloured cub and decided to take it as a mascot. They got as far as putting a noose around its neck and were leading it away when the mother bear came to its rescue. The footballers beat a hasty retreat and the cub scrambled up a tree. But here the real drama began when, in the words of one warden: "One of the townspeople reported to the Administration Office later in the day that the cub was entangled in the top branches of a pine tree and the mother was raging around the base of the tree being unable to free the cub which was loudly protesting every time the noose tightened on its throat."[179] The cub was rescued when a telephone lineman bravely climbed a neighbouring tree and, with a knife attached to a pole, cut the cub free.

Despite the potential danger of the situation, foolish luck allowed this Arcadian ideal of the friendly harmless bear to survive into the 1950s. In part, this was because there were still not great numbers of tourists visiting the park, and most of those who did come travelled in organized groups— in contrast to the later automobile tourists who toured in family units. For most visitors to the park, bears were not seen as a problem. Backcountry travel during this early period was still typically organized by the horse outfitters. The outfitters were experienced enough to know how to behave around bears and the number of people and horses in their expeditions tended to ensure that there were no unfortunate surprises. In this period, pernicious encounters with bears tended to be experienced more by locals: town residents whose property was raided and wardens whose backcoun-try cabins were broken into. The wardens' cabins were especially vulnerable to grizzly attacks. Percy Goodair had had his cabin broken into by a griz-zly that was later blamed for his death in 1929. By the 1940s, the wardens reported a virtual state of siege:

These bears seem to have changed their normal way of life,
to become very troublesome in the Rocky River and Maligne

districts. All of the cabins in these districts were repeatedly broken into. Doors, roofs and windows were renewed several times on most of the cabins ... For a time it was a question of whether the grizzly or the warden was going to stay in the districts. On one occasion a grizzly attempted to break into the Medicine Lake cabin while the warden was occupying the place, and it was necessary to shoot the animal through the window.[180]

As with town properties, bears were likely attracted to the wardens' cabins by the smell of garbage. It was the practice in these days for the wardens to dig a pit behind the cabin for his and his family's garbage. Although the refuse was frequently burned, there was still residual food to attract the animals. Some old wardens have also theorized that the bears were attracted to the pack rats that often lived under the floors of the cabins.

Clowns of the Park

There are many newspaper reports of the cute and funny bears that roamed around Jasper townsite. An item in the *Edmonton Journal* for 13 July 1939 thought it newsworthy to describe the antics of some bears on the Jasper Park Lodge golf course:

Bears who call this mountain resort home and add to 'local color' discovered last year the trick of turning on water sprinklers dotting the golf course. For a week during the warmer part of the summer, the bears enjoyed mid-afternoon showerbaths and watery siestas on the fairways, then adjourned to evening meals at the town refuse dump miles away.

Such news items just further encouraged tourists to get up close to these loveable and therefore harmless creatures.

Park officials started talking about the bear problem in the late 1930s. In 1938 Controller F. H. H. Williamson, who had succeeded Harkin as head of the national parks service, wrote to the mountain park superintendents instructing them to post signs advising people not to feed the bears.[181] In the 1940s there was growing concern in the mountain parks about the threat of grizzly bears in particular. There had been a mauling at Lake Louise of a Swiss guide and a well-known photographer in 1939 that caused some discussion of an emerging problem. Frank Williamson commented on the Lake Louise attack in a memo to the superintendents of Banff and Jasper in 1939: "The great amount of publicity which has been given to Nick Morant and Christian Haasler with a grizzly bear in Banff National Park raises a question as to steps which should be taken to warn the public from contact with dangerous animals or animals which are dangerous at certain seasons of the year."[182] There was more discussion in 1943 when the superintendent of Yoho was attacked by a grizzly. Following the Yoho attack, national park headquarters introduced a policy requiring that grizzlies near settlements or dumps be destroyed.[183] In spite of this directive, the park wardens seemed reluctant to wage war on the animals, with exceptions being made for those that were an obvious threat. There is some anecdotal evidence that wardens were less tolerant of bears that broke into their cabins.[184] Still, the bear issue continued to simmer through the 1940s and 1950s.

By 1947, with the resumption of tourism, the park superintendents were becoming increasingly concerned about the bear issue. There was particular concern in Jasper, where automobile tourism was expanding rapidly as a result of the opening of the Banff–Jasper Highway. Bears along the route were stopping cars to beg for food. The new bungalow camps and auto-campgrounds that were opening up along the route brought their own garbage problems and resident bears. In 1943 a mother bear brought her cubs into town, where they cavorted for the tourists in return for treats. On at least one occasion the cubs were seen rolling on the grassy lawn of the town park with children.[185] The mother had already learned how to entertain in return for food and was teaching her cubs. The public seemed eager to make the animals into pets. They fed them and gave the cute ones names. Park officials were worried, and stepped up the educational campaign to try to stop people from feeding the bears.

In the 1940s and 1950s national parks management clung to the notion that only a small proportion of the bears were causing most of the problems, and that most of the bears behaved in a friendly manner, showing up at the dumps to feed and then disappearing into the forest. This was the view taken at Yellowstone from the 1920s, where the solution there was to identify the "bad" bears and dispose of them.[186] Ottawa, too, adopted this approach and instituted a new policy where problem bears would be trapped and relocated. Problem bears were marked with paint on their posteriors, and if they were found back in their old haunts then they could be destroyed. Park Superintendent Harry Dempster found this policy inefficient and felt that the park needed to take steps to better protect the public. In a letter to headquarters in 1950, the superintendent warned that the wildlife biologists were going too far in protecting bears and not enough was being done to protect visitors. He added: "I feel that the Wild Life personnel, in some cases, are too prone to take to the view that the animals were here first, and if people visit our Parks they must be prepared to cope with it."[187]

Frank Banfield was asked to look into the matter in 1947. His report to the head of the Canadian Wildlife Service (CWS) pointed out that the root of the problem lay in the garbage dumps.[188] Once the bears had become familiar with the garbage dumps, they would travel long distances to get at them. Banfield also agreed with Dempster that the trap-and-relocate policy was ineffective. However, Banfield argued that destroying the bears would not solve the underlying problem. This was not what the parks service wanted to hear, and the branch director merely reiterated the existing policy, stressing that the final solution lay in the destruction of the "problem" bear: "Undoubtedly these bears are a considerable tourist attraction but they do get spoiled and they cannot be cured."[189]

The bear problem worsened in Jasper through the 1950s. In June 1950 a student was mauled by a bear after he had stopped to admire her cubs beside a lake.[190] That same year, Superintendent Dempster asked Banfield to look at the problem again. His report written the following year emphasized that "the final control of bear problems lies in the removal of fresh refuse."[191] Banfield also took the superintendent to the dumps to show him the problem. In another memo Banfield commented on his visit to the dump: "I cannot see what is attractive about bears wallowing in an odiferous garbage dump amid clouds of flies. This is what I was shown with pride at Jasper Park Lodge in October."[192] Following Banfield's second report in 1953, the park finally began to attack the issue of the garbage dumps, introducing incinerators to burn the refuse before it was dumped. In 1951 national park headquarters had also passed regulations making it illegal to feed the bears. The organization was encouraged to do this by the United States Parks Service, which seemed incredulous that the Canadians could curtail human behaviour by merely posting signs.[193] But though the regulations were passed, they were not enforced until the end of the decade.

The Jasper bear census of 1953 underscored the significance of the town and Jasper Park Lodge dump sites to the bear population. In that year, each of the thirteen backcountry warden districts reported the number of bears they had seen during the year. The total was fourteen black and five grizzly bears in the entire backcountry of the park; in contrast, twelve black and three grizzlies were counted at the two dump sites.[194]

The 1953 census brought about a further tightening of garbage burning procedures and a more serious attempt to discourage bear viewing at the dumps. At first these measures seemed successful—so much so that hungry bears roamed the townsite looking for garbage. CWS agreed that this was a dangerous situation, and the wardens were authorized to shoot up to twenty "destructive" bears in 1954.[195] The Jasper Park Lodge dump site continued to be a problem, however, and in 1957 and 1958 it was reported that between fourteen and fifteen grizzlies regularly visited the dump.[196] Based on the earlier bear census figure, this would have represented virtually the entire grizzly population of the park. The Jasper Park Lodge dump continued to be a source of trouble until its closure in the 1960s.

The bear problem was made worse by the burgeoning numbers of tourists visiting the park. Through the 1950s the number of park visitors grew twenty times over the pre-war records. A significant shift in the pat-

A black bear begging on the highway. JNP, A 681

tern of visitor use further increased the chances of bear/human encounters. Now, most people arrived by car. There were more hiking trails developed around the townsite and more people were camping. Meanwhile, much of the Jasper bear population had learned to associate humans with food. With the growth of auto-camping, bears soon came to associate tents with food and regularly tore them up. This was such a common occurrence that in 1959 Superintendent John Pettis proposed acquiring a commercial sewing machine for use by campers who wished to repair their torn tents.[197] The bears learned to stand along the Banff-Jasper Highway to beg for food from passing cars. When cars stopped to look at the bears, as they still do today, causing the inevitable "bear jam," the bears would come up to the cars, standing up to reach the windows.

Tragedy struck in August 1958 when "Victor" the bear met a seven-year-old girl named Barbara and forgot to play his part. Victor was about four years old and had grown up begging along the highway and raiding the bungalow camp garbage dumps. He was well known to the tourists and the young people who worked at the Sunwapta bungalow camp, and it was they who had given him his name. On that particular day, Victor was engaged in a more traditional pastime of eating berries from a bush near the camp. The bush was near the back of a cabin where a little girl was playing with her dolls on the back porch. Wanting some berries, perhaps for her tea party, Barbara went to the bush and did not at first see the bear. But when she suddenly saw him close up, she ran back to the cabin screaming. This provoked an instinctive attack by the bear, and he was mauling her when he was finally shot by the camp owner. The little girl died en route to the hospital.

The event caused a crisis within the parks organization. There was a lot of press coverage, a coroner's inquest was called, and the minister responsible for national parks, Alvin Hamilton, answered questions in Parliament. There was considerable soul-searching on the part of the park officials. In a long memorandum to headquarters, Superintendent Pettis pointed out that he considered tourists feeding the bears to have contributed to a serious situation.[198] A subsequent departmental investigation agreed with this analysis, and recommended that the park regulations be enforced. Subsequently, park wardens issued tickets to tourists who fed the bears, and a greater effort was made to discourage begging bears and garbage feeding. But the bears paid a bigger price. In 1959 and 1960, fifty-five black and twelve grizzly bears were destroyed in Jasper National Park.

Although scientists had identified garbage dumps as being an underlying cause of problem bears, the parks were slow to deal with this problem effectively, preferring to treat the symptoms either by relocating or destroying the offending animals. It was not until 1969 that a new national parks policy directed park managers to consider the rights of the animal over the convenience of humans:

> Conflicts between wildlife and other park interests including human safety should be resolved if possible without destruction of wildlife. For example adequate handling of garbage should replace destruction of garbage-fed bears, and feeding of bears by visitors should be stopped.[199]

Following this directive, Jasper closed all outlying dumps and all garbage was trucked to a sanitary landfill located four kilometres east of the townsite. Still, it attracted bears despite the addition of a chain-link fence until the addition of an improved incinerator and an electric fence took care of the problem. Also at this time, backcountry campers were instructed to pack out their garbage instead of the previous burn-and-bury custom.

Jasper town dump and incinerator, c. 1960. JYMA, 35.02.04

Park Superintendent Jim Christakos and Warden Max Winkler award prizes for a children's garbage collection project, 1970. The children are standing on plastic trash bags. Note the figure of Jasper the Bear on one of the trophies. JNP

Pamphlets were distributed to visitors to educate the public on better habits of garbage disposal.

Today, the appearance of bears along the Icefields Parkway can still cause a bear jam as tourists stop to take pictures, but now most people know enough to stay in their cars with the windows up. Gradually, through the number of well-publicized bear attacks and the visitor education in the park, people came to appreciate that these are potentially dangerous wild animals, not cute comedians to be posed beside one's child.

Building a Better Garbage Can

Throughout the 1960s and 1970s, park officials sought a design for a bear-resistant garbage receptacle. They tried burying them in the ground, hanging them from chains, and encasing them in concrete. At busy sites, such as automobile campgrounds, park officials tried using large industrial-style dumpsters. However, these only attracted more bears because, as they held more refuse, they smelled even better. The animals soon learned to rock them over, the sound of which kept many a worried camper awake at night. The present garbage cans in the park made their appearance in 1985, and have proven to be largely effective in keeping bears out. Built of heavy-duty steel, they are mounted on an angle on a wooden or concrete platform and are covered by self-closing steel lids.

The new policies greatly lessened the incidence of problem bears. Still, with the increase in backcountry use, the chances of bear-human encounters are still real. In 1992 a young British couple camped in the Tonquin Valley met with tragedy while out for an after-dinner stroll. They encountered an old grizzly and beat a hasty retreat. Sensing food, the hungry bear went after them and tried to get at the young woman who had taken refuge in a tree. The man tried to distract the bear, but was himself killed and

Bubbling Springs bear. Yes, that is a bear tipping the can! LEO BILODEAU, JNP

partly eaten. The woman was able to climb out of the tree and alert another camper, who ran fifteen kilometres to the trailhead for help. By the time the wardens returned in a helicopter, the woman had herself run thirteen kilometres and was suffering from immense physical and emotional stress. The bear was destroyed and was found to have been an old and ailing animal that likely had been unable to hunt.

CHAPTER TEN

Highway Travellers

In 1930 a typical tourist arrived in Jasper by train, stayed at the Jasper Park Lodge, and rode horses to the various sites. In 1950, although many people still came by train, increasing numbers were arriving in their own vehicles. Moreover, travel around the park was now largely by automobile—even the train travellers were being toured around the park in hired cars. Many of the automobile tourists were staying at other places besides Jasper Park Lodge, choosing the economy and informality of the new roadside bungalow camps and campgrounds. Jasper National Park had been transformed in the 1930s by the construction of two major highways into the park, and a network of secondary roads and facilities that opened up new sites to mass tourism: Miette Hot Springs, Athabasca Falls, and the Columbia Icefields.

These physical changes to the landscape influenced other transformations as well. First, the new roads brought many more tourists: the number of annual visitors grew from under 14,000 in 1930 to almost 85,000 by 1950. In 1968 park attendance jumped by 28 per cent from the previous year to 835,000 visitors. By 1970 a million visitors a year came to the park, many on the new highways. Second, the highways and roads influenced how and where people would experience the park. Visitors were funnelled along predetermined routes to a series of compacted sites.

Before the 1930s there were very few automobile tourists in the park. There were some roads, including scenic roads to Maligne Canyon, Mount Edith Cavell, and Athabasca Falls. There were roads to Pyramid and Patricia lakes, and to Jasper Park Lodge. And there were roads around town. The difficulty was road access to the park. Until 1940 the only access from the south and the west was by horse or by foot. A route existed from the east, but it was fairly rudimentary through the 1940s. Before this time, people wishing to use their vehicle in the park would generally have it shipped from Edmonton by train. Then as now, people travelling by car in the park needed a vehicle pass, and the statistics show how exotic vehicles were in the park in the early days: in 1927 only ten licenses were sold; in 1931 there were 188; and in 1933 park officials sold 716.[200] Part of the reason for the increase in vehicle traffic—besides just the growing popularity of automobiles in the period—was the opening of a motor route to Edmonton. The route was pioneered in 1923 by members of the Edmonton Automobile and Good Roads Association. One of the participants, Charles Grant, later recounted the work that had gone into preparing the route, much of which followed abandoned rail lines:

> Mr. Frank Wright, who was then Secretary of the Edmonton Automobile and Good Roads Association, and I left Edmonton on the 4th of November 1923, after the Motor Association had collected and spent $4000.00 for the taking up of the ties on the part of the abandoned grade where they would still be trouble-some and placing poles between the ties and trestles over ravines and creeks and clearing out the wind-falls on old tote roads constructed when the Grand Trunk Pacific Railway was being built, so as to complete a road which could be traversed from Edmonton to Jasper.[201]

A car that travelled to Jasper in 1922. Note the planks tied to the side of the vehicle and the oversized pickaxe on the running board for getting through difficult spots.
JYMA, 86.12.02.03

They crossed into Jasper three days later. The pioneers were surprised to find another vehicle in the park. Paul Welch had had his McLaughlin shipped in on a flat car.[202] With the encouragement of the Good Roads Association, the province improved the route until it became accessible to regular tourists. Still, by the beginning of the 1930s it was still a rudimentary dirt road, susceptible to washouts. The onset of the Depression halted any subsequent improvement until later in the 1940s.

National Parks Highway Engineers

Until the 1950s the national parks service had the most experienced, and some of the best-trained, highway engineers in western Canada. They were adept at building scenic routes and meeting the engineering challenges posed by the mountain terrain. Their abilities and the large projects that they managed gave engineers a superior position in the organization. Jim Wardle, hired at the end of World War I as one of the department's first university-trained engineers, headed the

The first government automobile in Jasper National Park, c. 1923. A right-hand drive Ford climbs Mile 10 of the Cavell Road. JYMA, PA 18-70

construction projects in the west through the 1920s and 1930s, and for a time served as superintendent at Banff. Jim Wood, who held a degree in engineering from McGill University, was associate superintendent at Banff, then the first superintendent of Riding Mountain National Park, before coming to Jasper as superintendent in 1938. Wood's World War I service was remarkably similar to that of Fred Brewster. He, too, had been·a major with the Royal Canadian engineers and had been awarded the Military Cross for bravery at Vimy. Wood was succeeded in 1949 by Harry Dempster, who had a master's degree in Engineering from the University of Saskatchewan. This was still at a time when practically no other member of the park staff, save the resident engineer, would have had a university degree. Dempster went on to become superintendent of Banff and then regional manager of all the western parks in 1960.

At the beginning of the 1930s Jasper Park was relatively quiet, with few signs of the activity that would transform the park later in the decade. In terms of development, Canadian National Railways (CNR) was by far the leading player in the area. Jasper Park Lodge remained the tourist centre of the park and the CNR embarked on an ambitious expansion program there. Colonel Rogers returned to the park as superintendent in 1931 after a two-year absence, and the park administration ticked along much as it had done in the 1920s. If anything, things became even quieter as the economic slowdown took its toll of tourists. Rogers reported that during fiscal year 1931–1932 the number of tourists had fallen off by 20 per cent and that the park had gotten only slightly more than eleven thousand tourists, of whom only 630 had arrived by car. Life became quieter in the park as the Depression deepened. Road-building projects would soon shatter this silence.

When the Great Depression began in the autumn of 1929 Canadians were ill-prepared to deal with it. Accustomed to periodic economic slumps, many people at first believed that the hard winter of 1929–1930 would be followed by recovery in the summer. But the summer of 1930 came and went and things seemed to go from bad to worse. The economic situation became an issue in the general federal election of the fall of that year. R. B. Bennett's Conservatives were elected to form the government largely because of his promises to do something about the Depression. The trouble was that, at this point in history, the government had few tools to deal with a problem that it scarcely understood. World financial markets were in disarray, the price of wheat, like that of minerals and lumber, had collapsed, and a prolonged drought on the prairies was ruining farms.

The traditional approach to dealing with economic downturns was to sit back and let private industry and capital deal with the problem. However, as the Depression deepened, Canada began to experience serious social problems with the thousands of unemployed men, destitute families, and hungry children. Social services in Canada at this time were rudimentary at best. Relief for the poor was the responsibility of municipalities, and as more and more people drifted into the towns and cities looking for work and handouts, their meagre resources were quickly overwhelmed. Cities turned to their provincial governments for assistance, and they in turn sought federal aid. Without any clear plan of what it was doing, the Bennett government nonetheless allocated $20 million to help local and provincial agencies establish emergency relief projects in the winter of 1930–1931. Public works projects funded by the three levels of government continued through the following winter of 1931–1932. However, as economic recovery was still nowhere in sight and unemployment figures continued to rise, local and provincial governments in hard-hit western Canada found themselves facing bankruptcy.[203]

It was against this backdrop of economic and social chaos that national parks emerged as important agents of government relief work. The western national parks had a huge backlog of projects, many of which involved road construction to attract the increasing numbers of automobile tourists. Moreover, there was plenty of space to establish work camps in out-of-the-way places, where social problems could be hidden in attractive but remote places. In the process, western national parks benefitted enormously from injections of government spending at a time when other government organizations were experiencing serious cutbacks. In Saskatchewan and Manitoba, the two new national parks of Prince Albert and Riding Mountain had virtually their entire infrastructures created through relief spending, including the building of their townsites and roads. Jasper benefitted as well—Depression-relief spending financed the building of roads and highways, initiating a new era of automobile touring in the park.

The first emergency relief projects in Jasper were aimed at employing out-of-work men from the town of Jasper who had been laid off by the railway. During 1931 some three hundred men toiled at make-work projects, fixing up the town streets as well as improving the Maligne Canyon, Edith Cavell, Pyramid, and Miette Hot Springs roads.[204] Meanwhile, both the government and the national parks branch were devising bigger plans for Jasper. A serious issue facing all levels of government as the Depression worsened during the winter of 1930–1931 was the growing number of single unemployed men drifting into the cities such as Edmonton and Calgary, seeking some kind of support. Unable to find work there and unable to meet the residency requirements for municipal relief, the men posed a threat of criminal or civil disorder. Consequently, the federal government began exploring the possibility of military-type camps to diffuse the problem. The national parks had already had the precedent during World War I of providing work for interned enemy aliens. Harkin and his lieutenants therefore began to think up uses for similar types of labour camps.

A highway link from Lake Louise to Jasper had long been the dream of the parks service. It had been mentioned as early as 1914 and, as highway links between Rocky Mountains, Yoho, and Kootenay national parks were developed in the 1920s, the idea gathered momentum and was a factor in the extension of the Jasper border to join with Rocky Mountains Park to the south in 1927. A highway connection would allow Jasper to join with the other parks to form a four-mountain park tourist system. It would divert tourist traffic north from the east-west highway through Banff, and it would give the four-mountain park block a gateway to the north and Edmonton. Finally, it would create a scenic highway of considerable beauty, giving motorists access to the heartland of the Rockies that was previously accessible only by pack horse.

Although there was already a well-established horse trail in place, there were formidable obstacles along this mountainous route that made it a costly undertaking: Bow Summit, the Big Hill leading up to Parker Ridge, Sunwapta Pass, as well as many river and creek crossings. However, with manpower available from the ranks of the unemployed in Calgary and Edmonton, the highway project suddenly became a possibility and Commissioner Harkin and his engineers submitted their proposal in the fall of 1931. Approval was immediate and through the rest of the season men were taken on, camps were built, and the route surveyed. The plan was to begin construction of the 140-mile highway from both the Lake Louise and Jasper Park ends and so four work camps were established in Rocky Mountains Park and three in Jasper.

Bunkhouse Men

Ted White, who worked as a surveyor on the Banff-Jasper project, remembered the men who lived in the work camps: "As can be imagined, the crews consisted of types from all walks of life. They were made up of ex-army officers, engineers, teachers, office clerks, and all down the line to the general roustabout. Patriots and communists, God-fearing men and atheists, politicians and those who couldn't care less but were generally good Canadians, temporarily up against it due to no fault of theirs."[205]

A Banff-Jasper Highway construction camp, 1930s. JNP, H2585

A typical camp housed fifty men and came equipped with bunkhouses, a cookhouse, a washhouse, and even an infirmary. About 350 men were employed in the Jasper camps through the winter of 1931, until about February or March when provincial funding dried up and the project was suspended. However, the desperate situation of the unemployed men caused the provincial and federal governments to renegotiate funding of the project, and work resumed later in 1932. From the governments' perspective, the priority was to employ as many men as possible while spending as little as possible. Efficiency was not a particular concern, and so the project dragged on for several years.

In Jasper there were five camps of sixty men each. Each camp was responsible for a fifteen-mile section of road, and as the work was completed, the camp would leapfrog down the line to commence work on a new section. To keep costs down, each section of road was limited in the amount of earth that could be moved. Therefore, if too much work was required filling depressions or removing hills, then the line was relocated to follow a more level contour.[206] Each camp was allocated ten teams of horses and only one caterpillar tractor, which meant that most of the work was done by pick and shovel. The horses pulled scrapers or graders and wagonloads of earth. The tractors also pulled wagons and, in the early years at least, were not equipped with a blade for moving earth. As a result, progress was slow. By the spring of 1933, only a twenty-three-mile stretch of the forty-foot right-of-way had been cleared at the Jasper end—and that was along the relatively flat opening section.

Construction proceeded more quickly following the passage of the 1934 *Public Works Construction Act* and its supplementary budget in 1935. CNR also helped by building the trestle bridge over the Athabasca near the

A Banff-Jasper Highway road gang, 1930s. JNP, H4522

Maligne Canyon road. This facilitated a new entrance to Jasper Park Lodge, separating general park traffic from that going to the lodge. Before this, the old road to the south leading to Mount Edith Cavell had passed through Jasper Park Lodge and crossed the Athabasca by Old Fort Point. With an influx of motorists projected from the south, this arrangement was no longer acceptable, and so CNR made arrangements for the second crossing of the river that is still used today along Highway 93A.

The completion of the Banff–Jasper Highway in 1940 called for the establishment of camp and picnic grounds along the route. Banff National Park established campgrounds at Bow Summit, Waterfowl Lakes, and Mosquito Creek and picnic sites at Hillside and Baker Creek. Jasper established primitive campgrounds at Jonas Creek and the Columbia Icefields and picnic sites at Honeymoon Lake and Athabasca Falls. Initial work on the campsites and picnic grounds was carried out in the 1940s, while more substantial development was completed in 1950–1951. The kitchen shelter at the Columbia Icefields campground was among the earliest of those built. Although it was small and contained only one stove, it was enclosed on three sides by shingle-clad walls with large multi-paned windows, a

Fred Brewster's Columbia Icefields Chalet and highway, c. 1940s. CSTM, CN X8839

concession to the more extreme weather at that high elevation. By contrast, the Bow Summit shelter at Banff was more crudely sheathed with vertical boards ending three-quarters of the way up the sides.

More substantial stopping places were also developed along the route by private entrepreneurs. Jasper Park licensed a bungalow camp at Sunwapta Falls and two more near the townsite. The Sunwapta bungalow camp consisted of a main lodge and a series of simple one-room cabins. It also provided a gas station, an important highway oasis in those days of early motoring when new drivers were still beginning to understand gas mileage and tire wear. The most substantial tourist development along the route was Fred Brewster's Columbia Icefields Chalet, built in 1939—just in time for the new highway's opening. The chalet provided a base for exploring the Athabasca Glacier, a major tourist attraction along the route.

The opening of the new highway in 1940 received national attention, muted only by the larger war news. Fred Brewster spoke on the radio and reminisced about travelling the route on pack horse before World War I. Where once it took weeks, now the route could be travelled in just seven hours. A federal government brochure published in 1950 advertised the route as "scenic beyond description," and claimed it to be "among the great 'highroads of the world.'"[207]

Meanwhile, the Jasper work camps began work on a series of other highway projects. Next in importance to the Lake Louse–Jasper Highway was the Jasper East Highway. An auto route had been established along the old right-of-way of the Grand Trunk Pacific Railway to the park gate. The hope was that this would connect with an all-weather highway being built west from Edmonton, now known as Highway 16, the Yellowhead route stretching from Selkirk, Manitoba, to Prince Rupert, British Columbia. Although this work was delayed by a lack of provincial resources, the park continued to widen and improve the route, building steel bridges and culverts. The Edmonton–Jasper Highway was officially opened in 1937, and brought increased motor traffic from the east; the opening of the Banff–Jasper highway brought even more cars from the south. The number of annual visitors to the park climbed from fifteen thousand in 1932, to ninety-one thousand in 1940.

As early as the 1920s the Edmonton Automobile and Good Road Association, along with other similar-minded groups, had pushed for an extension of the highway west into British Columbia. Some work in this direction had been started by the relief workers of the early 1930s, but not much progress was made before attention was shifted to completing the other two highway projects. The decade, with its accompanying Depression-relief spending, came to an end with virtually no progress having been made on the Yellowhead Highway, as it came to be known. With the outbreak of war in September 1939, it would seem that government money would be diverted from the parks and the project had missed its chance. But, once again, the park benefitted from the federal government's wish to employ troublesome men away from the cities.

The government was faced with two successive problems in the 1940s: what to do with the conscientious objectors who refused military service and, beginning in 1942, what to do with displaced Japanese-Canadians forced from their Pacific Coast homes following the panic and prejudice that erupted after the Japanese attack on Pearl Harbor. The national parks had previous experience hosting enemy alien camps during World War I, and had then operated a much larger program of relief camps through the 1930s, so Jasper park was a natural venue for wartime work camps. In the summer of 1941, two main camps for "alternate service workers," as the conscientious objectors were termed, were established in Jasper: one at Geikie, a station on the CNR line west of the town of Jasper, and the other near Sixth Bridge beside Maligne Canyon. The men at Geikie camp were put to work clearing the road right-of-way through the Yellowhead Pass.[208] The men at Maligne Canyon began working on improving the road to Medicine Lake, a link on the way to Maligne Lake. The Yellowhead Highway project foundered because of a lack of machinery, and less than three miles of roadway was passable by car. The Geikie camp was therefore closed, and the men transferred to smaller camps along the Banff–Jasper Highway where they were put to work clearing trails and campgrounds.

The national parks organization seemed cool to the suggestion that Jasper employ exiled Japanese-Canadians in the park. Certainly Jasper Superintendent Jim Wood was opposed to their presence, fearing their capacity to create all sorts of mayhem—from burning the forests to poaching fish. But the new federal surveys and engineering branch had no such qualms. Its director, Jim Wardle, had long contemplated a highway west of Jasper, through the Yellowhead Pass and along the CNR line to Kamloops. The availability of forced labour now made the project possible. In February 1942, his engineers were locating the route and identifying possible work campsites along the way. Subsequently, three camps were established in the park: one beside the old alternate service workers camp at Geikie, and two at Decoigne, another CNR station farther west. In all, about 175 men worked out of the three camps during the summer of 1942. But the venture was not a success: the men were deeply unhappy at being separated from their families and with their working conditions and staged slowdowns and sit-down strikes. Also, as with the Depression relief workers, machinery was in short supply. The project was therefore abandoned, and the workers moved to communities in the interior of British Columbia.

The highways that had been built in the 1930s were soon found to be inadequate as highway construction standards were raised with the introduction of better and faster cars and as highways across the continent became better engineered to allow faster speeds. Even as these roads were being built there was a revolution underway in highway construction. In the 1920s, when automobile travelling first started to become popular, cars and roads were fairly simple. Roads were often just graded tracks and mass-produced vehicles like the Ford Model T would be lucky to cruise along at twenty to thirty miles per hour with their twenty-horsepower motors. The Model A, which began to appear in 1928, had twice the horsepower of the

A Jasper Park Lodge touring car at Columbia Icefields, c. 1950s. CSTM, CN X21862

Model T and at least had the potential for highway speeds. In the 1930s, mass-produced autos became more powerful—for example, the Ford flat head V-8, which was capable of faster and safer highway travel, was introduced in 1932. This in turn increased pressure for the creation of highways that could be travelled at speeds approaching sixty miles per hour. Roads had to be widened, curves had to be made more gradual, and intersections needed to be controlled. As a consequence, upgrading the existing Jasper highways became a priority after World War II. In 1948 improvements were made along the Edmonton–Jasper Highway. Steel bridges were built across the Fiddle, Rocky, and Athabasca rivers and the whole roadway widened to thirty-two feet. The Banff–Jasper Highway was also improved. It was widened to twenty-six feet and "grades and alignments were extensively revised."[209]

Even with the improvements of 1949, the Icefields Parkway was still far from being of highway standard. Even before the Trans-Canada Highway through Banff and Yoho national parks was opened in 1960, that route had set a new standard for highway travel through the parks: it was paved, was engineered for highway speeds, and had pull-offs. The old parkway, by contrast, was still gravelled, not maintained in winter, and had many narrow winding sections. Rebuilding the parkway became a major priority of the national parks service in the 1950s. The work was undertaken by the federal Department of Public Works between 1958 and 1961 and, in contrast to the

Icefields Parkway construction, c. 1950s. JNP

earlier enterprise, it was built with great engineering efficiency. The steep winding stretches at the Jasper end were abandoned completely in favour of a straight right-of-way that followed the other side of the Athabasca River. The old highway was left as a scenic route to Mount Edith Cavell and Athabasca Falls and renamed Highway 93A. The new all-season route along the parkway was opened with a ceremony in August 1961, and a commemorative plaque erected at a pull-off on the Banff-Jasper boundary.

Façade Management

The creation of major auto routes through Jasper constituted a major investment on the part of the federal government. Where before the major transportation route had been maintained by the railway, highways were now the park's responsibility. It was not only the roads and bridges that needed maintenance. The roads were not just access routes into the park, they were important scenic outlets in their own right. The scenery along these routes became more valuable as a result, leading the park to implement a program that some would later describe as "façade management." Forest fire protection became a prime consideration of this approach, as blackened trees were considered unsightly. So it was natural, then, that the parks should deem that the protection of the forests along the new highways was a major priority. An important new development in this area came with the building of forest fire lookouts in the 1940s.

Through the 1960s, the park was busy finishing two more important highway projects: the completion of the Yellowhead Highway through Jasper and the building of a paved road to Maligne Lake. The opening of the Yellowhead in 1966 greatly reduced the driving time between Edmonton and the park while making winter travel along that road much more reliable. The Yellowhead also provided another gateway into British Columbia and made the park part of an important scenic highway system into northeastern BC. The Maligne Road, opened in 1970, served to make an important Jasper attraction accessible to auto tourists. All of this brought tourists to the park in increasing numbers.

CHAPTER ELEVEN

Skiers

Although Jasper did not emerge as a serious winter destination until the 1950s, its frozen charms had been appreciated by a lucky few for many years before that, and the local community had established a strong and thriving centre of winter sports since at least the 1920s. In the early years, frozen ponds were cleared for skating and curling. Annual curling bonspiels were held from at least the early 1930s, and there were hockey teams active in the interwar period as well. After World War II, an indoor rink became the winter community centre for the town. The community also formed hockey leagues to play local and district games. But the sport that garnered the greatest attention from people who lived outside the park was skiing. The local Jasper people took to this sport with great enthusiasm beginning in the 1920s, and by the following decade had popularized routes that attracted other skiers from across North America.

The popularity of skiing in Jasper developed gradually over many years, beginning with the development of local experts, exploring new ski areas and routes, and then building its international reputation as a skiing destination. One of the earliest recreational skiers was Pete Withers who came to the park to work as a warden in 1920. He later described having only the second set of skis in the park, the other pair belonging to the son of the chief warden. Lacking any particular skills, that first year the two ventured only two or three miles out of town. But Withers began to use his skis for getting around while carrying out his warden patrols in winter and became considerably more adept.[210] He was encouraged the following year by the return of two teenage boys who had been away attending school in Revelstoke. Vern and Doug Jeffery, the sons of the local shop owner, had had the opportunity to learn skiing while in Revelstoke where the sport had a long history through the many Norwegian immigrants living there. Skiing at this time was not like it is today, dominated as it is by alpine downhill runs, specialized equipment, and focus on parallel turns. Back then, skiing was dominated by Nordic events, which today are known as cross-country skiing, telemark skiing, and ski jumping.

Skis were introduced into North America by Norwegian immigrants

and it was their approach to the sport that defined it from the 1890s through
the 1920s. For many, skiing meant walking with boards over snow, hence
the early nickname for skis, "Norwegian snowshoes." However, skilled skiers knew how to kick and glide. They could go down steep trails, turning
by using either the stem christie (pushing out with the outside ski) or telemark techniques, and they could slow down or stop using the snowplow.
As well, proficient skiers learned how to wax their skis for different conditions and perhaps use seal skins for climbing hills. It was these learned skills
that enabled Withers and the Jeffery boys to venture farther and farther out
into the park. In 1923 they travelled past Maligne Lake. In 1927 they first
explored the Tonquin Valley on skis. It is likely that the Jeffery brothers also
built a ski jump near the edge of the golf course at Lac Beauvert.[211]

The arrival of Joe Weiss from Switzerland in 1926 expanded Jasper's
skiing expertise and introduced a different perspective: the Alps. The Swiss
and Austrian approach to skiing was slightly different from that of the Nor-
wegians. In Norway, people lived in scattered homesteads and used skis to
travel from point to point. They were accustomed to travelling along forest
trails and developed their techniques and approach to the sport accordingly. In the Swiss and Austrian Alps, on the other hand, people lived in valley bottoms and grazed cattle on the alpine slopes above the treeline. They
liked to climb the hills in winter to ski down the open alpine slopes. Joe
Weiss embodied this new Swiss perspective. Weiss looked for alpine cirques
where skiers could climb up using their seal skins and then take them off
to ski down. For this reason he was interested in the possibilities of the
Tonquin area, but in the late 1920s he explored the east face of Marmot
Mountain and recognized its potential. He called the area Marmot Basin
and by the early 1930s had blazed a trail to it by way of Whistler Creek and
Caribou Ridge.

Another thing that Weiss introduced to Jasper was the commercial
possibilities of the sport. Weiss was the first professional ski guide to work
in the area. Soon, the old horse outfitters saw the potential for ski guiding
as a way to keep customers coming in the off-season. Fred Brewster got into
the business, guiding parties to Tonquin Valley or to Maligne Lake. Curley
Phillips, too, became interested in the possibilities of the sport and was
apparently exploring a new alpine area when he was killed in an avalanche
in 1938. In the end, it was Brewster who took the ski-guiding business the
furthest, establishing a winter camp beside Amethyst Lake in the Tonquin
Valley. In 1940 he built a log chalet there to serve as kitchen-cum-dining-

Fred Brewster and his homemade snowmobile en route to Maligne Lake with skiers. JYMA, 994.45.71.3

Skiing at the warden cabin in the Tonquin Valley, February 1927. From left to right: Frank Burstrom, Dave Hartley, Doug Jeffreys, Sam Possum, and Percy Goodair.
PETER WITHERS, JNP, H3535

room for the camp. Brewster also took skiers out to his Maligne Lake Lodge in a homemade snowmobile. However, Joe Weiss was the real pioneer.

Another proficient skier from the 1920s was Frank Burstrom. Born in Tromsoe, Norway, he gained a reputation as a skilled and tireless skier. He may have used skis while working as a surveyor, and then after he joined the warden service in 1938. Although he participated in the pioneering Jasper to Banff trek of 1930, he tended to remain quietly in the background. But those who knew the sport knew Burstrom as something of a local legend.

Erling Strom was a professional skier who had taught skiing in Vermont before coming to the Rockies to help establish Assiniboine Lodge in the late 1920s. He had many American contacts and it was with a party of Americans that Strom first travelled to Jasper to ski the high country in 1931. Travelling with Joe Weiss and the Americans, he skied out to the warden cabin at Maligne Lake, a journey of some fifty kilometres that took them two days. From there they planned to travel over Poboktan Pass into the Columbia Icefields. However, going into Maligne, Weiss broke the tip of his ski. While a temporary repair could be rigged enabling him to reach the Maligne warden cabin, continuing on was problematic without getting a new ski. Upon reaching the cabin in late afternoon, the party telephoned Burstrom back in town. Although at first reluctant to come, Burstrom agreed to travel out that evening. This he did, and then, stopping only to warm himself by the stove in the cabin, he exchanged Weiss's broken skis and skied the fifty kilometres back to town. It seemed that he was getting married the next day and did not want to be late![212]

The pioneers who most publicized the sport in Jasper in the early days were Withers, Weiss, and the Jeffery brothers. In January 1930, these four skied to Banff in fifteen days of bitterly cold weather. They had established food caches along the way that previous autumn and stayed at the occasional warden cabin, but it was a remarkable achievement that received attention in the newspapers and journals of the day. The following year, Weiss and Strom travelled to the Columbia Icefields with Strom's American companions. The year after that, Withers and Weiss repeated the Jasper to Banff trip, this time accompanied by R. M. Bennett from Minneapolis and Clifford White from Banff. This time they travelled across the Athabasca Glacier, reaching elevations of almost four thousand metres.[213] The Columbia Icefields trip was repeated by Withers, Weiss, and the Jefferys in March 1933.[214] It took the group fifteen days during which they crossed three mountain passes and travelled almost three hundred kilometres

The start of the Jasper to Banff ski trip, 1930. The participants are wearing crests that identify them as members of the Jasper Ski Club. From the right: Frank Burstrom, Pete Withers, Joe Weiss, and Doug and Vern Jeffery. JYMA, 001.17.01

of unbroken trail during what was described as "bitterly cold weather."[215]

The activities of the hard-core enthusiasts helped spread the popularity of the sport among Jasper residents. Weiss and the Jefferys, with the help of Curly Phillips, built a cabin near Maligne Lake for the use of local skiers in 1936. Phillips devised an elaborate roof support structure for the cabin to strengthen it against the massive snow loads in the area. Called "Shangri-la," it was booked by locals who formed the Maligne Ski Club in order to justify the lease from the federal government. It was also used by Weiss as a base for guided ski tours. He charged $7.50 a day for beds, meals, and guiding.[216] Later, the British Lovat Scouts used the cabin as a base during World War II. It is still in use today and architectural historian Ted Mills described it as "a rare surviving example of a small-scale private venture in a backcountry location."[217]

More accessible ski trails were established around Pyramid and Patricia lakes in the 1920s. Here, a popular variety of cross-country skiing was ski-joring, where skiers were pulled across the lakes by horses. The Jasper

Ski Club was formed about 1930 to help organize activities for both beginner and expert skiers in the town. Leading members of the club were Withers, the Jefferys, and Fred Brewster. The club gradually became associated with the new craze—downhill skiing. Consequently, sometime around the mid-1930s, the club became focused on developing a downhill ski slope at Whistlers Mountain.

The Whistlers ski hill project marked a new phase in the development of the sport of skiing, not just in Jasper but throughout North America. Until the 1930s, the alpine skiers had been distinguished more by a difference of approach rather than by technique or equipment. Scandinavian-style skiers and Swiss- and Austrian-style skiers looked for different terrain, but essentially the style was interchangeable. Both groups wore what were essentially work boots on eight-foot skis. Gradually, though, alpine downhill skiing emerged as a distinct activity. Downhill skiers invented new types of competitions—slalom and downhill races—as opposed to the piste skiing and jumping events of Nordic skiing.

Differences in the two forms of skiing became more pronounced with the growing popularity of the Arlberg school of alpine skiing in Austria in the interwar period. Skiing became increasingly popular in North America after the winter Olympics held at Lake Placid, New York, in 1932. Although downhill events were not included in the Olympic skiing events, there was growing momentum for alpine skiing amongst younger people taking up the sport. The first ski resort devoted to the new craze opened at Sun Valley, Idaho, in 1935. Over the next ten years similar resorts opened at Aspen, Stowe, and Squaw Valley. The resorts shared similar features: open ski slopes cleared of trees, with gentle pitches for beginners and steeper ones for more expert skiers. Lodges were built to provide shelter and food. Ski lifts were introduced to make it easier and faster to get skiers up the slopes. The first lifts were simple rope tows, but T-bars and chairlifts began to appear in North America in the 1940s.[218]

Whistlers was an early prototype of these big American ski resorts. It offered two slopes, one above the other, each separated from the other by a bench. The slopes were cleared by local volunteers and by Depression-relief workers during the 1930s. Instead of lodges, it had tents on wooden platforms. And while there was no road access to the bottom of the hill, for most locals it was an easy ski from town. Unlike the Tonquin skiing area, Whistlers allowed for day skiing from the town. In this way it was much more accessible than the even earlier downhill ski locales pioneered

A Whistlers ski meet, 1951. PAA, PA 220.1

by people like Joe Weiss at Marmot and Skoki Lodge in Banff. The need for a rope tow was discussed by the Jasper Ski Club in 1939, but the outbreak of war precluded further effort in this direction until 1943 when a local railway employee, Ken Cook, got it going. He bought 1,500 feet of cable, scavenged a steel sheave from an abandoned rock quarry, and borrowed an old cat engine from the park. As Cook admitted, it was "a little dangerous so a year or two later we abandoned it and built the first of two rope tows on the lower hill."[219]

The extraordinary thing about Whistlers hill was that for the most part it was a community effort. There was no machinery to groom the runs, so squads of volunteers would sidestep up the hill to pack down the snow. Pete Withers led other volunteer teams to set up the shack tents and make sure that there was wood for the stoves. When the Jasper Ski Club wanted to erect a permanent lodge in the early 1950s, two members had to undertake to be responsible for the licence of occupation from the government. A cosy community hill, the place nevertheless received important support from both the park and the CNR. Both these sponsors saw the importance of Whistlers as a destination for winter tourists, something that both CNR and the national parks wished to encourage. In 1939, Jasper hosted an interclub ski meet, intended, so it was said, to promote the park as a winter playground.[220]

The Evolution of Downhill Skiing

The Jasper ski pioneers were advanced even by international standards of the day. Cable bindings were only invented in Switzerland in 1931. Steel edges were introduced three years later. These inventions, along with better, purpose-designed boots, allowed for better control of the skis on downhill runs and during the 1930s the parallel turn was developed in Austria. Still, downhill skiing did not really catch on in North America until after World War II. Although the 1932 Winter Olympic Games held in Lake Placid, New York, did much to popularize the sport, they did not include any alpine events. It was the 1960 Winter Olympic Games, held in Squaw Valley, California, that spurred the craze for downhill skiing in the US and Canada. After this, the technology for both skis and lifts improved dramatically. Toni Klettl described his first ski boots in the 1930s as a pair of work boots secured with leather straps. By contrast, his daughter Loni wore rigid plastic boots and step-in bindings when competing with the Canadian national ski team in the 1970s.

The popularity of skiing expanded during the war years as Jasper was used for training alpine troops. The British territorial unit known as the Lovat Scouts was stationed at the park for two years during the war. They stayed at Jasper Park Lodge, which was closed to regular tourists, and became the first guests to actually use the place during the winter. The scouts, who specialized in mountain warfare, established outlying camps at the Columbia Icefields and Tonquin Valley. Along with boosting interest in skiing, the troops introduced new ways of getting around in winter, including motorized toboggans—prototypes of the Bombardier ski-doos.

Following World War II, many thought that Whistlers would lead Jasper into becoming a major winter tourist destination. The park built a road access to the Whistlers Lodge. The railway promoted the advantages of a ski train, taking people from Edmonton for a weekend's skiing. In 1953–1954, a new rope tow was built and the club relocated its lodge farther up the mountain. The facilities continued to be improved through the 1950s. The runs were extended farther up the slope and in 1959–1960 a new chalet was constructed.[221] Designed by an Edmonton architectural firm, the building reflected the confidence that the locals had in making Jasper a downhill ski destination. Whistlers was promoted as a serious skiing destination, and it gained national recognition when the Canadian Junior Ski Championships were held there in 1961.[222] There was also a ski jump associated with the hill, and locals perfected their skills at this rare variation of skiing.

However, despite the enthusiasm, improvements, and promotions, Whistlers never really succeeded as a ski hill. In part this was because the snow was unreliable and, with the advent of chairlifts as the industry standard, the hill could not compete without a lot of capital investment. As skiing continued to grow in popularity following the 1960 Winter Olympics at Squaw Valley, California, park officials began to consider other venues for the sport in Jasper. They were especially interested in the possibilities of Marmot Basin. A cat road had been pushed into the area in the 1940s and snowmobiles were taking backcountry skiers there as it became renowned for its slopes and good snow. So, in 1963 the parks branch called for proposals to develop lifts and related facilities at Marmot. The bid from the company Marmot Lifts was accepted and development began the following year. By 1965 two T-bars and a chalet had been built. A lower chalet and chairlift were completed in 1969, and the park constructed modern highway access to Marmot in 1970.[223]

The emergence of Jasper as a year-round tourist destination was accompanied by tourist facilities designed to accommodate visitors in relative comfort. Park officials discouraged the planning of slope-side accommodation like that in vogue at the big American ski resorts. Instead, resort development was focused in the town. Motels and hotels supplanted the traditional bungalow camps in the 1960s. Only Jasper Park Lodge was able to winterize its cabins to make them suitable for winter weather. The combination of Marmot Basin and the new winter tourist business in the town created momentum for further winter tourist marketing. A feature of this new force was the invention of the Jasper carnival tradition. Beginning around 1989, some local Jasper businessmen joined forces with the Marmot Basin ski resort to promote "Jasper in January," a promotion specifically targeting a usually slow time of year because of cold weather and post–Christmas holiday retrenchment. "Jasper in January" began by offering reduced rates and lift ticket prices but added extra attractions associated with winter carnivals, such as ice sculpting, skating parties, and curling bonspiels.

A Jasper ski train, 1960s. CSTM, CN 69090/9

CHAPTER TWELVE

Wardens at the Crossroads

As late as the 1960s, the structure of a warden's life in Jasper had changed little since 1920. There were as many as fourteen park districts, each with a resident warden who spent much of the year at his district headquarters, or visiting a series of smaller patrol cabins. Much of the warden's routine involved travelling: moving up and down the boundaries of his district on horseback or snowshoes, noting the condition of the game, maintaining trails and telephone lines, and watching out for forest fires and poachers. There was a hierarchy among the wardens. The junior men would spend a summer or two assisting an old hand in his district before being sent out alone. A warden's first district was usually among the more remote stations, such as Blue Creek, out along the north boundary, or Brazeau, which looked after the south. As the warden acquired more seniority, he would be moved into districts that were closer to town until he reached the summit of his career as town warden. Not much was required in the way of qualifications: the warden was expected to know something about horses and the backcountry, be used to being on his own, and get along with the chief. No special training was required.

Yet, by the end of the 1960s, these prerequisites had radically changed as the position shifted from being that of the romantic backwoodsman to being a more conventional civil servant with specialized training and duties. This revolution was experienced by several young wardens who joined the park service in the 1950s and found their jobs radically different twenty years later. All of them shared a love for the backcountry and a sense that the old ways were best. Just as stories told around the campfire in the 1920s united the backwoodsman with the nineteenth-century explorers, so too the stories told around the stove in the 1950s tied the new wardens to the customs and beliefs of his predecessors. Values like toughness, self-reliance, courage, and a love of nature formed a common bond between old and new. And yet, as the modern world encroached more deeply into the mountains in the post-war years, the new generation had to adapt to new-fangled ideas. A scientific approach toward wildlife management was but one aspect of this transformation. Wardens in the 1950s and 1960s also were dealing with increasing numbers of unguided travellers in the backcountry, ski hills were presenting new dangers for public safety and the automobile campgrounds and highways required policing for infractions of the criminal code and the *National Parks Act.*

The 1950s introduced a period of transition for the Jasper warden service as many of the old-timers recruited in the 1920s retired. The new recruits represented both old and new trends. Frank Camp and Alfie Burstrom were both sons of old wardens. Clarence Wilkins was the nephew of Curly Phillips and the son-in-law of Frank "Cougar" Wells. Toni Klettl and Max Winkler were new Canadians, from Austria and Germany respectively. All learned to get along and adapt to the mixture of new and old ways.

In some ways, Toni Klettl was a typical warden of the 1950s. He had grown up on a farm in Austria and worked as a logger, surveyor, and powderman before being hired as an assistant warden in 1956. He was stationed at Maligne Lake where he worked for Larry McGuire. There he perfected his skills as a packer and horseman and learned to go out on patrol. McGuire had been a warden for many years and had worked as an outfitter before the war, and Klettl described him as "a tremendous horseman."[224] Klettl got further advice from the Moberly brothers, Frank and Dave, who were still working as packers in the area, providing the new Canadian with a tangible link back to the early traditions of Jasper. He spent the following summer in the Brazeau District, helping Mike Schintz, another young warden who had joined the park just a couple of years ahead of Toni, learning more of the ropes of being a district warden.

In the fall of 1957 Klettl was assigned his own district way out at Blue Creek, looking after the remote northern district of the park. At the end of October, loaded down with winter supplies and accompanied by his wife and small child, he made the two-day trek to his district headquarters. The Klettls spent the winter alone out there, with no electricity or running water, their only link to civilization being the telephone line to park headquarters. His district comprised four or five hundred square miles and so his patrols required extensive absences from his already isolated headquarters. His wife, Shirley, often found herself alone with only an infant for company for as long as twenty days at a time. This was typical of the era: wardens Mike Schintz, Frank Camp, and Max Winkler describe similar experiences at Brazeau.[225] In 1960 Klettl was transferred to the Whirlpool District, with headquarters at Cavell Cabin, near where Highway 93A crosses the Whirlpool River today. This cut the isolation considerably, but Shirley Klettl still home-schooled the children.[226]

Moving the Warden's Family

Retired wardens Max Winkler, Toni Klettl, and Mike Schintz all
spoke of the adventures they had getting their families into the
remote district cabins. As Klettl remarked, one did not want to make
a mistake when transporting an infant in sub-zero weather, far from
any help! The old wardens devised many ingenious ways of moving
their families around the backcountry. Children were a particular
challenge—they were often tied to horses, loaded on purpose-built
sleighs pulled by dogs, or carried in papooses. The "homemade"
sleighs and skids for travel and gathering firewood built by district
wardens were both unique and ingenious for the ways in which they
"eased" winter travels by warden families. Warden John Macklin
carried his children in boxes slung on either side of a packhorse.

Yet, already the winds of change were blowing. Tourism in the park was
mushrooming. More and more people were travelling on unguided tours,
taking advantage of the new motor highways and driving their own cars.
Skiing was becoming more popular, especially the downhill variety. Whistlers ski hill was expanded in the 1950s and Marmot Basin opened in the
1960s. In the summer, more people were hiking and backcountry camping.
Rock climbing was also becoming more popular, spurred on by the many
post-war immigrants from Europe. It fell to the wardens to take care of this
new wave of post-war tourists and in so doing they had to move with the
times. They learned about new ways of getting around the backcountry
and wardens stationed at highway cabins like Pocahontas and Sunwapta
learned more than they ever wanted to about motor vehicle accidents.

In some ways, Jasper wardens were extremely conservative and resisted
many of the new-fangled ideas that permeated the national parks service.
In other instances, they were very progressive. Even before World War II,
Jasper wardens had become proficient with European skiing techniques,
and men like Pete Withers and Frank Burstrom were pioneer cross-country
skiers. After the war, with the development of Whistlers and Marmot Basin
as alpine skiing destinations, the Jasper wardens became keen advocates of
the sport and, unlike their Banff counterparts, undertook responsibility
for ski patrol and avalanche safety. Recognizing that this work required
trained skills, Jasper became one of the first national parks in Canada to
initiate warden ski schools. The park held its first Ski and Snowcraft School

Warden John Micklin moving his family to their backcountry cabin in 1922. The boxes on the pack horse in front of his wife reputedly held infants. Wardens still moved their families this way in the 1960s. JNP

Warden John Macklin's children riding to their backcountry cabin, 1922. JNP

in March 1952. Here, instructors Alex Neumann and Tom Ross taught traditional horse wardens like Larry McGuire, Clarence Wilkins, and Frank Camp the rudiments of downhill skiing.[227] A more advanced course was held at Lake Louise in 1953 under instructor Noel Gardner from Mount Revelstoke National Park. Ross, Wilkins, and Camp attended this course.[228] The hiring of men like Toni Klettl and Max Winkler with European alpine backgrounds reflected in part this growing interest in warden involvement in the downhill ski industry.

The mountaineering skills of the Jasper wardens evolved from these rudimentary ski lessons. They were encouraged to expand this knowledge by Noel Gardner, who was beginning to take responsibility for mountaineering expertise in the mountain parks, and by the park's superintendent, Harry Dempster, who, as an engineer, was quick to appreciate the dangers of the ski slopes. Although Marmot Basin did not have lifts until the mid-1960s, there was snowmobile access into the bowl and adventurous backcountry skiers were keen to try what Joe Weiss had pioneered. But this area was also especially prone to avalanches. In a letter to national park headquarters in 1954, Superintendent Dempster wrote:

> I am firmly convinced that wherever any large numbers of skiers are involved, the marking of danger areas is not sufficient, because it is impossible to mark them so that a skier could not miss the danger signs.
>
> The answer, in my opinion, is stabilization of the slopes by causing the avalanches using explosives, and similarly doing away with the dangerous cornices in the same manner.[229]

Following Dempster's recommendation, three national park wardens, one of whom was from Jasper, were sent to the Advanced Snow and Avalanche Training School in Alta, Utah, run by the United States Department of Agriculture in 1954. After this exposure to more sophisticated methods of managing avalanche dangers, Jasper wardens began planting explosives in snow packs on mountain ridges. The early methods used were hair-raising. Three wardens would rope themselves together and one would crawl out onto the ledge of the mountain snow pack to drill holes for the dynamite. Toni Klettl described once having the cornice give way beneath his feet while he was attempting this manoeuvre—he was saved in the nick of time by half jumping and half being pulled to safety.[230] Later, the wardens

Avalanche control at Marmot Basin, c, 1970, using the 105-mm recoilless rifle. Toni Klettl is shown wearing ear protectors. JNP

used cannons to fire explosives into the snow pack, which was less danger-ous than climbing out onto a cornice, but caused anxious moments if the projectile froze in the barrel. After this, they tried army cannons. Some of the old wardens, like Klettl today, are consequently hard of hearing.

Beginning in 1955, the Jasper wardens were instructed in mountain-eering techniques at the annual search-and-rescue school held at an old wartime camp in Banff. It was called Cuthead College and was near Flint's Peak and other terrain suitable to learn the skills of technical climbing. There, they were taught by a Swiss mountain guide named Walter Perren. Perren had been part of a group of Swiss guides brought to Lake Louise by the Canadian Pacific Railway to guide people wanting to climb in the area until the program was cancelled in 1954.

National park headquarters had become convinced of the need for wardens to develop mountain rescue skills following two well-publicized climbing accidents in the Lake Louise area in 1954 and 1955. In one of these, four Mexican women had fallen to their deaths on Mount Victoria in Banff the summer before.[231] The parks branch was at first going to appoint Noel Gardner to the job, but the temperamental ski instructor suddenly

Walter Perren shows rooky climber O. Hermanrude the ropes. BRUNO ENGLER, PARKS
CANADA, CALGARY

quit, and someone had the inspired idea of giving the job to the extremely capable Perren. In the Cuthead College file there is a photograph of a very relaxed-looking Perren, standing on a narrow ledge on a cliff face, wearing a peaked cap, his hands almost in his pockets as he talks to a worried-looking warden wearing a Stetson and twenty pounds of rope. This was the situation that the wardens Larry McGuire, Clarence Wilkins, Mike Schintz, and Frank Camp faced when they took the course that fall of 1955. Although helicopters were around in those early days, they were not powerful enough to carry out sling rescues; that evolution occurred in the 1970s. Perren taught his students how to get a basket up the face of a cliff, get the injured climber into the basket, and then cable-winch him down to the bottom of the cliff face. Few liked to play the role of victim in the training exercises.

Despite some early misgivings, the Jasper wardens became avid climbers, mixing experienced hands like Klettl and Winkler with the old cowboys. They were encouraged by a growing community of European alpinists who had been attracted to the area's unspoiled mountain terrain. One such individual was Willi Pfisterer, who opened up a ski shop in Jasper in 1956. He was an accomplished skier, having been a member of the Austrian national team, and soon became an expert climber as well. He established his reputation as a climber by making sixty ascents in the Jasper area alone. In 1961 Pfisterer joined the parks service to work as an avalanche specialist in Rogers Pass. The Trans-Canada Highway was just being built through the pass, and Glacier National Park was developing ways to manage the huge snowfall in the area. From there, Pfisterer began working with Perren as a trainer at the Mountain Rescue School.[232] Following Perren's death in 1967, the duties of the regional alpine specialist were divided in two and Pfisterer was given responsibility for co-ordinating search-and-rescue operations in Jasper, Mount Revelstoke/Glacier, and Waterton national parks. Peter Fuhrman looked after the other parks, including Banff.

Following up on their role as mountain search-and-rescue specialists, the wardens began to use dogs for specialized tacking. Jasper wardens had used dogs to hunt wolves and cougars in the 1920s and 1930s, but that practice had been relatively unsophisticated. In a search-and-rescue application, the dog and his handler had to be specially trained to work together to track lost hikers or buried avalanche victims. Each of the mountain parks came to have a trained dog master, but the first was Jasper Warden Alfie Burstrom. It is claimed that his dog Ginger was a cross between a German Shepherd and a coyote.[233]

Mountain rescue training, c. 1970. JNP

Avalanche control, ski patrol and search and rescue were some of the new roles that wardens were taking on in the 1960s. As the park became overwhelmed with tourists in the summer months, they took on visitor service activities such as campground management and advising hikers, as well as an increasingly complex law enforcement role. In the early day, transgressors were poachers or people feeding the bears. As the campgrounds became like self-contained villages and the park roads became major thoroughfares, the wardens acted as local constables, patrolling against various minor and sometimes more serious infractions of the law. A memo from 1962 noted that Jasper wardens were involved in building construction (backcountry cabins), trail and forestry telephone line maintenance, and patrolled the town campgrounds. As well, "they supervised the park sawmill, cared for animals and were responsible for mosquito control measures and the operation of park ski patrols."[234] Jacks of all trades, they were in danger of being masters of none as their key functions were becoming increasingly complex.

It was perhaps inevitable that the development of specialized warden skills in the 1950s and 1960s should lead to the reorganization of the warden service in the 1970s. Throughout the 1960s, there had been a general reform of the federal public service and, when compared to most of the other federal occupations, the wardens must have appeared like something from another age. Two parks service reports produced in 1968 led to big changes for the Jasper wardens: the Sime-Schuler Report, and one from the ominous sounding "Management Utilization Study Team (MUST)." The first report emphasized the need for increased training and specialization in the warden service. At this time in Ottawa, the personnel-types were arguing that wardens should be in the general labour category. Yoho National Park Chief Park Warden Jim Sime argued that their duties required more technical training. However, his argument was undermined by statistics showing that only 80 per cent of wardens had even a grade ten education—hence his urging for increased standards. Another recommendation of the Sime-Schuler report was that wardens should focus on four key roles: natural resource management, public relations, public safety, and law enforcement. No longer having to be responsible for things such as trail maintenance or telephone line repair not only allowed the wardens to concentrate on more important duties, it improved their image as technicians instead of park labourers.

The issue of law enforcement was a thorny one for the Sime-Schuler report, as it remains for Parks Canada today. It was recognized that wardens were a symbol of authority in the park, they wore a distinctive uniform with a police-like badge on their Stetsons and were charged with enforcing the regulations of the *National Parks Act*. But, while recognizing that law enforcement was a main function of the wardens, the Sime-Schuler report was careful to point out that wardens were not law enforcement officers. Wardens enforced laws concerning the interaction of people and resources. Laws concerning the interaction of people and people should remain the responsibility of the police.[235] Unfortunately, the ambiguity of this interpretation crept into subsequent practice. For many years park wardens were trained in law enforcement at the Palisades Centre, and then in 1993 they began training at the RCMP Regina depot.

A study produced by the MUST group in 1968 recommended the abolition of the district system and proposed instead the creation of six resource management areas in Jasper.[236] Wardens were no longer based in their districts, but in town from where they would make periodic strategic patrols into their assigned resource management areas. Others were assigned specialty areas of law enforcement, public safety, or resource conservation. The proposal had a number of benefits. It dealt with the growing problem of imposing a pioneer lifestyle on a modern, largely urban workforce. While allowing the bulk of the warden service to remain generalists, it provided specialized support in the key areas. It also prepared the way for reformed labour practices where an already underpaid warden was expected to be on 24-hour call for the duration of his backcountry assignment. As with the Sime-Schuler report, many of the MUST report recommendations were accepted by senior management and guided the development of the warden service through to the beginning of the next century.

Naturally, there was some resistance from some of the old-timers. Micky McGuire, the chief park warden at the time, held out against these changes but by 1970 the change-over to centralization and specialization had begun. Veteran Warden Clarence Wilkins seemed to have had enough and resigned in 1969. Others followed suit. Many others, on the other hand, adapted to the new situation. Toni Klettl stayed on and at the end of his career in the late 1970s had a desk job as the public safety supervisor. Other Jasper wardens who had begun their careers in the 1950s went on to become chief park wardens elsewhere: Frank Camp, Mac Elder, Bob Haney, Mike Schintz, and Max Winkler.

Max Winkler became assistant chief park warden in 1970 and area

Dick Langford (right), chief park warden of Yoho National Park and former chief park warden of Jasper, modelling the new warden uniform in 1938. A distinctive warden uniform with badges of authority and service would be worn from this year until 2008. Yoho warden Joe Burkitt appears here with Langford. PARKS CANADA, CALGARY manager of Area One the following year. His meticulous reports from the 1970s document the many new areas in which wardens were now involved: removing nuisance bears, monitoring range conditions, advising on new hiking routes, and registering backcountry hikers. Some of his wardens were involved in their own special projects, such as John Turnbull's study of small animals in the park and Schintz and Bill Frey's area land use study.[237] In 1972 Frey was given leave to take a course in applied biology at the Northern Institute of Technology in Edmonton.[238] This was cutting-edge stuff for that time. Ten years later, Warden John Taylor would be on leave pursuing graduate studies at the University of Calgary.[239]

At the local pub, where some of the wardens sometimes gather, some of the old sweats feel that something was lost by taking the wardens out of the backcountry. Retired warden Rod Wallace writes:

> The end of year round backcountry presence by wardens led to a significant change in warden duties concerning the backcountry. The switch to skis and snowmobile patrol by more "modern" wardens of the sixties and seventies, and then the almost complete abandonment of the backcountry patrol in the nineties needs explanation. Today we are left with rare, sporadic, and short duration trips to the backcountry by wardens on skis, sometimes supported by helicopter access.[240]

Some of the younger men and women working in Jasper may find this opinion overly harsh. First, the specialization of wardens in areas of law enforcement, public safety, and conservation enabled them to develop the skills necessary to deal with the increasing complexities of managing a national park. Second, some would also argue that the attachment of many young wardens to the backcountry has not lessened, and that there is a continuing tradition of horse use in the park. The centre of this tradition remains the Jasper horse range with its broader attachment to the federal government's Ya Ha Tinda Horse Ranch. At the Jasper tack shed, the old saddles are lovingly restored and the legends of horses and riders of long ago kept alive.

While the warden service is proud of its history and traditions in the mountain parks, it has continued to evolve to meet the demands of the larger organization and the changing realities of work in places like Jasper while reflecting changes in the wider Canadian society. The 1950s saw the appearance of recent immigrants like Toni Klettl and Max Winkler, and the 1960s brought reorganization and increased involvement with park visitors. The 1970s saw the end of the old district system and the appearance of specialized functions of law enforcement, public safety, and resource conservation. With this came increased specialization and raised educational standards. By the 1970s men and women were coming to work in Jasper with university or college accreditation in Biology and Resource Conservation or with advanced skills in mountain rescue. The Jasper warden service ended its days as an exclusively male domain when Bette Beswick was hired as a seasonal park warden in 1978.[241] Naturally, tensions arose from this change: the new generation was critical of some of the hidebound ideas of their superiors, many of those hired before the revolution in the warden service had difficulty accepting women as colleagues. Still, the old traditions and ideals continued to bind new and old together in a common purpose of taking care of the park and its inhabitants.

Because old traditions continue to influence the service, the decision in 2008 to take the wardens out of their distinctive uniforms and blend them in with the rest of the park staff caused much unhappiness. The decision stemmed from a protracted union grievance demanding that wardens be permitted to carry side arms while carrying out law enforcement duties. The request was stubbornly resisted by Parks Canada headquarters and, rather than allow them side arms, instead eliminated their special functions and distinctive dress as peace officers. Jasper wardens, it seems, had arrived at another crossroads. At the end of 2008, headquarters created a special category of armed wardens to carry out law enforcement duties in the parks. Other wardens were re-named Resource Management and Public Safety Specialists. Only the law enforcement wardens are now entitled to wear the distinctive uniform and badges.

CHAPTER THIRTEEN

"Visitation"

Visitation (-z-) *n.*
 3. (Zool.) Unusual and large migration of animals
 —*Concise Oxford Dictionary of Current English*
Visitation (-z-) *n.*
 5. "A Passing influence (as of something intangible or
 supernatural . . .)"
 —*Webster's Third New International Dictionary*

By the end of the 1950s national parks across North America were being overwhelmed by increasing numbers of visitors. The figures, carefully collected and analyzed by park officials, were referred to as park visitation, giving rise to ironic allusions to alien hordes or divine rapture. By the mid-1950s economic prosperity, improvements in provincial highways, and the baby boom encouraged people to take to the highways in unprecedented numbers and the national parks became a favourite vacation destination. In Jasper, the increase in numbers was even more dramatic because the highways were a relatively new phenomenon. Before World War II most people arrived by train; it was not until the early 1950s that automobile tourists began to outnumber train visitors. Although the Banff–Jasper Highway and the Edmonton–Jasper road existed before the war, they were rough gravel routes that were not comparable to modern highways. But the Banff–Jasper route, renamed the Icefields Parkway, was reopened in 1961 as a paved all-season route and the Yellowhead Highway opened as an interprovincial highway across western Canada in 1968. Jasper tourism was also boosted by the opening of the Marmot ski hill in 1965, which made the park a popular winter destination. These developments are reflected in the huge increases in people coming to the park. In 1955 just over 150,000 visited Jasper. In 1960 the number had grown to over 350,000, and in 1965 it reached over half a million and in 1970 a million people visited the park. The shift to automobile tourism also changed the way in which people experienced the park, and there was increasing pressure to open more areas up to vehicular traffic.

Another factor influencing the growth of Jasper tourism was the growing popularity of getting out and appreciating nature. Although horseback riding faded in popularity, hiking was in. Beginning in the late 1960s, there was a surge of interest in backcountry hiking and camping fuelled by the maturing of the baby boom, a growing public demand for wilderness experiences, and the development of lightweight camping equipment such as packs, bedding tents, and cooking paraphernalia. Between 1969 and 1973 backcountry hiking registrations doubled in number to reflect about ten thousand visitors a year.

The increasing numbers of park visitors to the park and the increasing demands they placed on facilities and the environment presented enormous challenges to the park management. As Jasper emerged as second only to Banff in the number of visitors it handled and the amount of its annual budget, these challenges attracted a lot of attention from national office in Ottawa and the new regional office in Calgary, as well as inspiring superhuman efforts from the park staff. Their problems were made more difficult by the dual mandate of national parks as custodians of pristine nature and as tourist attractions. For a place like Jasper National Park, which encompassed a huge territory, this was not much of a challenge as long as it had relatively few visitors. But as numbers increased, the contradictions

Hikers at Columbia Icefields Chalet, c. 1950s. CSTM, CN X8986

inherent in the mandate became glaringly evident. These contradictions led to some contradictory responses that reflected different perspectives in the various parts of the organization and an evolution toward being more focused on protecting the environment. These contradictions and shifting opinions further complicated the already difficult work of the parks administrators, but for us it makes an interesting story.

In the early 1960s the park administrators—that is, the head of the parks service in Ottawa and his assistants in operations, planning, and engineering, along with the park superintendent and his resident engineer—had only a few options: they could build to accommodate more visitors, or they could limit growth. At first, increased expansion of facilities seemed to be the preferred option. Scenic drives around the park were expanded and upgraded. The realignment of the Icefields Parkway allowed parts of the old highway, renamed Highway 93A, to be developed along these lines, providing a scenic drive to Whirlpool Falls. A new highway was begun to provide easy access to Maligne Lake. New campgrounds, picnic sites, and highway rest stops were constructed. In 1964 the government granted permission to a private consortium to build a gondola to the top of Whistlers Mountain, thus opening up a sensitive alpine area to mass tourism. Also in the spring of 1964, the federal government announced tenders for the development of the Marmot Basin ski area. The parks branch built a gravel road, permitting bus travel to the base of the ski area, which was developed by private interests. Marmot Basin opened in 1965 and was visited by a reported 12,000 skiers that first year.[242] In the 1966–1967 season, this number had grown to over 45,000.[243] In 1967 the park approved the further expansion of the Marmot Basin ski facility, including the improvement of the road to the base of the hill that permitted private vehicle access and the installation of new lifts. Park wardens began to build trails to accommodate the back-country hikers and campers, erecting official-looking signs to supplant the old outfitters' way signs.

Increasing visitor numbers also meant a necessary expansion of the tourist facilities in the town of Jasper and the park granted an unprecedented number of building permits in this period. In 1957 it got its first motel, with twenty-eight units, and a new gas station. In 1959, another motel and gas station opened, as did a new hotel. The traditional bungalow camp facilities also expanded outside the town. Patricia Lake Bungalows was established in 1954 on the site of the old auto-campground at that lake. Pocahontas Bungalows, near the east gate at the Yellowhead Highway's junction with the road to Miette Hot Springs, opened in 1955; Jasper House Bungalows opened in 1958; and the Pyramid Lake Motel opened in 1959.

The boom continued through the 1960s, and by 1968 the *Jasper Gateway* newspaper was reporting that "the general trend has been more business for everybody. Hotels and motels report full houses every night and residences which offer approved accommodation report a similar situation."[244] Increased visitors brought more building: In 1967 construction started on two motel developments to add 127 units to the accommodation already available.[245] More tourists also meant that the town had to grow to accommodate the increased service sector, the people working in the hotels and restaurants and for the park. The department's *Annual Report* for 1973–1974 noted that "at Jasper, garden homes and a mobile trailer court have been constructed and the development of single- and two-family homes has been proposed."[246] Growth of the town demanded related expansion. For example, construction of a large sewage treatment plant was begun in the fall of 1971 at the mouth of Cottonwood Creek.

The era of the big projects in the 1960s encouraged the continuing ascendancy of engineers in the organization. They held key posts, commanded large budgets, and managed large projects, and therefore their views began to influence the direction of development. While the engineers held sway at the field level, their influence was mitigated at headquarters by the planning division, which since 1957 had endeavoured to balance new development with the protection of the park's natural assets. They prepared plans to separate the spheres of tourist development and natural assets and to ensure that buildings adhered to aesthetic guidelines, incorporating landscape and architectural design. Lloyd Brooks and his staff introduced a new professional perspective to park management as he and his staff were mostly all university-trained planners.[247] Versed in the burgeoning literature relating to American park planning, they brought to the program the optimism popular at that time, that expertise and rational thought could overcome most difficulties. Recognizing that demand for outdoor recreation could rapidly outstrip the supply of suitable wilderness areas, they believed that, given sufficient information and knowledge, rational choices could be made to satisfy these concerns. As one of Brooks' staff said: "The logical approach was to determine what the pressures generated by an increasingly affluent society would be and what rational resource development policies could be established to achieve the joint goals of scenic preservation and recreational use."[248]

During the first years of its existence, Brooks' planning division was tied up in immediate planning issues relating to a string of problems ranging from new park facilities in the maritime parks, to townsite development in Jasper. In this last regard, it commissioned a far-reaching town planning study prepared in 1963 by Dr. Peter Oberlander, professor of town planning at the University of British Columbia.[249] Oberlander and his engineer colleague R. J. Cave examined the various problems of the town, including its lack of capacity, especially for the growing numbers of winter tourists, and its chronic traffic problems. The report recommended some sweeping changes, including the introduction of new motels and other visitor services, and a beautification and redevelopment of Connaught Drive. One of the report's most significant recommendations was the construction of a highway bypass that would take the Yellowhead Highway around the town instead of along Connaught as it was planned for in the 1960s. This new route followed the abandoned Canadian Northern Railway right-of-way.

By the early 1960s, though, the planning division was working on comprehensive management plans for each national park, termed "master plans" at the time. The planners believed that the adverse affects of more building in the parks could be mitigated if it was confined to specific areas. This led to the idea of development zones, delimiting specific areas where new building could occur, and zoning became the cornerstone of the planning process. The planners surveyed each park and laid out a system of zones that prescribed an authorized level of development for each. Specific appropriate projects were then described for each zone. This scheme was then enshrined in the management or master plan that authorized new building in the park over the next few years. The advantage of the approach, at least in theory, is that it kept development from sprawling through the park and limited the blight of unplanned building along the highway corridors.

Completed in 1967, the Jasper Provisional Master Plan delineated five management zones. A distinction was made between front country and back country. The former was deemed to be that part of the park, such as along the Yellowhead Highway and in the townsite, that was developed for people. The latter implied wilderness where development and building was more strictly controlled. The Parks Canada planners believed that zoning using this distinction allowed the park to meet the conflicting objectives of use and preservation.[250] Numbers one and two were labelled as wilderness area, three was a transition zone, with limited development but accessible by road, four was a developed outdoor recreation area such as Marmot ski hill, and five was an intensive use area such as a townsite or service centre. While the plan promised to balance protection with visitor use, it was clearly on the side of managing more development, not managing natural areas. Emphasis was placed on identifying visitor statistics to better prepare for future demand. Thus the plan said: "This is the start of a systems planning approach. Where possible accent is on long range view of problems such as information management or the saturation of a park's known camping facility."[251]

With its emphasis on accommodating increasing numbers of tourists, the Jasper provisional master plan proposed an alarming level of new construction, especially scenic roads. While the town of Jasper was to remain the centre of development in the park, the plan proposed developing a second visitor services centre nearer the east gate at Pocahontas.[252] Other developments were also on the drawing board. The Provisional Master Plan proposed continuing the Maligne Lake Road around the west side of the lake and then cutting across Maligne Pass to Poboktan Creek to follow this route back down to the Icefields Parkway. The same plan called for a road to be constructed out to Sunwapta Falls and then along the Chaba River to Fortress Lake, outside the west boundary of the park. Long-range considerations proposed allowing public access to fire roads up the Whirl-pool and Snake Indian rivers.[253] While the plans called for further study, this implied further social science research to identify future tourist trends, not environmental impact studies.

In the late 1960s snowmobiles were considered to be an appropriate activity in the national parks, and were encouraged because they got people into the backcountry. While the sport was still in its infancy in 1967, the Provisional Master Plan called for further development along these lines. Typical of the sensibilities of park management at this time was the notion that further demand could be met with increased development. The master plan called for developing snowmobile trails into the Tonquin Valley. It concluded: "Seven trails have been laid out and as demand increases further trails will be marked."[254]

The provisional master plans for Banff and Jasper, both which proposed high levels of road building and encouraged motorized activities such as snowmobiling, met with considerable opposition from the growing environmental lobby in Canada. Led by the National and Provincial Parks Association and joined by university academics, this group mounted an articulate and effective campaign against what it saw as inappropriate levels of development, especially in the mountain parks. The year 1968 marked a watershed in public opinion about the role of national parks as natural preserves. Before this date, the emphasis was on building visitor facilities: afterward, the national parks service gave greater attention to the protection of natural values. The Canadian National Parks Today and Tomorrow Conference, held at the University of Calgary in 1968, was in the middle of this transformation and the Banff and Jasper provisional master plans became the hot button topics behind much of the discussion at the conference. The proposals of the Banff plan were attacked by Gordon Nelson in his paper, "Man and Landscape Change in Banff National Park: A national park problem in perspective." In this paper Nelson focused a lot of his criticism on the proposed new scenic roads.

> These roads seem to be intended to provide access by auto,
> rather than by foot or horse, to areas of outstanding beauty as
> well as to ease heavy automobile tourist pressure in Banff Town-
> site and other congested areas by spreading traffic and visitors
> over large 'undeveloped' areas of the park.[255]

While criticizing the projects themselves, Nelson also attacked the planning process that produced the master plan. In a few instances he referred to the lack of public consultation that excluded outside expert views and he objected to the lack of balance that favoured automobile tourists over the protection of wilderness areas. His harshest comments about planners were delivered in the discussion that occurred later in the conference. Adopting a deliberately combative tone he said: "I have been appalled at the way in which planning has been carried out in the past few years. I would hesitate to use the word 'planning' in any sense for what has been done as far as Banff National Park is concerned."[256]

Another articulate critic of the national park development mentality at the conference was Ian McTaggart-Cowan, professor of Zoology and dean of Graduate Studies at the University of British Columbia. Subsequent to his field work in the mountain parks in the 1940s, he provided occasional advice to the program's headquarters. His paper, entitled "The Role of Ecology in the National Parks," like Nelson's paper at the beginning of the conference, was harshly critical of the national parks' existing development and proposed plans. Like Nelson, he focused on development in the mountain national parks. He differed from Nelson, in focusing less on social issues and more on the lack of scientific understanding behind the proposed projects. He opened his paper by answering the question implied in the title, that is, "ecological considerations had almost no part in the establishment or design of any of the Canadian National Parks."[257] He went on the make a number of observations that, while they may seem commonplace now, were highly original at the time. By focusing on ecological zones rather than scenery or bits of wilderness, he revealed a fundamental flaw in the planner's approach: that the parks' high use or front country zones often occupied river valleys or montane areas that were also important habitat for wildlife. He made a number of other observations that were revolutionary for that time: that the protection of forests from fire was allowing forests to spread into natural grassland, and that increased public use of sensitive grazing areas was further threatening the environmental health of the parks. While not directly critical of the park planners, he did take aim at the engineering culture of park management, saying: "After thirty-eight years spent in our parks I have become progressively depressed by the complete failure of the highway engineers to respond to the unique demands inherent in the national park roadways." As with Nelson, McTaggart-Cowan decried the proposed scenic roads, asking rhetorically, "is this any longer the best way of taking people quietly into the right environment to see the things we want them to see … "[258]

The planners had a very good defence against this criticism: they merely described actions for consideration, they did not actually build things. They likely considered it a mark of success that their plans had provoked so much discussion. Nonetheless, the program quietly dropped many of the more contentious development proposals as it did with its support for snowmobiling.

Incremental as it may have been and as incomplete as some argue it still is, the organization underwent a sea change in attitude. At the second Canadian National Parks Conference held in Banff ten years later, Al Davidson summed up the changes in direction of the parks organization.

In 1968, we were about to start the public hearings programme on park master plans. That programme had a profound impact on our planning emphasis and public participation leading to decision making. Look back at some of the provisional master plans, at the emphasis on road building, at the catering to the *arm chair* tourists, and compare them with our present emphasis on programmes which will provide park experiences uniquely attuned to the natural environment.[259]

Davidson's remarks underline another aspect of the resistance to park development: that some kinds of activities such as snowmobiling and water-skiing were incompatible with the ideal of what a national park should be. Highways were regarded as a necessary evil but new development would be scaled down. Downhill skiing remained a divisive issue, with some arguing that it had a long and genuine association with outdoor experience in the mountains, others that it was elitist and required too much infrastructure to justify.

Too Much of a Good Thing

When snowmobiling first became popular in the 1960s, the national parks sought to encourage this outdoor activity. But the parks reversed this policy in the 1970s, believing snowmobiles were

Snowmobilers on the Signal Mountain fire road, c. 1970. JNP

incompatible with wilderness protection and now they are only occasionally used by the warden service or for emergencies or by outfitters for packing in supplies to the backcountry lodges.

The notion that national parks should encourage a range of healthy outdoor pursuits, and were incompatible with some of the development countenanced in the early 1960s, was recognized by some of the national park mangers well before the reaction of 1968. At an address to the fifth annual Naturalists' Workshop held in Jasper in 1964, superintendent Bruce Mitchell raised the alarm about increased tourist numbers leading to pressure for inappropriate activities. He cited two examples in particular as having unfortunate consequences for the park: the construction of the Whistlers gondola that was underway at the time, and the snowmobile tours on the Athabasca Glacier. Mitchell argued that national parks should maintain ideals of wilderness activity that had been lost in the current era of mass tourism. The answer, he felt, was to educate park users and the public generally in the values of national parks: "There is no question but that we must have an informed public who will get behind us and fight for the integrity of the Parks to ensure that their purpose is being met and that commercial developments are being held to a minimum."[260]

The idea of national park values was elaborated on by Winston Mair, chief of the national parks division in Ottawa. Echoing the sentiments of John Muir, Mair saw parks as being important to people's physical, mental, and physical well-being. Not wishing to separate people from nature, he saw people as being important to parks as well.

I like to think of our National Parks as windows to the soul of our nation, or doors through which we may step into understanding of our relationship with nature and hence man's relationship with man. Thus our National Parks are doubly important; for themselves as precious fragments of our natural heritage and to the nation and the world for the opportunity they provide for recreation, reorientation in tune with nature and with man as an element of the ecosystem.[261]

The Prime Minister Plays in the Park

Pierre Trudeau visited Jasper twice on holiday while prime minister of Canada, first in 1968 and then again with his three sons in 1977. The visits underscored Trudeau's reputation as an outdoorsman. On his first visit, he rose at 3:00 a.m. to climb Mount Colin with Willi Pfisterer. He also climbed mounts Athabasca and Edith Cavell. In 1977, he went kayaking on the Athabasca River. Trudeau's visits likely also helped the federal government appreciate the importance of Jasper as a wilderness sanctuary.

Mitchell saw the park naturalist as being instrumental in instilling proper awareness of national park ideals in the visiting public. Others agreed with this assessment. Seasonal park naturalists had worked in Banff and Jasper since the early 1960s, showing films to interested tourists and leading nature walks. One such person was Jim Grieve, a teacher who worked his summers in Jasper. While he was diligent and creative, he could not reach more than a small fraction of the thousands of visitors coming to the park each week. In 1964, however, national park headquarters was contemplating the creation of a larger, more co-ordinated program to educate park visitors.

Under the direction of the energetic head of national park operations, Winston Mair, Ottawa created a separate interpretive division. He hired a fulltime naturalist for each of the large parks and then set about creating an organization around them. While there was an atmosphere of enthusiasm and missionary zeal about the appointment of a resident naturalist in Jasper, there were birth pangs. Peter Heron described arriving in Jasper early in 1965: "We had no job descriptions, the Superintendent of Jasper didn't know what to do with me when my wife and three kids arrived and there was no Chief Naturalist in Ottawa to oversee the whole new service."[262]

There were a number of roles this naturalist service could fill. First, they could enlarge on the work of the seasonal park naturalists, giving more illustrated talks and guided nature walks. They could also tell people about suitable hiking trails and appropriate behaviour in the backcountry. This was a role that had been picked up by the warden service, but as most of them lived in the backcountry, they were not well-situated to interact with the public arriving at the information centre. Assistant Chief Park Warden G. F. Campbell explained the new wave of tourists in 1964:

For the most part they are unprepared in knowledge of how to organize such a holiday and, unless they are personally acquainted, there are very limited information sources available to them. The result is they compromise and take "a bus tour" type of holiday, leaving the Park with the feeling of having missed much of what they came for. Alternatively, they start out on their own, ill-prepared and ill-advised.[263]

The park interpreters could assist the wardens by providing frontline service in answering practical questions on visiting nature in the park.

At their first national get-together, held in Calgary in November 1965, the new service reflected the idealistic aims of the national park managers. The minutes of their meeting noted that "naturalists should go out as salesmen to the city, to schools, to service clubs, to community organizations to promote the broad ideas of nature conservation and parks to the public."[264] Still, the naturalists had more than enough work to do on their own turf without initiating outreach programs. They became busy creating exhibits and outdoor activities, leading interpretive walks and hiring more staff. Peter Heron left in 1968 and was replaced by Dave Pick who

An interpretive walk led by park staff, c. 1970s. JYMA, JASPER PARK COLLECTION

assumed the title of chief park naturalist. By 1970, he had expanded his staff to include ten summer students who were out and about in the park meeting tourists, as well as manning the new information centre in the former superintendent's residence, now the park administrative centre. Eventually the interpreters, as the naturalists came to be called, took over the whole building, forcing the administrative staff to move elsewhere in the town. In the summer of 1969 Pick reported that his staff had led forty-seven public hikes attended by 1,123 people, had given twenty-three public slide talks attended by 3,622 people, and had showed seventeen film presentations attended by 2,880 people. As well, the naturalists established three self-guided trails that, in July of that year alone, were used by an estimated ten thousand visitors.[265] The naturalists tended to be young, keen, and at times a little earnest. Each park was supposed to have its own interpretive theme, which visitors were expected to learn about, all the while sharing in their teachers' enthusiasm. Jasper's was a bit of a hard sell—its main theme, according to Parks Canada headquarters, was "alpine glaciation."[266]

At first, some of the wardens worried that the university-educated naturalists would usurp their position of influence in the natural resource field. As Mike Schintz noted in a letter to his parents in 1964: "These fel-

Permanent and summer interpretive staff, Jasper, 1982. JNP

lows are all university graduates, and much better qualified on paper to step into the higher paid jobs."[267] He need not have worried: the naturalists were confined in the park organization to the visitor service sector. Thus, according to an organization chart of 1968 that distinguished the work of the two units, Dave Pick, who had a degree in Biology, was in charge of nature trails, films and talks, and the interpretive centre. Micky McGuire, who had graduated from the school of hard knocks, was in charge of public safety, forest management, fire protection, insect control, care of horses and wildlife management.[268]

Still, the park naturalists had so much to do just carrying out their education mandate that they had little capacity for looking after natural resources. They also found that they could not keep up with demands to manage the more general needs of park visitors. This became the role of the visitor services division. It origins were similar to the naturalist service. It began in Ottawa in 1968 and spread out to the parks. Doug Welleck experienced the transition from visitor service planner in Ottawa to frontline visitor service manager in the park. Hired as a visitor services specialist upon graduation from the University of British Columbia in 1968, he transferred to the regional office in Calgary where he worked as a kind of planner, trying to anticipate visitor trends and devising budgets for new park facilities. Anticipating future demands for visitor services was a main preoccupation of the Ottawa planning branch at this time. In 1968 planner Gordon Taylor gave a paper entitled "Demand for Recreation—An Essential Tool for Resource Planning."[269] In 1970 Welleck moved to Jasper as the park's first chief of visitor services. There he managed the campgrounds, pools, gates, and the information service.[270]

The new staff, park naturalists and visitor service planners, joined with a better-organized warden service and a large engineering office to manage the tourist invasion. Each summer season brought a series of battles, and at times the park seemed in danger of being overrun. In 1970 Superintendent John Christakos warned that "continued increases in volume and demands of visitors to Jasper National Park cannot reasonably be met under existing operational status."[271] Another report in 1973 began: "Another year has passed and the upward spiral of visitation continues with its accompanying problems of maintenance and operation with too little money."[272] Not only were visitors overwhelming park facilities but the landscape itself was taking a pounding. Superintendent Rory Flanagan reported in 1973 that "all the high visitor use areas are continuing to deteriorate as reported in 1971 and 1972. At the Athabasca Falls . . . all the cover is trampled and worn out. The top of Whistler Mountain is rapidly deteriorating ."[273]

There were limits to what the government was willing to spend and, as the park staff was beginning to realize, there were limits to what the park could handle without sustaining negative effects. In 1973 Doug Welleck pointed out that overcrowded campgrounds adversely affected the experience of visitors to the park, as well as threatened wildlife habitat. He proposed placing limits on the number of campers let into the park and inaugurating a reservation system as some US national parks had already instituted. At the same time park staff realized that some of the more popular backcountry areas had a carrying capacity as well and began implementing systems to limit the numbers of people that would be going into places at any one time.

Adding to the chaos already challenging Welleck's staff was the youth invasion. Beginning in the late 1960s, growing numbers of youths were enjoying the freedom of being on the road, some searching for alternative lifestyles, countercultures, and perhaps even the chance to "drop out" for a while. This trend accelerated following the "summer of love" in 1969 when growing masses of Canadian youth were encouraged by the federal government and the seemingly sympathetic Prime Minister Trudeau to get out and see the country.

An overflow campground, Jasper, c. 1970s. JNP

Jasper began to attract youths because it was on a major transportation route, it was already a big tourist destination, and there was plenty of free space. Many young people were already employed seasonally in the park, working in the various resorts and restaurants, and young people attracted others like them. When asked why he visited Jasper as a young man in 1973, one informant said it was because the fellow with whom he was travelling knew a girl who was working at the lodge, and she had a friend. Back then, that was reason enough to hit the road. Growing throngs of youths quickly became a problem for the park authorities and the town merchants as they loitered around the town in large groups. They were disrespectful of authority and they did not have a lot of money to spend. On the other hand, the establishment was desperate for cheap help to serve the growing numbers of respectable tourists visiting the park, so the townspeople were not completely hostile to the youth invasion.

The park administration responded to this new "visitation" with a remarkable amount of tolerance and flexibility. In part, this was because it understood youth travel to be a reflection of government policy. As Park Superintendent Christakos saw things in 1971, "The Federal Government during the fall and winter of 1970, supported the idea of youth travel on limited funds and began to predict a large increase in young people on the road for the summer of 1971."[274] Accordingly, park officials made plans to accommodate these travelling folk, quickly setting up a campground specifically to accommodate youth and adapting the former Whistlers ski lodge as a youth hostel. These were operated with a minimum of direct control "in order to antagonize the users of the area as little as possible."[275]

"Freakouts" and "Bummers"

During the summers of 1971 and 1972, the Jasper hospital sponsored a youth emergency services summer program called "If," which was operated out of a borrowed Parks Canada trailer. Run by Brian, Adrian, and Maureen, the clinic had a front area where visitors could read literature on the non-medical use of drugs, get advice on a range of topics, listen to music, or just "rap." In the back were areas where people could sleep off the adverse effects of intoxication. One such space was reserved for "freak outs," or extreme reactions to drugs, another for "bummers," unpleasant but not severe reactions to drugs.[276]

One area where the park administration had not evolved to manage the new Jasper was in the realm of townsite management. In Rogers's day the superintendent had ruled the town as a benign autocrat, issuing edicts about the use of automobiles and stray cats and passing along proclamations from the supreme dictator in Ottawa. These rules were enforced by the town warden who, in the early days, had acted like the village constable. Townspeople had little say in the larger issues of civic government or planning. Property rights were further circumscribed by the lack of freehold tenure. Properties were occupied by long-term leases. On the plus side, annual leases were low and so long as property values remained low, there were few real instances for conflict.

But by the 1960s Jasper had grown from a sleepy village to a bustling town and the growth and investment in Jasper's tourist facilities brought about conflict between the town's business community and park headquarters in Ottawa. The emergence of Jasper as a year-round international tourist destination created some wealthy businessmen in the town. These businessmen naturally sought to increase tourism and lobbied for more development approvals. Some felt that the government was not doing enough to develop adequate facilities, others felt that there was not enough authority to make decisions at the local level. Things began to come to a head in 1963 when the local Chamber of Commerce arranged a meeting with the minister responsible for the parks service. Superintendent Mitchell telegraphed Ottawa to alert the minister's office to the main points of discussion: "Number one, lack of authority delegated regional supervisor and superintendent to make decisions. Number two, town improvements and Dr. Oberlander's report. Number three, winter development and number four, construction of roads."[277] This led to small concessions, but the town businesses felt that Ottawa was not doing enough to encourage tourist facilities.

Resentment grew over the government's stalling to approve tourist expansion to cater to the new ski tourists, for example. The *Edmonton Journal* wrote in 1967: "The federal government simply must realize that skiers—and tourists generally—want a full complement of services in the parks and towns." The article added: "A grudging, reluctant, stingy spirit in government could stunt the healthy growth of Marmot Basin (and Jasper Park as a whole)."[278] But the government was also investing heavily in rebuilding the town infrastructure. The new sewage facility built in 1971 cost millions and Treasury Board analysts wondered if the locals should not be shouldering more of their share of the costs. Rates were indeed increased in 1970, leading to various forms of local protests in both Banff and Jasper.

Both sides became interested in exploring a possible solution to their difficulties through the adoption of local self-government, essentially transforming the towns of Banff and Jasper into self-governing municipalities. The issue was first presented in the form of a petition from the school boards of Banff and Jasper to the minister responsible for national parks in 1970. At this time, the school boards were the only locally elected administrative powers in each of the towns, and each had become a quasi-municipal advisory body. They presented what they believed to be the wishes of the majority of residents: "Because the school boards are democratically elected bodies, they consider it proper and in the interests of their electors to support in the strongest possible way, the wishes of Banff and Jasper residents for local autonomy."[279] The Alberta Legislature passed a resolution supporting the request for what it described as a basic civic right and this led to the province's Department of Municipal Affairs carrying out a feasibility study that it described in "The Banff-Jasper Autonomy Report" issued in 1972. More reports followed and local self-government became a topic of discussion in the deliberations surrounding the Jasper townsite master plan in 1977.

Eventually, the Town of Banff was accorded municipal powers in 1990. It was not until 2002 that Jasper was granted an elected municipal government, although with less powers than the Town of Banff. By this time, residents of both towns were paying land rents and utility fees based on market-based assessments of their properties, so the tax hikes that residents experienced were immense. By controlling development and limiting new construction, the federal government had encouraged house prices in both towns to skyrocket. This caused huge sticker shock when the new taxing scheme was introduced in the late 1990s. This also lent greater weight to the argument that Jasper residents needed their own elected government. However, the new municipality was equally powerless to reduce property taxes. By this time, both Parks Canada and local residents were beginning to wonder if too much growth was a good thing. Many Jasperites echoed the refrain from the 1980s: "We don't want to be another Banff."

Although the 1960s and 1970s brought unprecedented growth and turmoil to the park's environment, its staff and its residents, not to mention the many people who flocked to its attractions each season, the end of the 1970s brought considerable cause for optimism. The park now placed greater emphasis on environmental protection, the park bureaucracy had grown better organized with better trained staff than before, and the town had made some strides to gaining local self-government. Many of the achievements in the 1980s grew out of the struggles in the 1970s.

Century's End

The 1980s ushered in a period of relative peace in the park. The number of people coming to the park levelled off at about two million a year, economic downturn cooled many of the development pressures on both the town and the park, and the park organization had time to coalesce around the structure and roles that had been introduced in the previous decades. A big event for the park was the completion of a new management plan that would determine the direction of the park until the end of the century. Recognizing that park ecosystems ranged beyond park boundaries, the plan attempted to engage macro issues by looking at the four mountain park blocks of Banff, Jasper, Yoho, and Kootenay as a single entity. *In Trust for Tomorrow: A Management Framework for Four Mountain Parks* was the culmination of a research and consultation process that had begun in 1981. The plan attempted to reconcile the two opposing objectives of national parks: preservation and use. Given the vocal opposition to previous park development, the plan was remarkably sanguine on the subject, favouring further development but within stricter limits. There was no attempt to limit visitor numbers. Indeed, the plan encouraged the improvement of visitor services and transportation networks. However, the plan aimed at keeping the developed corridors in the parks within traditional lines and not expanding outward.

In Trust for Tomorrow was followed up by a specific plan for Jasper that was approved in 1988. Its statement of values articulated the new philosophy of national parks that was to take precedence over development:

> Resource protection will take precedence over visitor use and
> facility development where conflicts occur. Visitor use will be
> managed to safeguard natural and cultural resources, as well
> as the aesthetics of the park. Park resources will be managed
> on an ecological basis; cooperating and coordinating resource
> management with the other parks in the four mountain park
> block, and with provincial and private interests managing
> adjacent lands.[280]

Offering new direction, the document was written by planners, and also reflects their optimism about the ability of planning to adequately deal with threats caused by overuse.

By this time, the rapid growth of annual visitors had eased off somewhat, and the planners could realistically expect only moderate growth.[281] In Jasper, this meant focusing tourist facilities within the town and highway development along the Athabasca Valley. One new development that was permitted by the 1988 plan was the rebuilding in the 1990s of the Columbia Icefields Chalet into a massive visitor centre with one of the largest tour bus parking lots on the continent. Still, the four-mountain park plan coupled with subsequent national park policies has offered increased protection to backcountry corridors. Thus, it is still possible to travel the Maccarib Pass into the fabled Tonquin Valley, or follow the Skyline Trail into the Maligne much as the early outfitters like Curly Phillips and Fred Brewster did.

Peace to the organization was disrupted in the early 1990s by an organizational review carried out by the regional office in Calgary, but instigated by pressure in the Mulroney administration to effect budget cuts through downsizing. This was the era when Prime Minister Mulroney announced he was going to issue "pink slips and running shoes" to many public servants. Cost-cutting to reduce the federal deficit was also a priority of the Chretien administration following the Liberals' election in 1993. The regional office strove to comply by reviewing the national parks' operations and determining what core services should be and eliminating the rest. The main objective for national parks was identified as protecting "ecological integrity." Functions extraneous to this were in danger of being eliminated by the Organization Review Task Force (ORTF), whose work began in 1990. The interpretive service was an early casualty of this review, and many of the park naturalists were let go or reassigned to other functions. The planning component of visitor services was also eliminated and the rest of the visitor service functions absorbed into a unit called "Front Country" management. Although the warden service was spared the draconian measures suffered by other units, it was also hit with budget restraints and, besides, it had to pick up some of the slack caused by the elimination of other positions.

There were a few instances of benefit to the park that resulted from the revolution of the mid-1990s. The regional office was eliminated and more powers devolved to the park superintendent. As well, greater attention was given to cultural resources as the reorganization placed cultural resource management on a par with ecological integrity as one of the objectives of the program. The Historic Sites and Monuments Board of Canada had identified a string of sites in the park associated with the fur trade, notably Jasper House and Athabasca Pass, as being of national historic significance. Yellowhead Pass and the Jasper Information Centre were also named national historic sites, the latter for being an outstanding example of national park rustic architecture. More or less neglected in the previous organization, these national historic sites now received more attention for conservation and interpretation. And, given the focus placed on ecological integrity, management gave greater attention to science in the park. A new emphasis on cultural resource management in the park turned attention to other cultural resources as well as just those of national historic significance. This new orientation led the park to curtail a 1980s program that had aimed to reduce "man disturbed sites" in the backcountry, a program that had caused the destruction of many historic cabins and lookout towers. Further benefits followed the creation of Parks Canada as a Crown corporation in 1999, allowing it to use revenues derived from the selling of park passes. As Jasper continued to be counted as one of the most popular parks in the system, this helped justify its still large budget.

New appreciation of ecological systems, better application of scientific approaches, and more rigorous planning all helped to protect Jasper from being loved to death by its visitors. However, many problems remain. In the last decade there has been an increasing awareness of threats to sensitive species such as the caribou. The caribou population in the park has declined dramatically in recent years, most likely due to habitat change influenced by global warming. If Jasper marks the southern range of the mountain caribou, so the argument goes, then warming temperatures will push this range north, out of the protection of the park. But some have argued that human use has also affected the health of the species. For instance, at Maligne Lake snowmobiles have been used to set tracks for cross-country skiers during the winter. Some have speculated whether the packed snow of the trails has given wolves a better chance of getting closer to the caribou, who can usually outrun the predators in deep snow.[282]

Other problems persist as well. In his book, *Phantom Parks: The Struggle to Save Canada's National Parks*, author Rick Searle has argued that organizational changes in the 1990s encouraged a development mentality in the parks, and that, by placing too much emphasis on tourist development, ecological objectives had been lost sight of in places like Jasper. Part of the problem, Searle argued, was the restructuring of Parks Canada as an agency, which gave it operating money based on gate receipts. More tourists coming to places like Banff and Jasper created a bigger operating fund for the entire agency. Moreover, he argued that the culture of the organization was operational rather than science-based. Thus, he concluded, "The tendency is to place a low priority on ecological research and a higher priority on the provision of facilities for the benefit and safety of visitors."[283] This is an issue that has been debated in Jasper since the 1920s and no doubt will continue to be debated through the twenty-first century.

The story of Jasper National Park is never-ending. The struggle between developers and conservationists that has lasted for over one hundred years will undoubtedly continue for at least another hundred. But the story is not one just of conflict. Throughout, people and places have become intertwined, with people placing their stamp on the environment now known as Jasper National Park and yet drawing much of their own sense of place and personal identity from these same surroundings. And not just locals have been shaped by this environment: generations of visitors from across Canada and around the world have drawn inspiration and refreshment from their Jasper experiences. The park has become a national icon. It is also a symbol of the entire national parks system. Second only to Banff as a national park tourist destination, Jasper surpasses Banff in area. Like Banff, it embodies most of the issues that have characterized the history of most of Canada's national parks, except on a grander scale. It has tried, not always successfully, to conserve and protect the precious natural assets of the park while developing an internationally renowned tourist destination. It is the home of many interesting species of wildlife and yet has some significant engineering achievements such as the two mountain highways. These large issues have challenged, and will continue to challenge, Parks Canada's larger mission.

Note on Sources

The early chapters in the book were based on a wealth of secondary material, mainly unpublished historical reports prepared for Parks Canada. Principal among these are Brenda Gainer's "Human History of Jasper National Park" (1981); Gerhard Ens and Barry Potyondi's "History of the Upper Athabasca Valley in the Nineteenth Century" (1986); Rod Pickard's "Jasper National Park: Archaeological Resource Description and Analysis" (1989); and Michael Payne's "The Fur Trade in the Upper Athabasca River, 1810-1910," in I. S. MacLaren's *Culturing Wilderness in Jasper National Park: Studies in Two Centuries of Human History in the Upper Athabasca River Watershed* (2007). Another useful source was Peter J. Murphy et al's *A Hard Road to Travel: Land, Forests and People in the Upper Athabasca Region* (2007). Half-breed land scrip application by Evan Moberly and Susanne Moberly, at the Library and Archives Canada, Record Group 25, provided a useful glimpse into the genealogy of this important family.

Historians working on Jasper are fortunate to have available to them the extensive archive collection of the Jasper Museum and Archives. The archives hold extensive clipping files and a series of interviews and memoirs prepared by former Jasper residents. Its photograph collection is first rate and it has begun collecting some of the discards from the national park.

The history of the park era draws heavily from the annual reports of the national parks service. From 1911 through 1936 these are described as the "Report of the Commissioner of National Parks." After that date they are included in the annual reports of the various successors to the Department of the Interior: Mines and Resources, Resources and Development, Northern Affairs and National Resources, and, from 1967 to 1977, the Department of Indian Affairs and Northern Development. During this last administration, the annual reports became thinner and thinner until they petered out altogether. At their peak, from the 1920s through the 1950s, they are an enormously useful source for national park history. An even greater treasure trove is in the records of national parks held by the Library and Archives Canada in Record Group 84, which cover park establishment through such arcane topics as wolves and bears, sheep and goats, land administration, and visitors. There is an enormous catalogue of material relating to the history of Jasper. Much of these files are now available on microfilm, making the task of the out-of-town researcher easier. Many records of the park and regional office from the 1970s and 1980s are held in an administrative limbo, in a satellite of the national archives system designated the Edmonton Federal Records Centre. Since the mid-1990s, the records system of Parks Canada has become increasingly dispersed and the transfer agreement with the Library and Archives Canada has lapsed, making the job of future national park historians considerably more difficult than mine.

Two published memoirs of former Jasper wardens are Frank Camp, *Roots in the Rockies* (1993) and Mike Schintz, *Close Calls on High Walls* (2005). Stories of warden wives are told in Ann Dixon's *Silent Partners: Wives of National Park Wardens (Their Lives and History)* (1985). An invaluable contextual history of the national park warden service is Robert J. Burns's *Guardians of the Wild: A History of the Warden Service of Canada's National Parks* (2000).

Endnotes

Introduction: People and the Park

1 Lawrence J. Burpee, *On the Old Athabasca Trail* (London: Hurst and Blackett, 1927); *Jungling in Jasper* (Ottawa: Graphic, 1929).

2 M. B. Williams, *Jasper Trails* (Ottawa: Department of the Interior, c. 1930), 5.

3 Brenda Gainer, "The Human History of Jasper National Park," Manuscript Report Series, no. 441, Typescript (Ottawa: Parks Canada, 1981); Great Plains Research Consultants, "Jasper National Park: A Social and Economic History," Microfiche Report Series, no. 198, Typescript (Ottawa: Parks Canada, 1985).

4 James G. MacGregor, *Pack Saddles to Tete Jaune Cache* (Toronto: Macmillan, 1962; repr. Edmonton: Hurtig, 1973).

5 Peter J. Murphy, with Robert W. Udell, Robert E. Stevenson, and Thomas W. Peterson, *A Hard Road to Travel: Land, Forests and People in the Upper Athabasca Region* (Hinton: Foothills Model Forest, 2007); I. S. MacLaren, ed., *Culturing Wilderness in Jasper National Park: Studies in Two Centuries of Human History in the Upper Athabasca River Watershed* (Edmonton: The University of Alberta Press, 2007).

6 For an extensive description of this idea as it applies to Jasper, see I. S. MacLaren, "Cultured Wilderness in Jasper National Park," *Journal of Canadian Studies/Revue d'etudes canadiennes* 34, no. 3 (Fall 1999): 7–58.

Chapter One: Early Travellers

7 Victor M. Levson and Nathanial W. Rutter, "Pleistocene Stratigraphy of the Athabasca River Valley Region, Rocky Mountains, Alberta," *Geographie physique et Quartenaire* 99, no. 3 (1995): 382.

8 James Alexander Teit, "The Shushwap," in *The Jesup North Pacific Expedition*, vol. II, pt. VII (New York, 1909), 460n3.

9 D. Jenness, "The 'Snare' Indians," *Proceedings and Transactions of the Royal Society of Canada*, Series 3, vol. 33, (May 1939), 103–05.

10 Gertrude Cecilia Nicks, "Demographic Anthropology of Native Populations in Western Canada, 1800–1975," Ph.D. diss., University of Alberta, 1980, 23.

11 *Life, Letters and Travels of Father Pierre-Jean De Smet, S. J. 1801–1873*, ed. Hiram Martin Chittenden and Alfred Talbot Richardson, 4 vols. (New York: Francis P. Harper, 1905), 2:537.

12 Hudson's Bay Company Archives, Jasper House Post Journal, B 94/9/2.

13 Hudson's Bay Company Archives, Jasper House Post Journal, B 94/9/2.

14 Geographic Board of Canada, *Place Names of Alberta* (Ottawa: King's Printer, 1928), 117.

15 Gerhard Ens and Barry Potyondi, "A History of the Upper Athabasca Valley in the Nineteenth Century," Microfiche Report Series, no. 225, Typescript (Ottawa: Parks Canada, 1986), 11.

16 Ron Pelletier, personal communication, 11 February 2007.

17 Henry John Moberly, *When Fur Was King* (London: J. M. Dent, 1929), 52.

18 Samuel Hearne, *A Journey to the Northern Ocean* (Toronto: Macmillan, 1958), 35.

19 Ron Pelletier, personal communication, 15 February 2007.

20 W. Kaye Lamb, ed., *The Journal of Gabriel Franchère* (Toronto: Champlain Society, 1969), 160.

21 Michael Payne, "The Fur Trade on the Upper Athabasca River, 1810–1910," in *Culturing Wilderness in Jasper National Park: Studies in Two Centuries of Human History in the Upper Athabasca River Watershed*, ed. I. S. MacLaren (Edmonton: University of Alberta Press, 2007), 10.

22 Gabriel Franchère, *Narrative of a voyage to the Northwest coast of America, in the years 1811, 1812, 1813, and 1814 . . .*, trans. J. D. Huntingdon (New York, 1854), 293.

23 Paul Kane, *Wanderings of an Artist among the Indians of North America from Canada to Vancouver's Island and Oregon through the Hudson's Bay Company's Territory and back again* (London: Longman, Brown, Green, Longmans, and Roberts, 1859), 153.

24 Cited in Lawrence Burpee, *On the Old Athabasca Trail* (Toronto: Ryerson Press, 1926), 138.

25 Michael Payne, "The Fur Trade on the Upper Athabasca River 1810–1910," 24.

26 Frits Pannekoek, "On the Edge of the Great Transformation," in *Alberta Formed Alberta Transformed*, ed. Michael Payne et al. (Edmonton: University of Alberta Press, 2006), 200.

Chapter Two: Standing at the Crossroads of Time

27 George Monro Grant, *Ocean to Ocean: Sandford Fleming's Expedition through Canada in 1872, Being a Diary Kept During a Journey from the Atlantic to the Pacific with the Expedition of the Engineer-in-Chief of the Canadian Pacific and Intercolonial Railways* (Toronto: J. Campbell, 1873; repr. Toronto: Coles, c. 1970), 233.

28 Jan Grabowski and Nicole St-Onge, "Montreal Iroquois *Engagés* in the Western Fur Trade, 1800–1821," in *From Rupert's Land to Canada: Essays*

in Honour of John E. Foster, ed. Theodore Binnema, Gerhard Ens, and R.C. Macleod (Edmonton: University of Alberta Press, 2001), 44.

29 JYHS, Young File, George Camp memo, 11 July 1964; cited in Brenda Gainer, "The Human History of Jasper National Park," Manuscript Report Series, no. 441, Typescript (Ottawa: Parks Canada, 1981), 79.

30 Sandford Fleming, *Report on Surveys and Preliminary Operations on the Canadian Pacific Railway up to January 1877* (Ottawa: McLean, Roger, 1877), 30.

31 JYMA, "Lewis Swift" file, *Edmonton Journal*, 28 February 1939.

32 Mary T. S. Schäffer, *Old Indian Trails* (New York, 1912), 323–24.

33 LAC, RG84, vol. 1472, J16–1, pt. 1, "Statement made and confirmed by statutory declaration by E. Moberly and J. Adam concerning Evan Moberly's claim to S. W. ¼ Section 17, Township 47, Range 1," 21 August 1909.

34 LAC, RG84, vol. 1472, J16–1, pt. 1, J. W. McLaggan to P. G. Keyes, 7 March 1910. "Statement made and confirmed by statutory declaration by E. Moberly and J. Adam concerning Evan Moberly's claim to S. W. ¼ Section 17, Township 47, Range 1," 21 August 1909. LAC, RG84, vol. 1472, J16–1, pt. 1, "Statement made and confirmed by statutory declaration by Adolphus Moberly and J. Adam concerning Adolphus Moberly's claim to S. E. ¼ section 27, Township 46, Range 1," 4 September 1909.

35 LAC, RG84, vol. 1472, J16–1, pt. 1, "Statement made and confirmed by statutory declaration by J. Adam and E. Moberly concerning Joachim Adam's claim to N. E. ¼ Section 17, Township 47, Range 1," 21 August 1909.

Chapter Three: The Making of a National Park: 1907–1930

36 George Monro Grant, *Ocean to Ocean : Sandford Fleming's Expedition through Canada in 1872, Being a Diary Kept During a Journey from the Atlantic to the Pacific with the Expedition of the Engineer-in-Chief of the Canadian Pacific and Intercolonial Railways* (Toronto: J. Campbell, 1873; repr. Toronto: Coles, *c.*1970), 233.

37 LAC, RG 84, vol. 147, J2, pt. 1, R. H. Campbell to Frank Oliver, 9 March 1907.

38 LAC, RG84, vol. 1472, J16–1, pt. 1, J. W. McLaggan to P. G. Keyes, 7 March 1910.

39 Ibid., R. H. Campbell, head of the forestry branch, advised the deputy minister, 15 February 1910: "Mr. Swift apparently has decided that he will not consider any reasonable amount of compensation . . . I think that probably the only thing to do is to give him patent for his homestead, as under the ordinary provisions of the Dominion Lands Act he has certainly earned it."

40 James G. MacGregor, *Pack Saddles to Tete Jaune Cache* (Toronto: Macmillan, 1962), 152.

41 JYMA, 78.01.5, George Camp to Constance Peterson, 22 November 1966.

42 Judy Larmour, "The Mine Superintendent's House, Pocahontas, Jasper National Park: A Contextual History," Parks Canada, Calgary, unpublished report, 1997, 30–34.

43 Brenda Gainer, "The Human History of Jasper National Park," 135.

44 LAC, MG 26G, vol.55, p. 175094, Frank Oliver to Wilfrid Laurier, 24 September 1910.

45 *House of Commons Debates* (9 May 1911) at 8606 (Hon. Frank Oliver).

46 *House of Commons Debates* (28 April 1911) at 8084 (Hon. Frank Oliver).

47 W. N. Millar, "The Big Game of the Canadian Rockies: A Practical Method for its Preservation," in Canada. Commission of Conservation, *Conservation of Fish, Birds and Game, Proceedings at a meeting of the committee, November 1 and 2, 1915* (Toronto, 1916), 103–14.

48 "Report of the Commissioner of Dominion Parks," in *Annual Report of the Department of the Interior, 1913–14* (Ottawa: J. de Labroquerie Tache, 1915), 4.

49 "Report of the Commissioner of Dominion Parks," in *Annual Report of the Department of the Interior, 1914-15* (Ottawa: J. de Labroquerie Tache, 1916), 6.

50 LAC, RG 84, vol. 521, J2–1, pt. 1, Briefing Note to W. W. Cory and Minister, 19 March 1914.

51 LAC, RG 84, vol. 521, J2–1, pt.3, R. W. Langford to R. W. Cautley, 30 September 1927.

52 LAC, RG 84, vol. 521, J2–1, pt. 3, R. W. Cautley to L. C. Charlesworth, 27 October 1927.

53 Ibid., R. Lindsay to Minister, 26 January 1928.

54 RSC, 1–2 Geo. V, chap. 10, "An Act Respecting Forest Reserves and Parks," para. 18.

55 "Report of the Commissioner of Canadian National Parks," in *Annual Report of the Department of the Interior, 1921–22,* (Ottawa: F.A. Acland, 1923), 112.

56 John Muir, *Our National Parks* (New York: Houghton and Mifflin, 1901), 1; Department of the Interior, "Report of the Commissioner of Dominion Parks, 1912–13" (Ottawa: King's Printer, 1913), 3.

57 Lawrence J. Burpee, *Jungling in Jasper* (Ottawa: Graphic, 1929), 94.

58 Jasper Yellowhead Museum and Archives, "Maynard Rogers" file. Rogers had worked in civilian life as an undertaker and in the insurance business.

59 Frank Camp, *Roots in the Rockies* (privately printed, 1993).

Chapter Four: Backwoodsmen

60 Lawrence J. Burpee, *On the Old Athabasca Trail* (London: Hurst and Blackett, 1927); *Jungling in Jasper* (Ottawa: Graphic, 1929).

61 Burpee, *Jungling in Jasper*, 196.

62 E. J. Hart, *Diamond Hitch: The Early Outfitters and Guides of Banff and Jasper* (Banff, AB: Summerthought, 1979; Banff: EJH Literary Enterprises Ltd., 2001), 253.

63 Hart, *Diamond Hitch*, 142.

64 Ibid., 220.

65 Ibid., 190–91.

66 Shand-Harvey's story is told in James G. MacGregor, *Packsaddles to Tete Jaune Cache* (Edmonton: Hurtig, 1973).

67 Hart, *Diamond Hitch*, 195–97.

68 LAC, RG84, vol. 529, file J212, pt. 1, A. Driscoll to Commissioner, 28 April 1916.

69 Ibid., S. M. Rogers to J. B. Harkin, 3 May 1923.

70 Mike Schintz, *Close Calls on High Walls And Other Tales From The Warden Service* (Calgary: Rocky Mountain Books, 2005), 20.

71 LAC, RG 84, vol. 52, J2–1, pt. 2, Donald Phillips to J. Simpson, 26 March 1921.

72 JYHS, 994.22, box 7, Warden Summaries, Annual Report for the nine month period ending 31 December 1952.

73 Mike Schintz, *Close Calls on High Walls*, 33.

74 LAC, RG 84, vol. 529, J212, pt. 1, undated memo *c.* 1939.

75 Sid Marty, *Men for the Mountains* (Toronto: McClelland and Stewart, 1978), 145; Robert Burns, *Guardians of the Wild: A History of the Warden Service of Canada's National Parks* (Calgary: University of Calgary Press, 2000), 188.

76 Catriona Sandilands, "Where the Mountain Men meet the Lesbian Rangers: Contesting Gender in Banff National Park," Joint Annual Conference for Environmental History and the National Council on Public History, Victoria, BC, April 2004.

77 Ann Dixon, *Silent Partners: Wives of National Park Wardens (Their Lives and History)* (Pincher Creek: privately published, 1985).

78 Dixon, *Silent Partners*, 61.

79 Dixon, *Silent Partners*, 91.

80 Dixon, *Silent Partners*, 49.

Chapter Five: Jasper Builds

81 LAC, RG 84, vol. 523, J19, pt. 1, Howard Douglas to J. B. Harkin, 17 July 1912.

82 Ibid., P. C. Barnard-Hervey to J. B. Harkin, 6 November 1912.

83 Cyndi Smith, *Jasper Park Lodge in the Heart of the Canadian Rockies* (Jasper: privately published, 1985), 7–8.

84 David Smyth, "The Jasper Roundhouse (and Hanna Roundhouse)," Historic Sites and Monuments Board of Canada, Agenda Papers, 1991–16, 595.

85 Cited in Edward Mills, "Rustic Building Programs in Canada's National Parks, 1887–1950," Ottawa, Parks Canada, National Historic Sites Directorate, 1994, 301.

86 "Report of the Commissioner of Canadian National Parks," in *Annual Report of the Department of the Interior, 1925-26* (Ottawa: F.A. Acland, 1926), 7.

87 JYHS, J. B. Snape file, "J. B. Snape, Dominion Government Engineer, Jasper National Park, 1921–1949."

88 Brenda Gainer, "The Human History of Jasper National Park," Manuscript Report Series, no. 441, Typescript (Ottawa: Parks Canada, 1981), 145–46.

89 Gainer, "The Human History of Jasper National Park," 145.

90 "Report of the Commissioner, National Parks of Canada," in *Annual Report of the Department of the Interior, 1928–29,* (Ottawa: F.A. Acland, 1930), 20.

91 Michael Simpson, *Thomas Adams and the Modern Planning Movement: Britain, Canada and the United States, 1900–40* (London: Mansell, 1985), 88.

92 Simpson, *Thomas Adams* , 105.

93 LAC, RG 84, vol. 2004, U18, vol. 1, pt. 1, Thomas Adams, "Planning of Industrial and Park Regions in Canada, A Report," 1923.

94 "Report of the Commissioner of Canadian National Parks," in *Annual Report of the Department of the Interior, 1922–23,* (Ottawa: F.A. Acland, 1924), 73.

95 W. F. Lothian, *A History of Canada's National Parks,* vol. III, (Ottawa: Parks Canada, 1976), 67.

96 Norah Story, *The Oxford Companion to Canadian History and Literature* (Toronto: Oxford University Press, 1967), 440.

97 "Report of the Commissioner of Canadian National Parks," in *Annual Report of the Department of the Interior, 1921-22,* (Ottawa: F.A. Acland, 1923), 128.

98 JNP, C8606/J1/1–8–4. S. M. Rogers to A. Laut, June 1933.

99 JNP, C8606/J1/1–8–4, Wright to Harkin, December 1935.

100 Cited in Great Plains Research Consultants (Barry Potyondi), "Jasper National Park: A Social and Economic History," Microfiche Report Series, no. 198, Typescript (Ottawa: Parks Canada, 1985), 269.

101 The same can be said of other western parks, and this last statement repeats a claim made for Riding Mountain National Park. C. J. Taylor et al., "Riding Mountain National Park of Canada: Built Heritage Resource Description and Analysis," unpublished manuscript, Parks Canada, 2001.

Chapter Six: Campers

102 Horace Kephart, *Camping and Woodcraft: A Handbook for Vacation Campers and for Travelers in the Wilderness* (New York: Macmillan, 1917), 20.
103 Lawrence J. Burpee, *Jungling in Jasper* (Ottawa: Graphic, 1929), 125; 193.
104 LAC, RG 84, vol. 1604, J36, pt. 2, Jack W. Brewster to S. M. Rogers, 28 October 1932.
105 LAC, RG 84, vol. 2016, U36–5, pt. 5, Lloyd Brooks to J. R. B. Coleman, 21 January 1960.
106 LAC, RG 84, vol. 498, B-36–6, A. R. Mile to Alvin Hamilton, 30 August 1960.
107 LAC, RG 84, vol. 525, J36, pt. 5, Lloyd Brooks to J. R. B. Coleman, 14 August 1961.
108 EFRC, Acc. 87–06, file J36, pt. 1, Richard F. Hillyer to Director, 18 August 1968.
109 EFRC, Acc. 87–06, file 90/1c6, G. J. Raby to Dr. R. P. Heron, 22 August 1973.
110 *Toronto Star*, 21 July 1973.
111 EFRC, F. J. Mcguire to G. Balding, 8 April 1971.
112 EFRC, F. J. Mcguire to G. Balding, 8 April 1971.
113 Mike Schintz, *Close Calls on High Walls and Other Tales from the Warden Service* (Calgary: Rocky Mountain Books, 2005), 168.
114 Robert J. Haney, "Back country management plan and usage limitations for Tonquin Valley, Jasper National Park," unpublished manuscript, Jasper, February 1974.
115 Bob Haney, personal communication, 18 April 2007.

Chapter Seven: Game in the Garden

116 Alan MacEachern, "Rationality and Rationalization in Canadian National Parks Predator Policy," in *Consuming Canada: Readings in Environmental History*, ed. Chad and Pam Gaffield (Toronto: Copp Clark, 1995), 199.
117 George Colpitts, *Game in the Garden: A Human History of Wildlife in Western Canada* (Vancouver: UBC Press, 2002).
118 W. N. Millar, "The Big Game of the Canadian Rockies," in Commission of Conservation Canada, *Conservation of Fish, Birds and Game* (Toronto: Methodist Book and Publishing House, 1916), 103.

119 "Report of the Commissioner of Dominion Parks," in *Annual Report of the Department of the Interior, 1918-19,* (Ottawa: Thomas Mulvey, 1920), 24.

120 "Report of the Commissioner of Canadian National Parks," Appendix no. 4,"Report of the Superintendent of Jasper," in *Annual Report of the Department of the Interior, 1921-22,* (Ottawa: F.A. Acland, 1923), 128.

121 LAC, RG 84, vol. 529, J212, pt. 1, J. B. Harkin to S. M. Rogers, 16 February 1921.

122 Colpitts, *Game in the Garden,* 160.

123 "Report of the Commissioner of Dominion Parks," in *Annual Report of the Department of the Interior, 1919-20,* (Ottawa: Thomas Mulvey, 1920), 20.

124 Harkin fed the story of the elk feeding to the CNR publicity agent. LAC, RG 84, vol. 529, J234 pt. 1, C. N. Higgins to J. B. Harkin, 30 April 1923. Mabel E. Ringland, "Jasper Park Wapiti Keep Scout to Bellow News of Wild Hay Treat," *Vancouver Sun,* 29 March 1924.

125 "Report of the Commissioner of Dominion Parks," in *Annual Report of the Department of the Interior, 1919-20,* (Ottawa: Thomas Mulvey, 1920), 26.

126 LAC, RG 84, vol. 529, J234, pt. 1, "Extract from Annual Report from Jasper National Park," 20 January 1931.

127 LAC, RG 84, vol. 14. J300. pt. 4, "Extract from Report of Supervising Warden Langford, April 1, 1931-December 31, 1931."

128 LAC, RG 84, vol. 14, J300, pt. 4, "Copy of resolution passed at semi-annual meeting of the Athabasca Guides and Trailmens' Association held on December 3d, 1932 in Otto's Hall."

129 LAC, RG 84, vol. 14, J300, pt. 4, H. H. Rowatt to Thomas. G. Murphy, 12 July 1933.

130 "Jasper Mourns 'Old Tubby,'" *Edmonton Journal,* 20 September 1933.

131 LAC, RG 84, vol. 14, J300, pt. 4, Hoyes Lloyd, draft memorandum to J. B. Harkin, 24 February 1933.

132 Ibid., Hoyes Lloyd, draft memorandum to J. B. Harkin, 16 January 1933.

133 LAC, RG 84, vol. 148, file J262, pt. 1, S. M. Rogers to J. B. Harkin, 16 January 1932.

134 "Report of the Commissioner of National Parks of Canada," in *Annual Report of the Department of the Interior, 1933-34,* (Ottawa: King's Printer, 1935), 25.

135 LAC, RG 84, vol. 14, J300, pt. 4, J. B. Harkin, draft memorandum to R. A. Gibson, 11 July 1933.

136 RG 84, vol. 14, J300, pt 4, H. H. Rowatt J. B. Harkin, 30 August 1933.

137 Ibid., pt. 5, H. H. Rowatt to J. B. Harkin, 22 February 1934.

138 LAC, RG 84, vol. 14, J300, pt. 4, R. W. Langford to Superintendent, 13 November 1933.

139 Ibid., C. W. Phillips, Supervising Warden, "Report of Predatory Animals killed during the month of March 1936."

140 LAC, RG 84, vol.14, J300, pt. 4, Bert Wilkins to S. M. Rogers, 24 December 1932.

141 LAC, RG 84, vol. 148, J229, pt. 1, J. B. Harkin to Superintendent, Jasper, 17 July 1935.

142 LAC, vol. 148, J261, A. C. Wright to Commissioner, 18 December 1935.

143 LAC, RG 84, vol. 148, J229, pt. 1, C. V. Phillips to Commissioner, 25 November 1935.

144 Ibid., A. C. Wright to Commissioner, 12 December 1935.

145 Ibid., J. B. Harkin to Edmonton Tannery, 29 January 1936.

146 LAC, RG 84, vol. 529, J210–1, pt. 1, J. Smart to Superintendent, Jasper National Park, 10 February 1953.

147 LAC, RG 84, vol. 1629, J300, pt. 8, Donald R. Flook, "Big Game Survey, South-east Jasper Park, Summer, 1955," unpublished report, 25 June 1956.

148 LAC, RG 84, vol. 1629, J300, pt. 8, J. A. Pettis to B. I. M. Strong, 18 November 1959.

Chapter Eight: Scientists Visit the Park

149 LAC, RG 84, vol. 15, pt. 6, R. M. Anderson, "Memorandum re Predators in Jasper National Park," 11 July 1940.

150 Rod Silver, "Renaisssance Man," *Discovery*, (Spring 2004).

151 James Hatter, *Politically Incorrect: the life and times of British Columbia's first game biologist* (Victoria: O & J Enterprises, 1997), 50.

152 Ian McTaggart-Cowan, *Preliminary report on wildlife in the mountain parks* (1943) cited in LAC, RG 84, vol. 15, J300, pt. 6, C. H. D. Clarke, memorandum to Hoyes Lloyd, December 1943.

153 James Hatter, "Canis latrons," "Field Notes" (Jasper, 1945), unpublished manuscript in library of Western and Northern Service Centre, Parks Canada, Calgary.

154 James Hatter, "Canis Lupus," "Field Notes" (Jasper, 1945), unpublished manuscript in library of Western and Northern Service Centre, Parks Canada, Calgary.

155 Ian McTaggart-Cowan, "Report of Wildlife Studies in the Rocky Mountain Parks in 1945," unpublished manuscript, National and Historic Parks Branch, 1946, 23.

156 Ibid.

157 James Hatter, "Field Notes," 18 December 1944.

158 Egbert Wheeler Pfeiffer, "Some factors affecting the winter ranges of Jasper National Park," M.Sc. diss., University of British Columbia, 1948, 54.

159 Ian McTaggart-Cowan, "Report of Wildlife Studies," 26.

160 LAC, RG 84, vol. 529, J234, pt. 1, Controller to Jasper Superintendent, 23 April 1947.

161 LAC, RG 84, vol. 15, J300 pt. 6, F. Banfield to H. Lewis, 20 September 1946.

162 Harrison F. Lewis, "Lively: a History of the Canadian Wildlife Service" (Ottawa: Canadian Wildlife Service, 1975). CWSC report no. 2018; A published history of the CWS based heavily on the Lewis manuscript similarly gives Banfield short shrift: J. Alexander Burnett, *A Passion for Wildlife: The History of the Canadian Wildlife Service* (Vancouver: University of British Columbia Press, 2003).

163 LAC, RG 84, vol. 1629, J262, R. A. Gibson to Controller, 30 August 1948.

164 LAC, RG 84, vol. 15, J300 pt. 6, N. D. Fisher, "Report on 1948 Wildlife Investigations, Jasper National Park."

165 LAC, RG 84, vol. 1629, J266, pt. 1, W. Winston Mair, to Director, 3 November 1952.

166 LAC, RG 84, vol. 15, J300, pt. 7, J. Smart, to Jasper superintendent, 6 February 1952.

167 LAC, RG 84, vol. 1629, J262, Robert H. Winters to Miss Gertrude Webber, 1 February 1951.

168 LAC, RG 84, vol. 1629, J262, Robert H. Winters to Miss Gertrude Webber, 7 February 1951.

169 Lewis, "Lively: A History of the Canadian Wildlife Service," 418–20.

170 LAC, RG 84, vol. 1622, pt. 6.

171 Wes Bradford, "A History of Elk in Jasper National Park with a reflection on the wolf history, the history of elk in the Willow Creek area and the history of elk/human encounters," unpublished manuscript, Jasper National Park, 1995,195.

172 Mike Dillon, personal communication, January 2008.

173 Lewis, *Lively*, 439.

174 JYHS, Warden Service Reports, "Month-end report to the Chief Park Warden," March 1972.

Chapter Nine: Jasper the Bear

175 LAC, RG 84, vol. 529, J212, pt. 1, J. B. Harkin to acting superintendent, 6 May 1916.

176 LAC, RG 84, vol. 529, J212, pt. 1, Maxwell Graham to J. B. Harkin, 15 July 1918.

177 "Feeding Bears Popular Pastime at Jasper Park," *Edmonton Journal*, 16 July 1921.

178 LAC, RG 84, vol. 529, J212, pt. 1, "Extract from interim annual report April 1–Dec. 31, 1924."

179 LAC, RG 84, vol. 529, J212, pt. 1, H. S. Davis, "A Few Facts About Bears" (1937).

180 JYHS, 994.22, box 7, "Annual Report for the Nine Months Ending December 31st, 1947."

181 LAC, RG 84, vol. 529, J212, pt. 1, F. H. H. Williamson to Jasper Superintendent, 24 August 1938.

182 LAC, RG 84, vol. 529, file J212, pt. 1, F. H. H. Williamson to superintendents, Banff and Jasper, 19 September 1939.

183 Lyle Barry Noble, "Man and Grizzly Bear in Banff National Park, Alberta," M.A. diss., University of Calgary, 1972, 81.

184 Ibid., 80.

185 LAC, RG 84, vol. 529, J212, pt. 1, press release, 1944.

186 James A. Pritchard, *Preserving Yellowstone's Natural Conditions* (Lincoln: University of Nebraska Press, 1999), 109.

187 LAC, RG 84, vol. 529, file J212, pt. 1, G. H. L. Dempster to Controller, 20 October 1950.

188 LAC, RG 84, vol. 529, J212, pt. 1, A. W. F. Banfield to H. Lewis, 20 September 1947.

189 LAC, RG 84, vol. 529, J212, pt. 1, R. A. Gibson to J. Smart, 25 September 1947.

190 "Stopped to admire cubs, student is mauled by mother," *Toronto Daily Star*, 14 June 1950.

191 LAC, RG 84, vol. 529, J212, pt. 1, A. W. F. Banfield to Chief, CWS, 2 September 1953.

192 LAC, RG 84, vol. 1629, J262, A. W. F. Banfield, "Wildlife Investigations Jasper National Park, February 26–28 1951." 12 April 1951.

193 LAC, RG 84, vol. 529, J212, pt. 1, H. C. Bryant, National Parks Service, United States Department of the Interior, to F. H. H. Williamson, 16 September 1938.

194 LAC, RG 84, vol. 529, J212, pt. 1, G. H. L. Dempster to Chief, National Parks and Historical Sites Division, 18 August 1953.

195 LAC, RG 84, vol. 529, J212, pt. 2, W. Winston Mair, Chief, CWS, to Chief, NPS, 28 July 1954.

196 LAC, RG 84, vol. 529, J212, pt. 2, J. A. Pettis to Chief, NPS, 13 Aug. 1957; B. I. M. Strong to Superintendent, 3 July 1958.

197 LAC, RG 84, vol. 529, J212, pt. 3, J. A. Pettis, "Damage to Campers Equipment by Bears." (1959).

198 LAC, RG 84, vol. 529, J212, pt. 2, "Preliminary Report by Supt. J. A. Pettis" transcribed from tape, 11 August 1958.

199 Parks Canada, Policy (1969), 5; cited in John Stuart Taylor, "Bear Management Plans in Canadian National parks: Fifteen Essential Elements," M.A. diss., University of Calgary, 1984, 36.

Chapter Ten: Highway Travellers

200 JYMA, file 86.19.01.08, K. B. Mitchell to Anne Richardson, 20 January 1966.

201 JYMA, file 86.19.01.05a, Charles H. Grant to Mrs. R. E. Richardson, 3 December 1965.

202 JYMA, file 86.19.01.17, Alber Baker to Mrs. Richardson, 10 March 1966.

203 James Struthers, "Canadian Unemployment Policy in the 1930s," in *Readings in Canadian History: Post-Confederation*, ed. R. Douglas Francis and Donald B. Smith (Toronto: Holt, Rinehart and Winston, 1990), 424–28.

204 Bill Waiser, *Park Prisoners: The Untold Story of Western Canada's National Parks, 1915–1948* (Saskatoon: Fifth House, 1995), 67.

205 JYHS, file 2006.77.01–04, Ted White, "The Banff-Jasper Highway," unpublished typescript, n.d.

206 Ibid.

207 LAC, RG 84, vol. 178, U-113–109, pt. 1, "Banff-Jasper Highway" pamphlet (*c.* 1950).

208 Waiser, *Park Prisoners*, 199.

209 Department of Mines and Resources, *Annual Report for Fiscal Year 1948–1949*, (Ottawa: King's Printer, 1949), 155.

Chapter Eleven: Skiers

210 Pete Withers, "Early Days of Sking [*sic*] in Jasper Park," unpublished typescript, Jasper Yellowhead Museum and Archives, n.d.

211 Joe Bryant to Mike Dillon, personal communication, 4 February 2008.

212 Erling Strom, *Pioneers on Skis* (New York: Smith Clove Books, 1977), 94.

213 "Report of the Commissioner of National Parks of Canada," in *Annual Report of the Department of the Interior, 1931-32*, (Ottawa: F.A. Acland, 1932), 15.

214 "Report of the Commssioner of National Parks," in *Annual Report of the Department of the Interior, 1933-34*, (Ottawa: J.O. Patenaude, 1935), 16.

215 "Report of the Commissioner of National Parks of Canada," in *Annual Report of the Department of the Interior, 1929-30*, (Ottawa: F.A. Acland, 1930), 18.

216 Nora Findlay, *Jasper: A Backward Glance* (Jasper: Parks And People, 1992), 30.

217 Edward Mills, "Rustic Building Programs in Canada's National Parks, 1887–1950." Unpublished report, National Historic Sites Directorate, Parks Canada, 1994, 104.

218 Hal Clifford, *Downhill Slide: Why the Corporate Ski Industry is Bad For Skiing, Ski Towns and the Environment* (San Francisco: Sierra Club Books, 2002), 12–14.

219 JYMA, file 997.07 415, "Ken Cook."

220 Brenda Gainer, "The Human History of Jasper National Park, Alberta," Parks Canada, unpublished manuscript, manuscript report series 441 (1981), 181.

221 This building became the Whistlers Youth Hostel in 1973. See Danielle Hamelin, "Whistlers Hostel, Whistlers Hostel Manager's Residence, Jasper National Park of Canada, Alberta (DFRP No. 15412)," unpublished report, Parks Canada, Federal Buildings Review Office, Building Report 87–014.

222 Hamelin, "Whistlers Hostel," 2.

223 Parks Canada, "Marmot Basin Ski Area, Jasper National Park: Long Range Proposals December 1981," unpublished report, 5.

Chapter Twelve: Wardens at the Crossroads

224 Toni Klettl, personal communication, 31 January 2007.

225 Frank Camp, *Roots in the Rockies* (privately published, 1993); Mike Schintz, *Close Calls on High Walls and Other Tales from the Warden Service* (Calgary: Rocky Mountain Books, 2005); Max Winkler, personal communication, 27 June 2006.

226 Toni Klettl, personal communication, 31 January 2007.

227 LAC, RG 84, vol. 49, U185–2, "Program: Proposed Wardens Ski and Snowcraft School, Jasper National Park, March 1st to March 31st, 1952."

228 Ibid., G. L. Dempster to Director, 28 March 1953.

229 Ibid., G. H. L. Dempster to Chief, 3 April 1954.

230 Toni Klettl, personal communication, 31 January 2007.

231 R. W. Sandford, *The Highest Calling: Canada's Elite National Park Mountain Rescue Program* (Canmore: Alpine Club of Canada, 2002), 5.

232 Sandford, *The Highest Calling*, 15.

233 Robert J. Burns, *Guardians of the Wild: A History of the Warden Service of Canada's National Parks* (Calgary: University of Calgary Press, 2000), 302.

234 Cited in Burns, *Guardians of the Wild*, 254.

235 Burns, *Guardians of the Wild*, 262.

236 Burns, *Guardians of the Wild*, 265.

237 JYHS, file 994.22, Max Winkler, Monthly Report to the Chief Park Warden, August 1971.
238 Ibid., "Month End Report from Lower Athabasca Area (M. Winkler), March 1972.
239 John Stuart Taylor, "Bear Management Plans in Canadian National Parks: Fifteen Essential Elements," M.A. diss., Faculty of Environmental Design, University of Calgary, 1984.
240 Burns, *Guardians of the Wild*, 262.
241 Burns, *Guardians of the Wild*, 309.

Chapter Thirteen: "Visitation"

242 *Jasper Tourist News* (1965), 17.
243 National Parks Service, "Jasper National Park: Provisional Master Plan–Plan Directeur Provisiore–1967," (Ottawa: National Parks Service, 1968), 42.
244 The *Jasper Gateway*, 14 August 1968.
245 Department of Indian Affairs and Northern Development, *Annual Report, 1967–68,* (Ottawa: Queen's Printer, 1968), 104.
246 Department of Indian and Northern Affairs, *Annual Report 1973–74,* (Ottawa: Queen's Printer, 1975),17.
247 Lloyd Brooks was not the first professional planner hired by the national parks organization. In 1921 the commissioner of national parks, J. B. Harkin, hired the pioneering town planner Thomas Adams to head up a town planning unit. His work was focussed on townsite development and after he was joined by an architect the unit was called the architecture and town planning division. Although the unit oversaw the development of aesthetically pleasing layouts of streets, green spaces, and buildings, Adams held strong ideas about the importance of functional zoning, a characteristic of the later generation of planners. Adams left in 1923 to head up a regional planning project in New York City, and his position was allowed to lapse.
248 Gordon D. Taylor, "Demand for Recreation—An Essential Tool for Resource Planning," in *The Canadian National Parks: Today and Tomorrow, Proceedings of a Conference Organized by the National and Provincial Parks Association of Canada and the University of Calgary October 9–15, 1968,* ed. J. G. Nelson and R. C. Scace, vol. II (Calgary: University of Calgary, 1969), 879.
249 H. Peter Oberlander and R. J. Cave, "Urban Development Plan: Jasper, Alberta," Typescript, National Parks Branch, Department of Northern Affairs and National Resources, Ottawa, 1963.
250 "Summaries and Discussion," in *The Canadian National Parks: Today and Tomorrow,* vol. II, 940.

251 Canada. National Parks Service, "Banff National Park Provisional Master Plan 1967" (Ottawa: National Parks Service, 1968), 3.

252 National Parks Service, "Jasper National Park: Provisional Master Plan–Plan Directeur Provisiore–1967," (Ottawa: National Parks Service, 1968), 27.

253 Ibid., 38–39.

254 Ibid., 42.

255 J. G. Nelson, "Man and Landscape Change in Banff National Park: A National Park Problem in Perspective," in *The Canadian National Parks: Today and Tomorrow*, vol. 1, 138.

256 "Summaries and Discussion," vol. II, 969.

257 Ian McTaggart-Cowan, "The Role of Ecology in the National Park," in *Canadian National Parks: Today and Tomorrow*, vol. II, 931.

258 "Summaries and Discussion," vol. II, 976.

259 A.T. Davidson, "Canada's National Parks: Past and Future," in *The Canadian National Parks: today and tomorrow conference II*, vol. 1 (Waterloo: University of Waterloo, 1979), 23.

260 K. B. Mitchell, "Natural History and Interpretation from the Park Superintendent's Viewpoint," in "Fifth Annual Naturalists' Workshop, Palisades National Park Training Centre, Jasper National Park, July 3, 4, 5 1964," unpublished typescript, Parks Canada Library, Calgary.

261 W. W. Mair, "Natural History Interpretation—Key to the Future of the National Parks," in Fifth Annual Naturalists' Workshop.

262 Larry Halverson, "Peter Heron," unpublished manuscript, courtesy of the author, n.d.

263 G. F. Campbell, "The Warden Service of the National Parks of Canada-Especially Jasper," in Fifth Annual Naturalists' Workshop.

264 Park Naturalists' Conference, National Parks of Canada, Calgary, Alberta, November 16–18, 1965," unpublished typescript, Parks Canada Library, Calgary.

265 LAC, RG 84, Acc. 86–87/350, file C-8373–2/J1, "Interpretive Statistics Jasper National Park," D. Williamson to Regional Park Naturalist, Monthly Report for July 1969.

266 Department of Indian Affairs and Northern Development, *Annual Report, 1969–70*, (Ottawa: Queen's Printer, 1971), 7.

267 Cited in Robert J. Burns, *Guardians of the Wild: A History of the Warden Service of Canada's National Parks* (Calgary: University of Calgary Press, 2000), 263.

268 JNP library, Jasper National Park Organization Chart, 1968/69.

269 Taylor, "Demand for Recreation," 879.

270 Personal communication, 28 January 1998.

271 LAC, RG 84, file C-1445–10/J1, pt. 1, "Semi-Annual Regional Report, Jasper National Park, April 1 to September 30 1970."

272 LAC, RG 84, vol. 2343, file C1445–101/J1, pt. 1, Jasper National Park superintendent's report, 1972.

273 Ibid.

274 EFRC, Acc. 87–06, file 65/1. w1.1, vol. 1, J. Christakos to Regional Director, 2 November 1971.

275 Ibid.

276 EFRC, Acc. 87–06, file 65/1. w.1.1, vol.1, "IF Youth Emergency Services Summer Program for Jasper (1971)."

277 LAC, vol. 1625, J172 pt. 1, K. B. Mitchell to chief, 16 September 1963.

278 "Jasper Still Needs Civilized Services," *Edmonton Journal*, 24 July 1967.

279 Alberta. Department of Municipal Affairs, "The Banff-Jasper Autonomy Report" (Edmonton: Department of Municipal Affairs, 1972), Appendix II.

Epilogue: Century's End

280 Canadian Parks Service, *Jasper National Park Management Plan*, 1988 (Ottawa: Environment Canada, 1988), 16.

281 "It is expected that, in the next 15 years, demand for opportunities to enjoy and use the Parks will grow at a modest but steady rate. Within the limits imposed by environmental and social considerations, such opportunities can be provided for a greater number of people and, where it is appropriate, increased use in non-peak period will be encouraged." Parks Canada, *In Trust for Tomorrow: A Management Framework for Four Mountain Parks* (Ottawa: Environment Canada, 1986), 25.

282 Kevin Van Tighem, "A Caribou Community," text of talk presented at Jasper, 27 February 2004.

283 Rick Searle, *Phantom Parks: The Struggle to Save Canada's National Parks* (Toronto: Key Porter, 2000), 128.

Index

Look for the following FIFTH HOUSE
titles at your local bookstore: